T5-CWK-090

ST. MARY'S COLLEGE OF MARYLAND
ST. MARY'S CITY, MARYLAND

Papers on
Capitalism, development and planning

By the same author

Political economy and capitalism: some essays in
    economic tradition

Studies in the development of capitalism

On economic theory and socialism: collected papers

An essay on economic growth and planning

Soviet economic development since 1917

38999

Papers on
Capitalism, development and planning

Maurice Dobb

INTERNATIONAL PUBLISHERS
NEW YORK

First United States Edition by
International Publishers Company, Inc., 1967
381 Park Avenue South
New York, New York 10016

© *Maurice Dobb 1967*

No part of this book may be reproduced
in any form without permission from
the publisher, except for the quotation
of brief passages in criticism

Printed in Great Britain

Contents

AUTHOR'S NOTE

The present collection, with the exception of the two Delhi lectures, consists of pieces written within the past ten years. In a collection of this kind from a variety of sources some repetition can scarcely be avoided. Rightly or wrongly it has been thought better on the whole to preserve the sequence of the original than to start omitting passages and abbreviating. Acknowledgment is made at the head of each chapter for permission to reprint. It should, perhaps, be explained that the publishers of *Soviet Studies* are Messrs Basil Blackwell of Oxford, and that publications of Polish Scientific Publishers (P.W.N.) are sold in this country by arrangement with the Pergamon Press.

M.D.

December 1966

One

Some problems in the history of capitalism: three lectures

Lectures delivered at the Institute of Statistics of the University of Bologna on 24th, 26th and 27th March 1962, and published in Italian in *Statistica*, April–June 1962 (N. 2, Anno XXII). They are reproduced here by kind permission of Professor P. Fortunati, Director of that journal and of the Institute. English versions of the lectures have appeared in *Our History*, Winter–Spring 1963, and in *Science and Society*, Winter and Spring 1964 (Vol. XXVIII, Nos. 1 and 2) respectively, and are used with the consent of their editors.

One

Transition from feudalism to capitalism

The question of what was the nature and what were the moving forces of the decline of Feudalism as an economic system, and what connection had this decline with the birth of modern Capitalism, is not entirely without interest, I think, for many underdeveloped countries today. However, it is in the context, rather, of historical interpretation that I want to deal with this question here. For historical interpretation, at any rate for one that attaches primary importance to distinctive modes of production in defining stages in the historical process, a true understanding of this crucial transition is, I believe, essential. Moreover, without it much in our definition of Capitalism as a mode of production, as well as of its origins, must inevitably remain blurred and unclear.

I should perhaps explain that when I talk about Feudalism, I am not referring to this as a juridical form or set of legal relations; I am speaking of it primarily as a socio-economic system. But in looking at it in this light, I do not wish to identify it with Schmoller's 'natural economy', even if it be true that trade and money-dealings (certainly long-distance trade) occupied a smaller place in this type of economy than in others, both preceding and succeeding it. I refer to it as a system under which economic status and authority were associated with land-tenure, and the direct producer (who was himself the holder of some land) was under obligation based on law or customary right to devote a certain quota of his labour or his produce to the benefit of his feudal superior. Regarded in this way, as a system of socio-economic relations, it is almost identical with what we generally mean by serfdom; provided that we do not confine the latter to the performance of direct labour services (on the lord's estate or in his household) but include in it the provision of tribute or feudal rent in produce or even in a money-form. Using Marc Bloch's phrase, it implies the existence of 'a subject peasantry': he goes on to say, 'the feudal system meant the rigorous economic subjection of a host of humble folk to a few powerful men . . . the land itself (being) valued because it enabled a lord to provide himself with "men" '. To which Bloch added: 'whatever the source of the noble's income, he always lived on the labour of other men'. Summing it up we can say that the differentiating feature of this type of exploitation is accordingly that the sanction behind it, whereby it is enforced and perpetuated, is so-called 'extra-economic compulsion' in some form.

As I see it, there are two central problems connected with the transition from Feudalism to Capitalism—from a system of production resting on serf-labour or 'a subject peasantry' to one based on hired wage-labour. These two problems correspond to two phases in the transition, an earlier phase and a later one. Firstly there is the question as to what historical motive-force it was that brought about the disintegration of the feudal system of exploitation, generating a virtual crisis of feudal society at the end of the mediaeval period in Western Europe; certainly in England, in the fifteenth century, and more widely also in France and Germany (*vide* Marc Bloch's 'crise des fortunes seigneuriales'). I would add that this question has to be answered, not only with reference to the unevenness of the process and to differences in the chronological sequence as between different regions, but also in close relation to the so-called 'second serfdom'—the reinforcement and extension of serfdom, including the imposition of a servile relationship on previously free cultivators, which occurred in parts of Europe in the fifteenth and sixteenth centuries. Secondly, there is the question as to the process whereby from this disintegration of Feudalism bourgeois or capitalist methods of production, based on wage-labour, arose. Did these new social relations of production spring up directly from the soil of feudal society, their appearance hastening the decline of the old system and directly supplanting it? Or was the process of burgeoning of Capitalism more complex and more long-drawn-out in time than this?

In considering these questions I must inevitably draw upon English experience since this is what I best know. This limitation has serious disadvantages, as I am well aware. But it has at least one advantage: in that England has always been treated, rightly or wrongly, as the classic case of the rise of Capitalism; and as a result of the Norman Conquest the Feudal System had previously been imposed on England in its most complete form. In connection with the second of the two questions that I have just emphasised, it is to be noted that in this 'classic' English case two whole centuries elapsed between the decline of labour services on the lord's estate as the main form of servile obligation (labour-rent as Marx called it) and the Bourgeois Revolution, and a further century and a half elapsed between the Bourgeois Revolution of the seventeenth century and the coming of the so-called 'Industrial Revolution' with power-machinery and factory production. Any answer we give to our second question must take full account of this elongation of the process of transition: must explain why there was so long an interval between the decline of Feudalism and the full maturing of Capitalism. If it were true that 'more or less complete forms of the capitalist order ripened in the womb of feudal society'[1] this long interval would be hard to explain.

The explanation of the decline of Feudalism with which we are commonly confronted (sometimes among 'Marxist' writers) is that a system rooted in so-called 'natural economy' was undermined, weakened and finally destroyed by the growth of trade and money dealings, which caused labour services to be commuted to a money-rent and encouraged commodity production for a wide market. We find, indeed, this antithesis between 'natural economy' and 'money economy', and the dissolvent influence of the latter upon the former, in the work of Gustav Schmoller and his school. Pirenne was to elaborate this into the view that it was the revival of long-distance trade from the twelfth century onwards, as a result of the revival of Mediterranean trade, that broke down the self-sufficient manorial economy of feudal Europe. The spread of commerce encouraged the demand among the aristocracy for imported luxuries; merchant caravans, forming permanent settlements at key points, stimulated a revival of town life and market exchange; feudal estates themselves were encouraged by the proximity of markets and of a thriving exchange to produce a surplus for sale outside the locality (whether a surplus of rural produce or of handicrafts), and feudal lords themselves became

[1] As was stated in the Soviet textbook on *Political Economy*, 2nd ed., p. 59.

increasingly reliant on trade and on the obtaining of a money income. In his discussion with me in the pages of the American journal *Science and Society*, some ten years ago, Dr Paul Sweezy was evidently basing his own position on this conception of Henri Pirenne.

The picture we get is, accordingly, one of trade as the primary solvent of feudal society: of trade operating on the feudal system of production and exploitation as an external force. As regards its internal structure, Feudalism tends to be regarded in this conception as an essentially stable system, which, but for this historical 'accident' of the revival of long-distance trade, might have continued indefinitely long.

Once, according to this view, trade and 'money economy' have become enthroned as the historical destroyers of Feudalism it is easy enough to regard them as the direct begetters of Capitalism. Here merchant capital plays the essential progenitive role. From the accumulated profits of expanding trade small capitals grow to become large capitals. Some of this capital, originating in the sphere of commerce, flows over first into the purchase of land and then into production—into the employment of free wage-labour in production. Thus the Soviet textbook of which I spoke a moment or two ago (and imitating it a recent volume edited by Otto Kuusinen) speaks of capitalist 'manufactories' (i.e. large handicraft workshops employing wage-labour) competing with and ousting the old craft guilds as being the crucial link—the form in which the metamorphosis of merchant capital into industrial capital was realised. Others (and I think this was essentially Sweezy's view) have seen the 'putting-out' system, or *Verlag-System*, organised by large merchants of the towns to employ craftsmen scattered in domestic workshops in the villages or suburbs, as the crucial road of transition to the matured factory system of the 'industrial revolution'.

There is much that can be shown, I believe, to be unsatisfactory about this view. Firstly, there is the difficulty I have mentioned about explaining the chronology of the process: if the process of transformation was as simple and direct as this conception represents it as being, why was not the transformation, once it had started, completed in a much shorter time—in the English case within one or two centuries instead of four or five? Secondly, the counterposing of 'money economy' and 'natural economy' as the direct antinomy responsible for the dissolution of Feudalism is not only far too abstract a formulation, but it ignores (partly if not wholly) the influence of internal contradictions and conflicts on the feudal mode of production, for example the peasant struggles and revolts (in a variety of forms) which were virtually endemic in the centuries of its decline. Moreover, it ignores the fact that the existence of trade and of production for the market were by no means always inconsistent with serfdom as a labour-system; and increase of trade and money dealings far from uniformly acted as a dissolvent of serfdom, even in the form of direct labour services on the lord's demesne. On the contrary, growth of trade was not infrequently accompanied by an actual intensification of serfdom, as the 'second serfdom' east of the Elbe, of which Friedrich Engels spoke, is witness. Even within England itself it was in the relatively backward north and west of England that direct labour services disappeared earliest, while in the more advanced south-east, close to town markets and ports such as London, labour services were most stubborn in survival; and it was in the thirteenth century when agricultural production for the market was at its highest for some centuries that labour services increased.

Reflection on this and on the situation in Eastern Europe, where intensification of serfdom was associated with the growth of export trade in grain, led me to go so far as to declare in my discussion with Dr Sweezy that in many parts of Europe 'the correlation was not between nearness to markets and feudal disintegration, but between nearness to markets and strengthening of serfdom'. I should mention, perhaps, that the late Professor Kosminsky summed up the matter more concretely by stating that 'the development of exchange in the peasant economy, whether it served the local market directly, or more distant markets through merchant middlemen, led to the development of money-rent. The development of exchange in the lords' economy, on the other hand, led to the growth of labour services.'

Thirdly, the conception of Merchant Capital growing up in the interstices of feudal society, and then evolving directly into Industrial Capital and becoming the pioneer of the new mode of production based on wage-labour is, I suggest, not only a gross oversimplification (for example, in its treatment of Merchant Capital as a homogeneous entity), but stands in direct conflict, again, with many of the facts concerning the actual role of the big merchant companies and merchant princes of the time. This conception of the essentially progressive role of Merchant Capital in the transition is difficult to square with the actual social alignments at the time of the Bourgeois Revolution. Far from being uniformly progressive, the larger merchant families were often found in alliance with the feudal ruling class (on whom, indeed, they often relied for their trading privileges as well as for their custom), and the powerful trading companies and guilds (especially those engaged in the export trade) often, in defence of their own monopolistic rights, pursued policies which brought them into conflict with those who were interested in the development of handicraft industry (e.g. the conflict between wool merchants and cloth-workers in England), and which hampered the growth of the latter. Moreover, it quite overlooks the important role, both in the economic transition and in the Bourgeois Revolution, of what one may call the 'democratic element' (as they were initially)—of the 'small men' who rose from the ranks of the petty producers themselves, alike in agriculture and in the handicrafts, who accumulated capital from small beginnings, battled for independence, later for dominance in the guilds and companies of the period, and also in town government, and became employers of wage-labour because having no stake in feudal society and no claim upon servile labour, they had nothing else but 'free labour' to draw upon.

There is, I believe, a fertile misconception associated with the idea that growth of trade necessarily leads to Capitalism: namely the idea that the presence of a *bourgeois* element in society (in the sense of persons using money-capital in trade) implies the presence of bourgeois methods and relations of production. As soon as one reflects upon the matter, it becomes clear that nothing could be more mistaken. All societies since the very primitive have been characterised by trade. Classical society is an example of this; and historians have now discovered that even in the heyday of the mediaeval period there was more trade than was formerly thought. Such trade nourished traders: in other words a social stratum of commercial bourgeoisie. But these were generally remote from production: they were excrescences upon the mode of production, not part of it, and their presence in no way altered the character of this mode of production whatever it might be. (Did not Marx say that 'merchants' capital in its supremacy everywhere stands for a system of robbery' and that 'in the antique world the effect of commerce and the development of merchants' capital always result in slave economy'?) Similarly the existence of a trading bourgeoisie in the late mediaeval period, who accumulated capital from the profits of trade and reinvested it as merchant capital, was not inconsistent with the existence of a predominantly feudal mode of production and exploitation. Its existence did not automatically dissolve the latter; nor were the interests of feudal nobility and traders necessarily in conflict with one another. Indeed, feudal *seigneurs* sometimes themselves engaged in trade (this was particularly true of monasteries), and their sons often went into partnership with merchants while the latter acquired land and titles of gentility. Only if Merchant Capital turned towards production, and sought ways of investing capital in new forms of production, did it serve as an instrument of transition to Capitalism. This is a matter to which we shall return.

Let us go back and consider what was the character of the system of production that formed the basis of feudal society. So far as the serf was attached to the land and had a holding of land from which he derived his own subsistence (as was true of all except household serfs), one can speak of the system of production as being the petty mode of production—individual or family labour with primitive implements on small plots of land. The same was true of handicraft production; and even when this was organised by the lord or his servants in large-scale workshops, production remained individual production with no more than a primitive division of labour and coordination of individual units. There was also, however, the lords' *demesne* or manorial estate; and in the heyday of feudalism the surplus labour of the serf took the form of work on this *demesne* or estate—work which was commonly organised as collective work on a larger scale. This can scarcely I think be embraced within the category of the 'petty mode of production'.

At a later stage of feudal economy, however, in the degree to which large-scale *demesne* or estate farming declined, surplus labour took the form of an obligation to deliver part of the produce of the serf's own holding (to which all or most of his labour-time was now devoted), or else its money-equivalent, to the feudal superior. Feudal exploitation, in other words, took the form of direct appropriation of a surplus product from the petty mode of production. In England this change commonly took the form of commuting labour service for a money-rent (often apparently with retention of the right to reconvert it into direct labour services at the lord's behest). The change, in other words, represented a transition from what Marx termed labour-rent to money-rent; but the latter was still a *feudal* rent, enforced by feudal law or custom, and not a contractual rent deriving in any sense from a free market in land. It is true, of course, that this implied the presence of a market and some element of money economy; and one result (though not an invariable result) of the spread of trade, as we have seen, was to encourage the change to money-rent. In France, however, the sixteenth century witnessed a growth of rent-in-kind or product-rent on a basis which anticipated the metayage system. In Asiatic forms of feudalism (for example, in India and in Japan) it may be noted that produce-rent or tribute was for centuries a predominant form of exaction.

Marx called money-rent, 'as a converted form of rent in kind', 'the last form and the dissolving form' of feudal rent. ('In its further development,' he says, 'money-rent must lead . . . either to the transformation of land into independent peasants' property or into the form corresponding to . . . rent paid by a capitalist tenant.') Evidently it is most likely to be a 'dissolving' and transitional form if the commutation of services into money-rent is achieved as a concession by the lord to pressure from the producer. This was widely true of the spread of commutation in England after 1300 and even of parts of France and Flanders after the Hundred Years War. Marc Bloch has said that 'to the eyes of the historian . . . agrarian revolt appeared as inseparable from the seigneurial regime as is, for example, the strike from large-scale capitalist enterprise'; and an English mediaeval historian, Rodney Hilton, in a study of 'Peasant Movements in England before 1381', has stated that 'peasant resistance to seigneurial pressure seems first to become significant in England in the thirteenth century', after which it seems to have increased both in frequency and in intensity. One form assumed by peasant resistance to feudal exaction was peasant flight from the land—flight into the towns or to the waste or borderlands, and on the continent of Europe into the forests or migration towards the less populated east. Such movements drained the estates of labour, and was a powerful factor in promoting commutation and encouraging the actual leasing of *demesne* lands. In this respect small estates were apt to react differently from large, since the former tended to be less well supplied with labour in the first place as well as possessing less power to assert their claims or to bring back fugitive serfs. It seems to have been this kind of situation which underlay what has been called the general crisis of feudal society in Western Europe in the fourteenth and fifteenth centuries; and it was the verdict of the late Professor Kosminsky (in his contribution to *Studi in Onore di Armando Sapori*) that it was not a decline of population 'but rather the liquidation of the seignorial economy, commutation and diminution of feudal rent' that underlay the economic decline of this period—a decline and crisis of feudal economy which had as the other side of the medal an 'improvement in the situation of the peasantry and an expansion of simple commodity production'.

It was precisely this improvement in the situation of the producers and an enlarged scope for simple commodity production that was to accelerate in these centuries that process of social differentiation within the petty mode of production which was to prepare the soil from which bourgeois relations of production were later to emerge. Some differentiation there had always been. To quote Mr Rodney Hilton again:

> The growth of a rich upper stratum among the peasants has been well enough documented in recent agrarian studies. Whether we look at peasant life in the south-east, in the Thames Valley, in East Anglia or in the Midlands, we find standing out from the ordinary run of tenants with their fifteen or twenty-acre holdings, a small group of families, sometimes free, more often serf, holding a hundred acres or more.[2]

[2] *Economic History Review*, Second Series, Vol. II, No. 2, p. 130.

And he goes on to point out that it was precisely these larger peasants (most likely to be commodity-producers for a market and ambitious to expand) who took the lead in revolt against feudal oppression. In the degree to which this revolt succeeded, however, and a portion of the surplus product of the petty mode of production was retained within it, and the greater the chance for peasant leasing of additional land, the more this process of social differentiation was able to develop, since there was now scope for a modest measure of accumulation in the hands of this upper stratum of well-to-do peasants. Here the influence of factors internal to feudal economy interacted with that of such factors as the growth of towns and of trade. It was these more prosperous elements in the petty mode of production, both in agriculture and in the urban handicrafts, who not only had direct links with the market, but sought to improve and extend production, and as they expanded became employers of wage-labour. As universally happens among small commodity-producers, the process of differentiation which breeds the nascent employer breeds also a supply of depressed, if not actually dispossessed, wage-labour available for employment. In later centuries enclosure and concentration of land ownership were to complete the process of dispossessing the poorest stratum of producers, separating them from the means of production and creating a proletariat. But the completion of this process was to take some time.

The picture we have then, in summary, is this. A main factor in the decline of Feudalism in Western Europe, and particularly in England which witnessed a crisis of feudal economy in the late fourteenth and the fifteenth century, was the struggle of the small producers to loosen the bonds of feudal exploitation. Particularly conscious of these bonds were the upper stratum of well-to-do peasants, who were in a position to extend cultivation onto new land and to improve it, and who accordingly tended to be the spearpoint of revolt. Such tendencies were both aided by and aided the spread of trade and of production for the market. But in the degree to which disintegration of the old order proceeded and the petty mode of production shook itself loose from feudal bonds and feudal exploitation, the process of social differentiation within the petty mode of production was accelerated; and it was from this process of social differentiation (with its double tendency to form a *kulak* class of richer peasants on the one hand, and a depressed class of poor 'cottagers' or landless 'squatters' on the other) that bourgeois relations of production were born. But the process both of disintegration and of differentiation took time; and for this very reason the new mode of production did not spring full-grown from the old, but could only develop when the decline of the old had reached a quite advanced stage.

This seems to be the point at which to remind you of an illuminating distinction to which Marx first drew attention between what he called 'two roads' of transition. According to the first of these 'the producer becomes a merchant and capitalist'. This he calls 'the really revolutionary way'. According to the second, it is the merchant who 'takes possession in a direct way of production': a way which though it 'serves historically as a mode of transition', 'nevertheless cannot by itself do much for the overthrow of the old mode of production, but rather preserves it and uses it as its premise'; and eventually becomes 'everywhere an obstacle to a real capitalist mode of production'.

This pregnant suggestion is, I believe, abundantly borne out by the facts of English economic development in these crucial centuries of transition from the fourteenth century to the sixteenth and seventeenth; and is an important key to understanding the complex developments that were occurring in the handicraft industries, with the proliferation of Livery Companies and Corporations as well as contests of divergent interests within them, and the spread of a country craft-industry (largely on the so-called 'putting-out system') outside the towns and outside the jurisdiction of the older town guilds. This extension of handicraft industry was evidently pioneered in two main ways. Firstly, a section of the merchants at the head of companies such as the Clothworkers, Drapers and Leather-sellers, Cordwainers, Cutlers and Pewterers began to turn their capital towards the encouragement of domestic handicraft production in the countryside and the suburbs of towns on the 'putting-out system'—advancing raw materials to the craftsmen (later supplying as well their actual working implements, as in hosiery knitting), and marketing the finished product.

Secondly, the more prosperous among the craftsmen as well as also the *kulak* element among peasant farmers established their own contacts with the market, and accumulating a little capital themselves organised the putting-out of work to poorer craftsmen on a half-wage, half-subcontracting basis. In the sixteenth and early seventeenth century there were also examples of production in larger workshops or 'manufactories', as well as of considerable capitals being invested in mining operations and some new industries like soap-boiling, paper, cannon-founding, brass-making and brewing, about which Professor Nef has written extensively; but in England at any rate such large enterprises were the exception rather than the rule (and their owners, incidentally, were apt to be on the side of the Crown rather than of Parliament in the English Civil War).

Thus small to middling-sized 'clothiers' were a feature of the small country towns in Tudor England; and it was the clothing towns and districts that were apt to be strongholds of the Parliamentary cause in the English Civil War—for example, the clothing districts of Gloucestershire in the West of England and in East Anglia. Similarly, a marked feature of this period was the prosperous 'improving' yeoman farmer, of whom Professor Tawney speaks, consolidating holdings and 'enclosing' them, and not uncommonly purchasing manors and setting up as minor country squires or gentry. On the continent, especially in Germany, there was a similar spread of the *verlag system*; but here it seems to have been more exclusively dominated and monopolised by large 'merchant manufacturers' of the cities, and to have represented accordingly Way No. 2 rather than Way No. 1.

Such contrasts, indeed, on an international scale seem to be crucial to any appreciation of the differences one finds in different countries, both in the historical genesis of Capitalism and in the character of Capitalism when it has finally emerged. In turn, the key to such contrasts is, I believe, to be found in the extent to which Feudalism had disintegrated and the petty mode of production attained a substantial degree of independence *before* some form of capitalist production first took the stage. This has been well emphasised by the Japanese economic historian Professor Kohachiro Takahashi with an eye particularly to the peculiarities of economic development in his own country. He expresses the contrast in this way:

> Certainly the way in which capitalism took form in every country was closely tied up with previous social structures, i.e. the internal intensity and organisation of feudal economy there. In England and France feudal land property and serfdom either disintegrated in the process of economic development, or were wiped out structurally and categorically in the bourgeois revolution . . . These revolutions in Western Europe, by the independence and the ascent of the petty commodity-producers and their differentiation, set free from among them the forces making for the development of capitalist production; while in Prussia and Japan this 'emancipation' was carried out in the opposite sense. The organisation of feudal land property remained intact and the classes of free and independent peasants and middle-class burghers were undeveloped . . . Since capitalism had to be erected on this kind of soil, on a basis of fusion rather than conflict with absolutism, the formation of capitalism took place in the opposite way to Western Europe, predominantly as a process of transformation of putting-out merchant capital into industrial capital . . . It can be said that in connection with varying world historical conditions the process of establishing capitalism takes different basic lines: in Western Europe, Way No. I (producer into merchant), in Eastern Europe and Asia, Way No II (merchant into manufacturer). There is a deep inner relationship between the agrarian question and industrial capital, which determines the characteristic structures of capitalism in the various countries.[3]

There is one further point. What has been said about the petty mode of production during the period of feudal decline must not be taken to mean that there was an intermediate mode of production which somehow filled the interval between the period of high feudalism and capitalism. This, or something close to it, has, indeed, been suggested at times: for example, again by Dr Sweezy in the above-mentioned discussion. What he suggests is that we call 'the system which prevailed in Western Europe during the fifteenth and sixteenth centuries "pre-capitalist commodity production" '. This I do not feel is either necessary or very satisfactory. It is true, as we have seen, that petty commodity production predominated in this period. But then so also was this the

[3] *Science and Society*, New York, Fall 1952, pp. 344–5.

case in varying degrees throughout the feudal period. Even if it be true that in these later centuries feudal revenue had declined and the form of feudal exaction had generally changed to that of money-rent, the subordination of petty commodity production to feudal fetters and exaction had not ended; and one could only speak of the situation correctly as being *non*-feudal if there were no longer a feudal ruling-class with its peculiar source of income still surviving. There can be no doubt, I think, that the ruling class in these centuries was still the feudal aristocracy, even in England where its ranks had been considerably thinned by the Wars of the Roses in the fifteenth century, and where in the Tudor period there was recruitment to its ranks from among the merchant princes (this constituting the *parvenu* element in the Tudor aristocracy, the new upstart families filling the gaps in the older families). This was the period of the growth of political absolutism —a State form different from the looser, more decentralised form of government of earlier centuries, which had seen considerable autonomy for the various territorial lords each within his own region. But it remained a *feudal* absolutism; and in England the Stuart period at the beginning of the seventeenth century saw power and influence (including economic influence and privileges, such as grants of monopoly) concentrated in the Court, up to the challenge of the bourgeois revolution in the 1640's.

Similar considerations apply to the quite common notion of a distinctive Merchant Capitalism preceding the rise of a matured Industrial Capitalism.[4] Now, if 'Merchant Capitalism' is intended merely as a descriptive term for that first and early stage of capitalism prior to the Industrial Revolution and to the arrival of machinofacture—then one need not quarrel simply about a word. But if the use of the term is intended to imply (as I think it generally is) the existence of a distinctive, and in some sense intermediate, system of production and of social relations of production (subsequent to feudalism but *prior* to the arrival on the scene of capitalism proper), then I suggest that this kind of classification is mistaken and misleading. We may well ask what

[4] A notion sponsored *inter alia* by Professor M. N. Pokrovsky in his *History of Russia from the Earliest Times to the Rise of Commercial Capitalism* of forty years ago.

special kind of animal this so-called 'Merchant Capitalism' was. That capitalist relations of production appeared on the scene some time before the Industrial Revolution; that there was an immature and undeveloped first stage of capitalism in England for two centuries before 1800—this is all quite true. But, if we understand the situation correctly, I believe we shall see it as a precursor stage, and not at all a separate system or mode of production.

Two

Prelude to the Industrial Revolution

Over the past ten years economists have returned to the question of the Industrial Revolution, and the conditions prerequisite to it. However, they no longer call it by its traditional name, since 'revolution' is considered to be a word of undesirable associations, especially in the United States. Instead, following the lead of the American Professor Rostow, the word 'take-off' is used. From one point of view the awakened interest in the crucial and (*pace* Rostow) revolutionary series of events is to be welcomed. It represents a reaction against the tendency among economic historians for several decades to play down or deny the crucial character of these changes by denying that there was anything that could be called a unique collection of interconnected and decisive changes, or by emphasising their gradualness and their extension in time. Moreover, renewed interest in the question has derived from discussion of the problems of underdeveloped countries, of the obstacles that exist there to the start of an industrialising process and of how the conditions for 'a truly self-reinforcing growth process' (Rostow) can be contrived. Professor Rostow speaks of 'seeking to isolate a period when the scale of productive economic activity reaches a critical level and produces changes which lead to a massive and progressive structural transformation in economies and the societies of which they are part, better viewed as changes in kind than merely in degree'.[1]

On the other hand, revival of interest in this crucial period has been accompanied by such a narrowed focus in viewing economic factors and economic problems as to make analysis of it a matter of mechanics rather than of history (as the very use of the term 'take-off' implies). The concept of Industrial Revolution as the

[1] W. W. Rostow, *The Stages of Economic Growth*, Cambridge, 1961, p. 40.

inauguration of a mature and developed stage of capitalism is thus emasculated; and the bashful change of terminology turns out to have been far from accidental. Attention is concentrated, in the first place, on a narrow set of readily quantifiable 'economic' factors, such as national product, trade returns, investment ratio, employment. This is part of the fashionable obsession with reducing historical development to statistical series. Secondly, the economic factors so defined are virtually endowed with a momentum of their own, and treated in isolation from such socio-economic factors as property relations and labour relations—the whole group of conditions and influences of which Marx spoke as the structure of class relations—the relevance of which is by implication denied. Indeed, it is a prime intention of Professor Rostow in his writings on growth to demonstrate that there is a universal sequence of stages in economic development quite independent of institutional differences and social structures (although there are some vague references to 'the existence of an institutional framework which exploits the impulses to expansion'). About the causation of development—why growth should proceed at different tempos at different times—he is again curiously vague. Here appeal is made to the mystery of various psychological 'propensities', such as the 'propensity to save' and the 'propensity to contrive'. This is to substitute verbal jugglery for interpretation.

There are still some who regard the Industrial Revolution, apparently, as the originator of capitalism. That it had extensive and crucial results for the structure of production and for the pattern of social life, as the name itself implies, is undoubtedly true: its concentration of production into relatively large-scale units (the factory, harnessed to mechanical power) and of population into the new industrial towns, its direct confrontation of Capital and Labour in the form of the captain of industry or the industrial company and the permanent wage-earner uprooted from the land and selling his labour-power as a commodity. Moreover, it unleashed a number of forces that were to give a new momentum to economic activity: technical innovation breeding new technical innovation under the spur of competition; capital accumulation by a snowball compound-interest process, ploughing back the fruit of capital investment into new investment. Yet, this climacteric is scarcely conceivable (except to those content with mysterious 'propensities') without a preceding stage of which this was the maturing and which laid the basis for it.

Subsequent research leaves little doubt that Marx was right when he spoke of capitalism as dating from the sixteenth century in England, 'although we came across the first beginnings of capitalist production as early as the fourteenth or fifteenth century sporadically in certain towns of the Mediterranean'. He might perhaps have added, had he known what we now do, Flanders and the Rhine district as examples of capitalism in these centuries. In what form, then, was capitalism already appearing at so early a date? I will confine myself to England, of which I am more competent (or less incompetent) to speak. Save exceptionally, it was not appearing at this date in large-scale forms. The records tell of a few cases of large-scale 'manufactories' like those of Jack of Newbery or Thomas Blanket of Bristol or William Stumpe in Wiltshire employing several hundred weavers in one building (if contemporary accounts do not exaggerate). As we have already noted on page 13 there were in Stuart times a number of new investments involving considerable capitals running into thousands in mining and some new industries; and at the *end* of the seventeenth century the English Copper Company had a capital approaching £40,000 divided into as many as 700 shares and a company known as Mine Adventure was trying to raise a capital of £100,000. But these were scarcely typical as yet, and were quite rare in the textile industry (at least in its main processes, apart from finishing). More characteristic of Tudor and Stuart England was the domestic or cottage industry organised on the 'putting-out' system, of which we have already spoken, on the initiative of 'merchant manufacturers' large or small. In the cloth industry the rise of merchant-employers dates from the fifteenth century, as is witnessed by occasional complaints of craft guilds in the towns about work being given to craftsmen dwelling outside the town boundaries and hence in evasion of the guild regulations about limitation of apprentices and control of entry to the trade. In the sixteenth century both the practice and the complaints multiplied; so much so that in the middle of the century Acts of Parliament were passed to restrict any further extension of weaving and cloth-making out-side 'a city, borough, town corporate or market town'. In the craft guilds of the time this movement coincided with attempts of the merchant-employer element to use their dominant position in the guild to subordinate the craft element to them and to nullify the traditional regulations about apprenticeship. Speaking of Europe generally, Dr Eric Hobsbawm has said (in an article to which we shall refer again) that 'as a general rule the transformation of crafts into "putting-out" industries began seriously during the boom of the later sixteenth century', and 'the seventeenth is clearly the century when such systems established themselves decisively'.[2]

The question arises as to why this domestic industry should have predominated over the large-scale manufactory at this period and should have lasted for so long. In the first place, it has to be borne in mind that before the invention of power-driven machinery there was little to be gained economically (i.e. from a productivity or a cost standpoint) in congregating workers together in large establish-ments. A somewhat improved division of labour, perhaps, some saving in transport expenses in delivering materials to craftsmen and collecting their work—that is about all the economy which concentration could have achieved. As long as the work was *indi-vidualised* in character, it could make little difference to the output rate whether the handicraftsmen worked side by side in one place or were scattered, each working in his own cottage or workshop.

An important contributory reason, if not the decisive one, is that, in England at any rate, labour available for wage employment outside its own village was still scarce; and it was scarce because even the poorest villagers still retained some attachment to the soil, even if a slender attachment. It is true that the Tudor period had migrant 'vagabonds and beggars' in considerable numbers (witness the brutal draconian legislation of the period), these being migrants uprooted by the earlier wave of 'enclosures', and possibly turned adrift by Henry VIII's spoliation and dissolution of the monasteries. Even so, their numbers were not large; and it seems probable that some part of them, at least, were in search of places where it was possible for cottagers to squat upon the commons or

[2] 'The General Crisis of the European Economy in the Seventeenth Century', *Past & Present*, No. 6, November 1954, p. 51.

on the edge of cultivated land, or to combine agricultural employment with some subsidiary employment. Moreover, legislation
sought to restrict the movement of labour in order to keep it
available for employment in the countryside (witness the Statute
of Artificers of 1563 which made service in agriculture compulsory
for unemployed persons and forbade hired servants to leave their
locality without a written licence). The fact that it was not easy to
obtain free labour in any quantity outside London and one or two
of the larger cities is suggested by the frequency with which compulsory impressment of labour was resorted to by large-scale
employers, for example capitalist entrepreneurs engaged in
mining.

A recent study of the location of handicraft industries in Tudor
and Stuart England has, indeed, suggested that their location was
commonly associated with the ratio of population to available land
in various districts and with the type of agriculture, according as
this affected the availability of labour, either seasonally or *in toto*,
for subsidiary employments.[3] According to this writer 'there seems
to be enough positive evidence to support the proposition that the
location of handicraft industries is . . . associated with certain
types of farming community and certain types of social organisation'. There is such an 'association between the rise of population
and pressure on the land in the sixteenth century and the rise of the
hand-knitting industry in the Yorkshire dales'; similarly with cloth-
making in Wiltshire and in Suffolk (where a weak manorial framework made possible a rapid growth of local population through
immigration from other districts). On the other hand, another
writer attributes the rise of the serge industry in Devonshire in
the seventeenth century, under the control of a few merchants of
the towns of Exeter and Tiverton, to the appearance of 'a considerable class of landless households'.[4] Somewhat analogously the
Polish historian Malowist finds a connection between the rise of
the cloth industry in Baltic countries in the fourteenth and fifteenth

[3] See Joan Thirsk's paper, 'Industries in the Countryside', in *Essays in
the Economic and Social History of Tudor and Stuart England in Honour
of R. H. Tawney*, edited by F. J. Fisher, Cambridge, 1961.
[4] W. G. Hoskins, *Industry, Trade and People in Exeter, 1688–1880*,
Manchester, 1935, pp. 12–14.

centuries and a crisis in agriculture,[5] and the question arises as to whether southern Germany and Italy provide similar examples.

We seem, therefore, to have this situation: that the rise of the first, predominantly domestic-handicraft, phase of capitalism owed its rise to the availability of cheap wage-labour, but to a *limited* availability of labour which still had some ties with the land. One could say that it was the product of a situation of *partial* proletarianisation; but so long as the labour force remained, for the most part, a *semi*-proletariat only, dispersed production of the domestic type, organised on a 'putting-out' basis, prevailed. Moreover, the small producer, as he retained some link with agriculture (if only as a small cottager or 'squatter'), so also he retained possession of the tools and implements of his handicraft.

This hold on the land and on his handicraft implements the craftsman of the domestic industry was eventually to lose. Starting as half-small-master and half-employee of the clothier or the capitalist putter-out, he was to become progressively more of an employee on a wage-contract. As regards his hold on the implements of production of his craft the main influences that loosened this hold were debt and the increasing complexity of these means of production themselves. Mantoux, historian of the English Industrial Revolution, speaks of the 'process of alienation, slow and unnoticed' as going on 'from the end of the seventeenth century'.[6] The craftsman's hold on land tended to be loosened by the increasing concentration of landholding in the course of the seventeenth and particularly the eighteenth century and through eviction by enclosures which reached a new *crescendo* towards the end of the eighteenth century. In the earlier half of the eighteenth century there was still complaint of shortage of labour; but some modern writers (e.g. Professor Chambers) have claimed that the rise in the natural rate of increase in the later decades of the century contributed more than did the enclosure movement to swelling the proletarian labour supply on the eve of the Industrial Revolution.

[5] M. Malowist, *Studia z Dziejow Rzemiosla w Okresie Kryzysu Feudalizmu w Zachodniej Europie w 14 i 15 Wieku*, Warsaw, 1954.
[6] P. J. Mantoux, *The Industrial Revolution in the Eighteenth Century*, London, 1928, p. 65.

In the evolution of the wage-labour : capital relationship within the system of domestic industry there are some interesting transitional stages which show the handicraftsman in process of conversion into a pure wage-earner. There were also gradations to be noticed at any one date within a given handicraft industry. Gaskell, for instance, an English writer of the time of the Industrial Revolution, speaks in his *Artisans and Machinery* of 'two very distinct classes . . . divided by a well-defined line of demarcation'. 'This division,' he goes on to explain, 'arose from the circumstance of their being landholders, or entirely dependent on weaving for their support. . . . The inferior class of artisans had at all times been sufferers from the impossibility of supplying themselves with materials for their labour.'

One fairly well-known example of these transitional forms was the hosiery industry. As early as 1589 there had been invented (by a Nottinghamshire curate called William Lee) a knitting frame, which although hand-operated and capable of being housed in a small workshop or room, was a complicated and fairly costly mechanism. Only fairly well-to-do master craftsmen were, therefore, in a position to own one. In the middle of the seventeenth century, however, a group of capitalists (drawn apparently from among merchant hosiers) secured incorporation as the Framework Knitters Company, and proceeded to hire out knitting frames to small craftsmen. In the following century there were complaints of 'shameless exactions on the workmen by their masters' through what seems to have been a monopolistic raising of frame-rents and the boycotting of such workmen as happened to own their own frames. In the cloth industry one finds weavers who fell into debt pledging their looms and finally surrendering them to the merchant and thereafter paying a rent for them. In the industry round Exeter which we have already mentioned, weavers in the eighteenth century often rented their looms from capitalists, and as a next step in the transition worked on the latter's own premises. Elsewhere in Devonshire there were examples of the weaver being compelled to 'live in the square of houses near the master's' and to do their work there.[7] In the old-established cloth industry of Wiltshire we hear in the first half of the eighteenth century of 'workers . . .

[7] Hoskins, op. cit., p. 55.

suffering from various oppressive practices', including truck payments, forming workers' associations and organising demonstrations that ended in riots.[8] Other much-quoted examples came from the iron trade, such as the industrial community of over a thousand inhabitants owned by a capitalist called Ambrose Crowley, where families worked in their own houses, but the houses and tools and materials alike were owned and supplied by Crowley, payment for work being made on a kind of piecework basis. Similar hybrid forms, half-factory, half-domestic-putting-out, probably characterised the famous Carron Iron Works in Scotland and parts of the Scottish weaving industry.

In laying emphasis on this labour situation as a primary influence, I do not wish to imply that one can handle the Industrial Revolution and its dating in terms of what one may call 'simple causation', or the causal influence of one single factor. Historical turning points of this kind obviously need to be interpreted in terms, rather, of 'complex causation'—of the simultaneous maturing of a whole situation, containing a group or collection of factors all of which are in some degree necessary if further and crucial change is to result. Something needs to be said about these other elements in the situation, the presence or absence of which could make a crucial difference to whether and when the early immature beginnings of capitalist production were able to make the transition to the fully developed capitalism of the nineteenth-century type.

This seems to be the place to mention an hypothesis advanced, in an interesting and stimulating manner, by Dr Eric Hobsbawm—that there was something which can be called an economic crisis over most of Europe in the seventeenth century: a crisis which itself represented a retardation in development of capitalism as it had flowered in the sixteenth century, and the very overcoming of which prepared the stage for the further breakthrough (Rostow's 'take-off') of the Industrial Revolution.

Dr Hobsbawm starts from what he regards as 'one of the fundamental questions about the rise of capitalism: why did the expansion of the later fifteenth and sixteenth centuries not lead straight

[8] J. DeLacy Mann in (edited by L. S. Pressnell), *Studies in the Industrial Revolution*, London, 1960, pp. 66 ff.

into the epoch of the eighteenth and nineteenth century Industrial Revolution? What, in other words, were the obstacles in the way of capitalist expansion?'[9] He thinks that there is 'a good deal of evidence for the "general crisis" ' and that 'it is perfectly clear that there *was* a good deal of retrogression in the seventeenth century'. A factor in this crisis and an obstacle to further growth on which he is inclined to lay special stress is the absence of a sufficiently large 'internal market'. There existed a restricted *luxury* market; but there was very little *mass* market; and the absence of the latter he is inclined to attribute to the fact that peasant production in agriculture remained predominantly *subsistence* farming (what was marketed being mainly devoted to raising money with which to pay rent, with little or no margin for buying industrial products in return). He writes: 'Except perhaps in England no "agrarian revolution" of a capitalist type accompanied industrial change, as it was to do in the eighteenth century; though there was plenty of upheaval in the countryside'; and he goes on to point out that in France the 'lords (often "bourgeois" who had bought themselves into feudal status) reversed the trend to peasant independence from the middle of the sixteenth century, and increasingly recovered lost ground'.[10] In other words, it was the slowness, or even failure, of capitalist relations to develop in agriculture that was a crucial retarding factor.

I am not competent to pass judgment on Dr Hobsbawm's claim about the evidence for an economic crisis in seventeenth-century Europe. Whether crisis or no, there seems to be a strong case for speaking of retrogression, or at least retardation, as regards the further development of capitalism. Of his particular emphasis—on markets, and in particular the agricultural market for industrial products—I will say only this. As I have elsewhere noted,[11] my own prejudice is to regard influences in the sphere of exchange (markets) as secondary to influences concerned with the social relations of production (e.g. the labour situation and the forces of production, technique, etc.). No one, however, could reasonably deny the importance of the growth of an internal market for the

[9] Op. cit., *Past & Present*, No. 5, May 1954, p. 39.
[10] Ibid., pp. 46–7.
[11] 'Transition from Feudalism to Capitalism', mentioned below.

development of capitalism: *vide* the importance attached to it by Lenin in his *Development of Capitalism in Russia*. Dr Hobsbawm is obviously quite right to stress its importance as one of the elements in the situation which needed to mature before the Industrial Revolution could occur. At the same time, in order to put this 'market factor' into correct perspective, one has to remember the emphasis which Lenin also laid upon the fact that the growth of an internal market was a product of the growth of capitalism itself—of growing social division of labour and growing labour productivity, yielding a surplus above the self-consumption or subsistence of the producers. Looked at in this way, I should regard what Dr Hobsbawm is emphasising as being the *other side* of those changing and developing relations of production to which I referred earlier. The stress he so rightly lays on agriculture draws attention to the important role played by developing capitalist relations in agriculture—by that process of social differentiation within the petty mode of production in agriculture which we have noted. The importance of this process viewed in one aspect appears as the growth of an internal market, in another aspect as the growth of a supply of wage-labour. Regarded in this light, 'the market' as a factor in development plays a different role from 'the market' as an *external* factor (independent and in a sense 'ultimate' and for that reason 'accidental') as this appears in Pirenne's theory of feudalism and as used by Sweezy.[12]

This is perhaps also the place to call attention to the so-called 'primitive accumulation of capital' to which Marx in *Capital* gave a prominent place in this early period of capitalism. The main instruments of this 'primitive accumulation' were direct and forcible appropriation of the property of small producers, of which the English land 'enclosures' afford the most vivid illustration. (Marx added also colonial loot and plunder, e.g. in the Orient). In its earlier period capitalism had need of such development to lay the basis for large-scale investment; once the foundations had been securely laid, further accumulation and expansion could proceed

---

[12] Cf. the Sweezy–Dobb debate, 'The Transition from Feudalism to Capitalism', *Science & Society*, Vol. XIV, No. 2, 1950; subsequently reissued as a booklet by *Science & Society* and by Fore Publications of London.

'normally' by the method of ploughing back the profits on existing capital in new investment.

The question at once arises as to what the essence of this process was. The word 'accumulation' implies the mere piling up of durable objects of wealth. In modern capitalism we have learned to visualise this as the constant creation of new means of production—industrial plants and equipment, means of communication, sources of power. But at the time of primitive beginnings fixed capital played a relatively minor role; investment was largely in stocks of more or less perishable raw materials or semi-finished goods; and the picture we have of accumulation (and as it has been represented by some writers) is that of a piling up of gold and silver plate or bullion, the building of country mansions or châteaux. Reflection creates an immediate doubt as to how such an accumulating process could aid the growth of capitalist production. May it not be, and has it not been at times, an actual *obstacle* by *diverting* wealth from productive investment? Is it not the case that gold and silver and *objets d'art* need to be *sold* before they can be made the means for investment in means of production—in other words, that their *dis*accumulation rather than their accumulation aids the growth of production?

I think we have to conclude that the essence of this preliminary and formative process cannot lie in the mere piling up of wealth (least of all in the form of barren precious metals and durable consumer goods). Take the case of land—land-purchase by the *parvenu* bourgeoisie: extension of the cultivated area by reclamation and drainage (e.g. in England the drainage of the Fens) is one thing; but a mere transfer of ownership of *existing* land can in no sense be treated as synonymous with the creation of real capital and with productive investment. Hence mere 'enrichment' cannot be treated (as Sombart, for example, was apt to do) as the essence of the process. Instead, we have to see it, not in a narrowly economic sense, but as a *social* process of *concentration* of ownership of existing assets: a concentration which had as its other aspect the *dispossession* of small producers. Thus viewed, it represents the progressive polarisation of society into the two modern classes of bourgeoisie and proletariat. This is a much fuller and more rounded historical conception than the simple creation of a few rich men.

CDP—C

Viewed concretely, one aspect of this process was reflected in the centuries of feudal decline, bourgeois enrichment, mainly in the hands of merchant capital, at the expense of feudal wealth, on the one hand (a transfer considerably aided and accelerated by the price inflation of the sixteenth century) and of the small peasant producer and craftsman, on the other hand. But this stage of the process, as we have seen, was not of itself enough. Bourgeois wealth so acquired was not necessarily used to promote the growth of production. Too often it sheltered behind and preserved surviving forms of feudal privilege, adapting these to its own ends, and even promoted a measure of feudal reaction and restoration, as in seventeenth-century France and Germany, or financed predatory commercial ventures overseas. A further deepening and extension of the process was needed in the shape of social polarization of the petty mode of production itself, especially in agriculture, and the enrichment and promotion from it of a numerous, active, thrifty *kulak* class (with the pushful, self-reliant qualities of the Artamanovs of Gorky's trilogy), simultaneously with the formation of a dispossessed class of potential wage-labourers. A too early and too great subordination of the petty mode of production to the big bourgeoisie of merchant capital might actually retard and smother the latter process: this is one of the paradoxes of capitalist development which many have been slow to appreciate.

In representing this formative period as a many-sided, interdependent internal process of development, I do not wish to deny the part played by foreign commerce and the export trade. This was undoubtedly an important influence, and is in a sense a separate story on its own—a story of bourgeois enrichment of whole countries or regions (for example, France and Holland and then England) at the expense of other regions, such as the Orient and India—or the small producers of the new transatlantic colonies of the period. This is one way, in particular, in which the national States of the period aided the process of primitive accumulation. All I wish to plead is that one should not get foreign commerce and the stimulating effect of export markets out of focus, giving to them exaggerated importance. (In 1700 the total tonnage of outgoing vessels from all English ports was scarcely more than 300,000.) Still less should one try to write the whole story of capitalist development in these terms. In this connection it is noteworthy that Mercantilism as a policy and a theory of this period was centred on the notion of national enrichment through State-regulated trade. As applied to stimulation of the demand for exports by protecting export markets from competition and limiting the intrusion of imports into home markets, it was simply the old laws of the Merchant Staple and the monopolistic rules of the Hansa or Company of Merchant Adventurers writ large in State policy: a policy of ensuring a sufficient degree of monopoly in markets of sale and markets of purchase to turn the terms of trade to the advantage of one's own trading community. Incidental to it was that 'fear of goods' which Heckscher, the historian of Mercantilism, thought to be so characteristic of this doctrine. In this connection may be noticed those striking modern parallels to it in the trading policies of our modern monopoly age with their lust for export surpluses, protected 'spheres of influence', regulated sales quotas and (in the conditions of modern capitalism) the all-pervading 'fear of productive capacity' in extension of Heckscher's 'fear of goods'.

In discussion of the process of capital accumulation in this period a further question has arisen which is deserving of mention. We have pointed out that in so far as previous enrichment was instrumental in preparing the Industrial Revolution, there must have been a final stage of 'realisation'. Was there in fact any such stage: a stage in which forms of bourgeois wealth previously accumulated were sold or realised in order to find the means for investing in industry and financing the new instruments of production of the period of technical innovation? If there was no such phase, then it would seem as though the whole notion of enrichment *per se* as a precursor of industrial revolution must be dismissed as a myth. I am not myself aware of any evidence that would enable one to answer this question. Evidence may possibly be lacking for the simple reason that until recently no one has posed this question and sought to answer it. But there is a general consideration which has some bearing upon it. If there had been a *general* tendency at any time to sell a particular type of asset (say, gold and silver plate or country houses), then these would have lost value for lack of buyers, and this very fall in value would have inhibited their sale. On the other hand, if the market for such assets had been supported by a plenitude of buyers of them— buyers who constituted presumably a new and rising *parvenu* bourgeois stratum—then prime significance would have attached to the enrichment of the latter, since it would have been they who were providing (at one remove) the investible funds for financing the Industrial Revolution.

My own inclination is, accordingly, to conclude that mere bourgeois enrichment *per se* two centuries earlier could have contributed little to the rise and extension of factory industry. Such a conclusion will have added plausibility if we remember that, in England at any rate, the new techniques were pioneered mainly by small men, often by previous small masters of the handicraft industry with comparatively little capital at their personal disposal. (Mining, on the other hand, and some early metal production was apt to be financed by local landowners.) What remains true, however, is that many of these pioneers of factory industry would have been severely restricted in their endeavours, initially at any rate, if there had not been some credit network (whether trade credit or bank credit) whereby capital was transferred to their hands. We know that many early enterprises (including that of Watt, one of the inventors of the steam engine) were handicapped for lack of capital. In the cotton industry a common source of funds for entrepreneurs of the new factory industry was cotton merchants of Liverpool with whom they had trade connections (one branch of the Rothschild family being engaged for a time in financing the Liverpool cotton trade). In other words, it was necessary that the innovating type of capitalist entrepreneur, or the potential innovator, should either himself be in possession of sufficient capital or else have easy access to loanable funds (through partnership or credit) in order to finance the new type of productive enterprise. As to the source of such funds and such financing, it seems to me that we still have too little detailed information to be in a position to generalise at all confidently.

How then are we to summarise the conditions (themselves composing a complex historical situation) the maturing of which explains the occurrence of the Industrial Revolution and the peculiar dating of it? Speaking again in terms of England as the classic case, there was, firstly, the maturing of capitalist relations in agriculture, the emergence of a class of considerable farmers, cultivating their 'enclosed' and improved farms with wage-labour; and a process of progressive concentration of land ownership in the course of the seventeenth and eighteenth centuries. The early decades of the eighteenth century saw something of a technical revolution in agricultural methods (largely pioneered by progressive landlords or large farmers like Jethro Tull and Townshend and Robert Bakewell and Thomas Coke), which served to increase productivity and to swell that marketable surplus of agricultural products to feed a growing urban population upon which modern theoretical discussion about preconditions of industrialisation have focused attention. Even so, wheat prices rose after 1760 and England became on balance a net importer of wheat by the end of the century. As twin products of these developments in agriculture went an expanding internal market (aided by extensive development of roads and of canals in the second half of the century) and the formation of a proletariat such as had not existed two centuries before. To the latter development the demographic situation in eighteenth-century England apparently contributed. Labour had become sufficiently plentiful to facilitate investment in factory production, but yet not so cheap as to leave no incentive to the introduction of labour-saving techniques.

Secondly, there had been developing over the seventeenth and eighteenth centuries, as we have seen, a broadly based handicraft industry with clearly-marked and developing wage-labour : capital relationships within it. Nurtured by this incipient capitalism of the domestic handicraft industry was a whole tribe of small ambitious entrepreneurs, possessed of initiative, close acquaintance with production and of small-sized or moderate-sized capitals, also of trade connections sufficient to supplement their own capital with credit from merchants.

Thirdly, to a widening internal market was to be added a rapid growth of export trade in eighteenth-century England. In this century England enjoyed an unusually strong commercial position, having succeeded to a number of the advantages enjoyed in the seventeenth century by Holland and after her by France; and although the straitjacket of Mercantilism was eventually to become a drag upon the expansion of trade (as Adam Smith arraigned it), there is little doubt that it contributed for some time to the profitableness of foreign commerce for those directly or indirectly connected with it. For at least some part of the eighteenth century (and often for the major part) trade in the main articles of commerce all showed a rising tendency: a rising tendency in trade which both reflected and simultaneously provided the impulse to increased production.

Perhaps as in part a by-product of this commercial prosperity of England we have the further fact that in the second half of the eighteenth century there was a considerable influx of Dutch capital to London. The immediate destination of most of these funds seems to have been investment in British Government bonds of the period. We do not know the extent to which Dutch investment in this way set free British capital for investment in industry that might otherwise have been absorbed into Government bonds. But it is a possibility that I think must be borne in mind.

There is a final question of interest to those who are specially concerned with the problems of underdeveloped countries or regions. How far do historical analogies drawn from the past of capitalism apply to such countries today? To what extent must one regard any of the aforementioned preparatory processes and preconditions as necessary prerequisites for industrialisation and economic growth in the underdeveloped countries of our present century? Can industry equipped with modern techniques only grow there to the extent that small-scale production, especially in agriculture, is first of all subordinated and exploited, enrichment of a *kulak* class is facilitated and something resembling Marx's 'primitive accumulation of capital' is promoted?

So far as the dispossession on which we have touched and the creation of a surplus population is concerned, most underdeveloped countries, at any rate in Asia and in Latin America, are characterised by large reserves of actual unemployed or by so-called 'disguised unemployment'. The problem essentially is that both existing industry and the rate of investment are too small to absorb these reserves of labour into employment. Lack of the will or the incentive or the means to invest (or some mixture of all three) is apparently the crux of the prevailing stagnation. But there is one element in the situation today which sharply differentiates the position of such countries from that of European countries three centuries ago standing at the threshold of capitalism. It is the possibility of State investment: of the State, by conscious intent and policy, framed in the national interest, mobilising economic resources and directing them towards the fulfilment of a State-controlled development plan, thereby providing the crucial impetus to growth that was previously lacking. It is even conceivable that development occurring in this way under the aegis of State Capitalism may succeed in by-passing altogether the capitalist stage of development as history has known it hitherto. But whether this is possible or likely or not will, of course, depend on the political character of the State in question and of the particular economic and class interests it serves. If we are to draw historical lessons from the past in order to illuminate problems of economic backwardness in the twentieth century, it must be with crucial reservations such as this in mind and with full awareness of historical differences of this kind.

Three

Some features of capitalism since the First World War

In this lecture I can hope to do no more, at best, than indicate a few features of the contemporary scene that strike one as novel, or significant or that have been the subject of discussion; to discuss them at all exhaustively or even to defend their selection, is impossible.

I scarcely need remind you, perhaps, that there are some who have claimed that capitalism in the twentieth century has undergone a sufficient transformation to have become an entirely different system, bearing little resemblance in its major features and its social tendencies to the capitalism of last century. Two American authors of a famous study of ownership in the interwar years,[1] while emphasising the growth (with the modern corporation) of 'a concentration of economic power which can compete on equal terms with the modern State . . . and may possibly supersede it', spoke also of a 'dissolution of the old atom of ownership into its component parts, control and beneficial ownership'—a dissolution which 'destroys the very foundation on which the economic order of the past three centuries has rested'. Mr Berle has more recently written a book entitled the *Twentieth Century Capitalist Revolution*. The English writer John Strachey has spoken of 'a new and distinct stage of our extant economic system' in which 'the laws of development of the older stage of the system no longer fully apply to the new stage'.[2] Of the so-called 'Managerial Revolution', at which Berle and Means hinted and which Burnham[3] was later to develop into a gospel, I have written on several occasions; and I will not repeat my verdict here, except to say quite summarily

[1] Adolf A. Berle, Jr, and Gardiner C. Means, *The Modern Corporation and Private Property*, New York, 1933.
[2] *Contemporary Capitalism*, London, 1956, p. 21.
[3] James Burnham, *The Managerial Revolution*, New York, 1941.

that, while some divorce of ownership and control is characteristic of the modern large joint stock company or corporation, it is nothing like so extensive or complete as the Burnhamites like to maintain, and its significance certainly does not amount to a social revolution.

It goes without saying, of course, that the modern business corporation is something very different as a form of economic and financial organisation from the business partnership or one-man business of the nineteenth-century type. And its growth has had some important consequences. From one aspect it is a product of the growing concentration of capital and ownership that is characteristic of this monopolistic age—product of the need to finance and to administer large-scale units. (We may recall that the American Federal Trade Commission announced that the 113 largest manufacturing corporations owned in 1946 almost a half of the 'property, plant and equipment employed in manufacturing'.) From another aspect this form of organisation itself facilitates the process of concentration, giving scope for mobilising capital in large aggregations and for such financial devices as holding companies and the 'pyramiding' of holding companies, 'take-over bids' and mergers. It certainly breeds an extensive bureaucracy of business executives, power-conscious and bent on aggrandisement, but still servants of the profit motive and not scorners of it, and by no means having a distinctive (allegedly non-capitalist) class interest of their own. What may be true of their financial strategies and of the motives influencing them is that they tend to plan investment policy with a fairly long time-horizon to their view and that they may attach more importance to business gains accruing as increment of capital values than as annually declared dividends. In times of prosperity, and more generally in periods of inflation, large corporations can accumulate financial reserves, which render them largely independent of banks and of monetary policy, and even of the capital market, and provide a basis for the 'internal financing' that has been such a feature of business finance since the Second World War.

One outstanding feature of a rather different kind is worth mention, concerning the relations on a world scale between the most advanced capitalist countries and the less advanced. For most of the nineteenth century capitalism widened its boundaries by the classic method of capital moving from sectors or geographical regions where the rate of profit was relatively low to where the rate of profit was relatively high. Capital thus *migrated*, as well as labour, as it did from England in the course of the nineteenth century across the Atlantic to America (both north and south), largely to finance railway building, and to India; and later from France and Germany into Eastern and South-eastern Europe. But in the monopoly age which has grown up since the end of last century, backward areas of the world, where capitalism was un-developed or weakly developed, came increasingly to be treated as colonial (or semi-colonial) preserves, like the colonies of the old Mercantilist period. Investment of capital in them was apt to have a bias towards the production of primary products for export to serve the needs of industries in the advanced metropolitan countries; and such capitalist development as was encouraged there tended to take the form of industrial enclaves geared primarily to export and constituting appendages of the metropolitan economy rather than self-developing elements of the colonial economy itself. The outstanding (and extreme) example of this is investment today in oil production; but there are analogous examples in the invest-ment by big monopoly groups, e.g. in the United States, in the exploitation of various minerals in various parts of the world. (Other examples are British capital in Rhodesian copper and Belgian in Katanga.) Thus, most advanced industrial countries have satellite economies attached to them, and the inequality between developed industrial countries and the underdeveloped have tended to get greater rather than less. As the well-known Polish economist, Oskar Lange, has put it:

> Investment in underdeveloped countries of capital from the highly developed countries acquired a specific character. It went chiefly into the exploitation of natural resources to be utilised as raw materials by the industries of the developed countries and into developing food production to feed the population of the developed capitalist coun-tries. . . . In consequence, the economies of the underdeveloped countries became one-sided, raw material and food-exporting econo-mies. The profits which were made by foreign capital in these countries were used not for re-investment in these countries but were exported

back to the countries where the capital came from. . . . This is the essential reason why the underdeveloped countries were not capable of following the classical capitalist path of economic development.[4]

How far this monopolistic relationship between metropolitan economy and satellite economy is reflected in a movement in the terms of trade between industrial countries and primary producing ones is not easy to say, since such movements are a complex result of changes in production costs (due to changes in productivity) and of shifts in the relationship of selling-prices to production costs. Most studies in terms-of-trade movement have failed to separate out these two distinct influences. In the interwar period the terms of trade went markedly in favour of industrial products, resuming the trend apparent in the final decades of the nineteenth century. It seems fairly clear that this partly reflected an increase in agricultural productivity (also some extension of cultivated acreage) and partly the monopolistic influence of industrial cartels in output restriction and price maintenance. For a number of years after the Second World War the terms of trade moved back in the opposite direction; since then it has fluctuated from time to time, mainly under the influence of short-period shifts in demand from the leading industrial countries. One of the recent sharp movements against the primary producing countries followed in the wake of the American 'recession' of 1957-8 when it was estimated that the primary producing countries lost some two billion dollars per annum (or as much as the total of loans from the International Bank for Reconstruction and Development over the previous six years). Whether behind these movements there is a trend, and if so in what direction, it is difficult at present to say.

If we divide the period of four decades with which we are concerned into two halves, we shall find one rather striking contrast between the interwar period and the period since the Second World War. The former witnessed the world-wide economic crisis of 1929-31, a crisis of unexampled severity during which the capitalist order suffered the most severe shock it has received apart from wartime. During the latter period no crisis approaching pre-war ones in severity has shown itself to date, and leading countries

[4] *Economic Development, Planning, and International Cooperation*, London and New York, 1963, pp. 10-11.

of Western Europe and America have generally suffered from persistent inflationary pressures rather than from deflationary ones. This is not to say that the so-called 'trade cycle' has disappeared and become a phenomenon of past history. There have, indeed, been four downturns in sixteen years—more frequently than ever before. But these downturns (or 'recessions' as it is fashionable to call them—in 1948-9, 1953-4, 1957-8 and 1960-1 in America) have been shallower and much more short-lived, not only by comparison with 1929, but by comparison with what had come to be considered normal prior to the First World War. Whether this is something temporary or is more than temporary, it certainly requires explanation. I believe that phrases like 'deformation of the cycle', and their attendant expectation that a new 1929 is just over the horizon, are *wrong*.

Looking again at our period as a whole, we notice two crucial developments which, it would seem, must inevitably have affected the working of the economic system in some major respects. Although these developments have frequently been the subject of comment in recent discussion, they evidently deserve some further attention from us here. I refer, firstly, to the fairly radical changes that have occurred in the technique of industry—changes which amount, I believe, to something like a technical revolution; and secondly to the much enlarged role in the economy played by the State.

As regards the first of these changes: it is a commonplace that the epoch of so-called 'mass production' methods started in the United States about the time of the First World War, after which they spread somewhat tardily and unevenly to the leading industrial countries of Europe, including Britain. The decade following the First World War also witnessed the rise of numerous new products and new industries, largely the offspring of modern chemistry (e.g. new synthetic products and fibres) and of the invention of the internal combustion engine. It is a curious feature of American statistical series of production and employment that the year 1919 constituted, apparently, a watershed. In the decades prior to this, expanded production had come predominantly from an expansion in the labour force, with higher productivity per man playing a subordinate role. After 1919 the roles were apparently reversed, and the expansion of production of the 1920's (a decade of American boom) was built mainly on higher productivity. Indeed, employment in *manufacturing* industry actually *fell* during the 1920's, even though there was a more than compensating rise in employment in other sectors such as services and distribution. This was the decade when so-called 'technological unemployment' became a leading theme of economic writing. Evidently something was happening either to the methods of production in individual industries or to the relative weight of different industries to exert a more labour-saving bias than before. Yet another curious fact is that statisticians are apt to choose this date as an indicator of when the capital–output ratio began (as they claim) to *fall*. (This ratio is, of course, not the same as the capital–labour ratio, or what Marx calls the 'organic composition of capital', the former being the ratio of capital to labour divided by the product per unit of labour.) But in an attempt to measure the movement of the composition of capital from decade to decade, Dr Joseph M. Gillman has cited 1919 as a turning point, after which he thinks that the composition of capital also began to fall.[5] If he is right, then the capital–output ratio must have fallen by more than the rise of labour productivity: either technical change or shifts in relative importance of different sectors and industries must have had what economists have called a 'capital-saving' bias. For this there are two possible reasons: that the new techniques involved in some way more simple or more economical equipment, or that capital goods had been abnormally cheapened because this sector of industry had been the main beneficiary of recent technical improvements.

These changes in methods of production between the wars can largely be regarded, I suggest, as a preliminary stage or threshold stage to the automation movement of which so much has been talked and written since the Second World War. I realise that the term 'automation' is variously used by different writers, and it is not easy to draw a line and say that beyond it automation begins. Automation in the full and complete sense of total supersession by the machine (with electronic controls and feed-back mechanisms) of human handling and control remains limited in its application, and its extensive adoption can be regarded as still a matter of the

[5] Cf. *The Falling Rate of Profit*, New York, 1958.

future. None the less, I think there can be no doubt that automation as a tendency—as a movement *towards* automatic control of
work-processes as well as the mechanisation of material-handling—
has set the tone and the pace for the extensive innovation and
re-equipment of industrial processes during the past decade, which
has constituted something of a technical epoch. I cannot help
thinking that this has had a good deal to do with intensifying the
investment booms of the 1950's, especially that of 1954–7 in the
United States and Western Europe, and in France, Italy and West
Germany in 1959–61. True, large-scale military expenditures have
been the largest single factor in causing the inflationary pressures
of the postwar period; but the stimulus of technical innovation
would seem to have been an important secondary influence, as a
boost to private business investment even at times when defence
expenditure was stationary or falling. At the same time, this very
drive to deepen and extend productive capacity has brought in its
train widespread excess capacity, which is showing signs, particularly in the United States, of acting as a drag upon further
expansion. Once more we have the phenomenon of output growing
in face of stationary employment, and signs even of the growth rate
of output (in the United States and Britain at least) declining.

   To come to the second of our two developments: State interference with the working of the economic system is, of course,
nothing new. It played a significant role in the early phase of
capitalism—during what Adam Smith called the period of the
Mercantile System and Marx the epoch of primitive accumulation.
In conditions of modern 'war economy' it is bound to assume a
prominent role once more. (It may be remembered that at the end
of the First World War Lenin was already speaking of elements of
State Monopoly Capitalism, as he termed it, in the contemporary
war economy, especially of Germany.) The prominence of war
economy in the present epoch (and during the past fifteen years of
a chronic 'Cold War economy') is no doubt a principal reason why
the economic functions of the State in the present century have
assumed dimensions altogether different from anything in the age
of *laissez-faire* and economic liberalism of the nineteenth century.

   While even in peacetime there was a good deal of State intervention during the interwar period (for instance, the law on

compulsory cartellisation and wage control in Nazi Germany, on the one hand, and President Roosevelt's New Deal in the United States, on the other), there is plenty of justification, I think, for regarding it as having reached since the Second World War something different both in extent and in kind. Moreover, State intervention today wields new instruments in its attempts to regulate and to steer the economy—some would call them the invention of Keynesian economics which politicians and bureaucrats have learned to use; but I do not think they can be explained simply as the artifact of an economic theory. Of course, there is considerable variation in different countries in both the extent and the forms of these elements of 'controlled economy' superimposed upon an essentially individualistic (perhaps one should say 'oligopolistic') market economy. There is, for example, more direct control of production and State ownership of capital in Italy and in Britain than there is in the United States or in West Germany. But, generally speaking, direct control over, or participation in, production is relatively unimportant. What has assumed unprecedented dimensions is State *expenditures*, including investment expenditures by State companies or State Boards, and the influence which these exert on the market, even in the vaunted 'free economy' of the United States. The question arises whether this development is explicable solely in terms of war and military needs—of 'militarisation' of the economy even in time of 'peace'. Evidently military expenditure must have a prominent place in any explanation. But I am going to suggest that this cannot constitute the whole explanation.

It is, I think, scarcely open to serious dispute that in most countries (although not in all) the organised working class has emerged from the Second World War stronger than at any previous period. In the immediate postwar years in Europe, partly as a product of anti-Fascist resistance struggle, this was true of its political influence as well as of its economic organisation. (Since then in a number of countries, including Britain, its political influence has declined.) One result has been that in a number of countries, although again not in all, the standard of living of wage-earners has risen to a higher level than in the prewar period. This does not mean that the proportionate share of wage-earners in the national income has increased: it means that in the face of rising productivity the real earnings of labour have been raised without encroaching on the share of profits. At the same time employment has tended to be at a higher level than in the years of extensive unemployment in the 1930's. For both these reasons total consumption-demand has increased.

It is a familiar fact that in the classic period of capitalism in the days before the First World War, as indeed also between the two wars, the labour market was characterised by a chronic state of surplus supply—by the existence of a reserve army of labour. Labour scarcity or full employment was an exceptional occurrence, even in years of boom. Moreover, the maintenance of this reserve army was the classic method whereby any upward pressure of wage-rates at the expense of profits was resisted. For the system, the existence (or if need be the re-creation) of this reserve acted as an automatic safety-valve. A leading characteristic of the situation since the Second World War has been that, for a number of reasons (some of which we have already touched upon), this condition of the labour market has radically changed. The unemployed reserve army has shrunk compared with prewar days; and even where it has persisted, trade unions have been in a sufficiently strong position to maintain or even raise wages in the organised sectors of the economy. It is true that, in this respect, we have a far from uniform picture. There are considerable differences, between Britain where the unemployment percentage for much of the decade has been near to 1 per cent (now it has gone above 2 per cent) and in the United States where it has been for a considerable part of the time above 5 per cent; in Western Germany, at least until recently, there has been considerable unemployment owing to the so-called refugee problem, while in Italy there is the special situation of chronic underdevelopment in the south, with consequent migration from south to north. None the less, I submit that there is in most countries a significant qualitative difference from former times in the balance of economic and social relations, and that this difference, combined with the high level of demand in product markets (due to high government spending, a high level of investment and a raised level of consumption) underlies the inflationary situation which has become chronic over so large a part of the so-called 'Western world'. Today, it would seem, fairly constant inflationary pressure instead of periodic deflationary tides has become the rule.

To this I believe we have to add another and more political influence which, though difficult to measure, would be hard to overestimate. The coexistence in the world of two rival socio-economic systems cannot fail to exert a fairly profound influence on the operation of traditional institutions, policies and social relations. Memories of the shattering effects of the crisis of 1929–31 upon the stability of the existing order are still fairly fresh; and it is, I think, no exaggeration to say that the magnitude and per-sistence of mass unemployment at that time exerted a more weaken-ing effect on traditional institutions and social relations than did the collapse of capital values and of profits.

But inflation, of course, brings its own problems and contradic-tions, if of a somewhat different kind; and especially if it gets out of hand and becomes a cumulative process it can exert a shattering effect on a market economy. In a country so dependent on foreign trade as is Britain, it holds the threat of recurring balance-of-payments crises; and these in turn, by encouraging speculative movements of foreign balances ('hot money'), exert a strongly destabilising effect on foreign exchange rates and international trade relations. Even at a milder stage than this, inflation can have drastic effects both upon the pattern of production and on the distribution of wealth and income. In its way it can be regarded as being as much an instrument of class struggle as was traditionally the existence of an unemployed reserve army, even though in the kind of setting here described it may appear, for the time being, a safer way of pruning the share of labour in total income to allow prices to rise than to force a reduction of money wage rates.

How does all this concern the tendency towards increased inter-ference by governments in the economy? I think one can say that it is because of these novel problems pushed to the forefront in a period of inflationary pressures—and because in the sphere of exchange relations (i.e. money and price relations) inflationary pressure can constitute a knife-edge instability—that government action is called for in an attempt to keep this instability within bounds. Needless to say, this does not imply that in taking such action the State operates as some neutral agency raised above a society of conflicting class and sectional interests, as instrument of some *mystique* of 'the interest of society as a whole'. Least of all could such a notion make sense in a society characterised by so great a concentration of economic power as is the society of today. However, even among warring monopoly groups (or oligopolists) there may be some consciousness of common interest in maintaining certain stability conditions as *sine qua non* of the system's survival. And in matters affecting the basic social production relations the policies pursued in capitalist societies have always shown a stubbornly conservative bias in face of signs of danger. An historical hypothesis which I once tentatively suggested is that periods of history characterised by actual or apprehended labour scarcity have been those when State policy has moved in the direction of economic regulation, and the spirit of economic liberalism has thrived only in periods when labour was sufficiently plentiful, or otherwise weak and compliant, to present no threat to the traditional stability of the labour market.[6] Put in this way, perhaps, such an hypothesis is an oversimplification even if it is not inconsistent with historical facts. In any case, it was advanced as no more than a hypothesis deserving of further enquiry. But if there is any truth at all in it, the present obviously qualifies for inclusion among periods when regulation of the economy by the State could be expected to increase: regulation which, although by no means confined to control of wages, will tend to regard the imposition of a ceiling on the rise of real wages as the fulcrum of its activities and its central (if unacknowledged) *raison d'être*.

I should like to conclude this paper with an observation of a rather different and more general character—different though connected with what has just been said. I believe that we have to recognise the present age as being one in which a dividing line can no longer be drawn (if it ever could be) between economic problems and political problems. A hundred years ago economists at least thought that they could achieve such a separation, and in the theories which they constructed of a competitive market system, operating 'automatically' according to special laws of its own, they

[6] See my *Studies in the Development of Capitalism*, London, 1946, pp. 23–4.

sought to create an 'autonomous' economic sphere of this kind. Those were the days when the economic functions of the State were minimised, and all relationships could be conceived of as contractual, products of a free market—even to the extent of ignoring social factors, such as property institutions, of which market relations were the reflection. But today it is manifest that most economic problems, involving as they are bound to do, not only the question of State action in some form, but the distribution of income, monopoly rights and property values, are *ipso facto* political problems. This interpenetration of political issues with economic factors has varied in degree in different historical epochs. Only the age of *laissez-faire* was to introduce the notion that money ruled all things and possession of capital was the sole measure of power and privilege.

Today we have not turned full circle, but I suggest that we have partly done so—turned back from what the English legal theorist Dicey would have called contract to status. This consideration is relevant for analysing or estimating business motivation: this may be at one time a mixture of profit maximisation in the simple sense and of motives of power and prestige. K. W. Rothschild in writing some years ago about theories of monopoly output and prices suggested that such theorising should preferably be cast in terms of military strategy rather than in the traditional terms of Bertrand and Cournot. 'The separation of the economic from the political', he wrote, 'must necessarily result in a very incomplete picture, which will not suffice for giving us a reasonable explanation of oligopoly price.'[7] The consideration is relevant to inflationary and deflationary policies and their comparative effects to which we referred earlier, as it is indeed to all questions of wage and price movements, and of shifts in productivity and in the other distributive shares in national income. It is relevant also to estimating both the feasibility and the effects of government policies: least of all can such policies today be regarded abstractly apart from the particular social interests which actuate them and whose ends they serve.

Thus alike at the level of national policy and of the large business enterprise or the cartel, methods of rivalry have long since passed

[7] *Economic Journal*, September 1947, p. 317.

beyond the traditional economic competition of the textbooks. Today they involve not only vast expenditures on propaganda campaigns and the 'psychological warfare' of the 'image creators' and the 'hidden persuaders', but such quasi-political, quasi-military measures as the elimination or browbeating of rivals, the creation of protected markets and privileged 'spheres of interest', and weapons such as the tying contract and the organised boycott. This is not to mention the competition for government contracts which are such an important market factor today. While in international economic relations Cold War motives clearly dominate, for example in export prohibitions and the political strings attaching to 'aid' and credits, there lies inherent in the formation of trade blocs and in currency and exchange policies a struggle for economic hegemony strongly reminiscent of two or three centuries ago, or even earlier. There was a time when the trading patriciate of Venice warred with that of Genoa, and Genoa with Pisa, and Florence warred with Siena and Pisa. Is it altogether fanciful to see the story of these rivalries writ large in the trading blocs and commercial and investment rivalries of the world today?

One thing can be said, I think, with some assurance: although the days of colonialism are by no means over (as recent events have shown), the days when the great industrial powers surrounded themselves with satellite economies—an underdeveloped primary-producing hinterland dependent on a highly developed 'metropolis'—are clearly passing, and with them is passing the old international division of labour between industrial and agricultural countries. Already this is evidenced by current international trade figures, which show that much the larger share of the trade of the highly industrialised countries is with *other* industrialised countries. This is not, of course, to say that international division of labour will disappear and individual countries tend to autarky: there are other patterns of international division of labour than the traditional one. But the change is bound to have important repercussions on the differential advantages and the terms of trade which the richer and more advanced economies formerly enjoyed. What the probable effects will be on the economic situation of such countries cannot be here explored. But the other side of the picture, as regards the previously backward, predominantly agrarian or primary-producing areas of the world, is already becoming apparent. In the coming decade or decades a growing number of previously underdeveloped countries are likely to take the road of independent industrial development, and in doing so to adopt both new social and economic forms and rates and patterns of economic growth quite different from the traditional ones. That their development path will be a simple imitation of that followed in the industrial revolutions of a century to a century-and-a-half ago is highly unlikely. In certain major respects it is bound to be different. (Here in particular I suggest that the generalisations and 'analogies' of a Rostow reveal themselves as essentially *un*historical.) What shape this development will have is sure to place its unique imprint, almost more than any other single factor, upon the character of the closing decades of the twentieth century (if the world survives to see them).

Two

Some aspects of economic development

These were two (of three) lectures delivered in January–
February 1951 at the Delhi School of Economics and
published as Occasional Paper No. 3 of that School.
They are here reproduced by kind permission of the
Delhi School of Economics, University of Delhi, India.

One

Economic development and its momentum under capitalism

In attempting to say anything that is worth saying about problems of economic development in various settings one must necessarily select one's theme with an eye towards a fairly drastic economy of words and of time. In so doing one may well give the impression of an abstraction which does injustice to reality. In other contexts I should be the first and most vehement in denying that economic factors, in particular factors in development, can be separated from their social background and from political implications. Yet in these three lectures I must of necessity make such a separation to a large extent, and can select for your attention certain strands only of economic development. I hope that, in dealing with *economic* development *per se*, the connection between it and the social and political background of events will not be absent from the picture: I intend to refer to this from time to time at places where that connection is of special significance. But it seemed advisable to mention the matter at the outset lest any of my audience should think I had forgotten it or should be in danger of overlooking it themselves.

It should perhaps be further added by way of explanation that in this first lecture, concerning the momentum of development in a capitalist economy, I shall be referring largely to British experience, both as the classic case of capitalist economy in its earlier stages and as the example upon which I am most capable of commenting. I am aware that this may restrict the interest of what I am going to say for an Indian audience and that what is said may require some qualification in its application to the environment of countries of Asia.

There are three main dynamic factors to which economists have given attention. Historically the first of these to be emphasised was the division of labour, which formed the cornerstone of Adam

Smith's study of the causes of the *Wealth of Nations*: a book which was written when the Industrial Revolution was still young and the division of labour rather than machinery accordingly appeared as the main factor upon which the productive power of labour, and its increase, depended. Secondly, there was the accumulation of capital, regarded initially as the amassing of funds with which employment could be given to labourers (the 'subsistence-fund' or 'advances to labourers' of classical Political Economy), and later as the creation of instruments of production, or mechanical equipment, in growing complexity and abundance. Finally there was technical change: the continual process of invention by which the mechanical instruments available as aids to labour were progressively extended and improved.

To a large extent, of course, these three factors are interdependent, and are facets of a single organic process of development. The second and third of them are specially close in their interconnection; so much so as to have led some to regard them as virtually one. I must say that there seems to me to be a great deal to be said for this view. While one can speak on the one hand of something like an autonomous growth of technical knowledge, product of the growth of science and research independently of growth of capital, the *application* of such knowledge in the concrete form of industrial improvements seems to have been overwhelmingly the product of *economic* initiative: i.e. it seems in the past to have been predominantly the result of deliberate searching by the entrepreneur for ways of ousting competitors and enhancing his profits. As regards capital accumulation *per se*: in the days of the Industrial Revolution, when the new capitalist industry was expanding at the expense of earlier forms of production (e.g. handicraft), and this expansion was feeding upon growing reserves of labour recruited from the decay of handicraft industry and the small producer, it was natural to think of capital accumulation as an independent process whereby growing funds of working capital were provided to enable a growing labour army to be set to work. Machinery and its improvement was then treated as something quite separate, even incidental (as what some modern methodologists would call an 'exogenous' change of 'data'). In more recent times such a separation is much less plausible. Deliberate searching by entrepreneurs for methods of cost-reduction nowadays takes the form, in large businesses at least, of financing research into particular projects; while the entry of new firms into an industry is increasingly associated with the introduction of some new process of manufacture or some new product or product-model rather than with a simple multiplication of existing processes. Thus technical innovation can, and should, I believe, be treated as the product or accompaniment of growth of capital; and the two processes in their forward movement can be regarded, without much damage to truth, as virtual Siamese twins.

A theoretical consequence of doing this, of some importance, is that new investment is regarded as generally involving some *qualitative* change in the coefficients of production as well as a quantitative change in the existing stock of capital (the fact that it does so is, incidentally, an added reason why this quantitative change in capital eludes measurement). Although it is not denied that new investment *can* take the form of what has been termed a mere 'widening' of capital of a given type, the possibilities of this at any given time are regarded as very limited, at any rate in face of a given level of consumption-demand. The result is that new investment, if it is to occur, must generally take the form of '*deepening*' capital—finding new ways of 'putting more power behind the human elbow', as Americans would say. This assumption, which may have been an implicit assumption among one or two of the *later* classical writers (though *not*, as we have seen, of the earlier ones), is one which seems to be appearing more explicitly in certain economic writings today. In this connection a fact of some considerable significance deserves to be mentioned. So far as one can gather from the available evidence, a fairly high degree of correlation apparently exists between capital per head and productivity in different countries and regions of the world. Of the stock of capital equipment there is, of course, no satisfactory measure, and one has to fall back upon approximate indices such as horse-power of mechanical power per worker. Differences in the value of output, both per head of the population and per worker, are sufficiently striking even inside a continent such as Europe. As one of the recent Surveys of the U.N. Economic Commission for Europe has shown, the net value of commodity production per head of population in countries of North-western Europe in 1948 was nearly twice the European average and as much as four times that of South and South-eastern Europe. Labour productivity in industry in the most developed countries of Europe was three times that of the less developed, and in agriculture (where labour productivity was universally lower than in industry) the difference was as great as six to seven times between the more developed and the less developed countries.[1] By comparison with U.S.A., the average productivity of labour in Europe was only one-third, and was no more than a half the American level even in the most developed areas; while in the least developed countries it stood at no more than one-fifth to one-sixth of the American level.[2] Such differences seem approximately to correspond to differences in capital equipment per head;[3] and as the *Survey* from which we have quoted concludes, 'there can be little doubt that the bulk of the difference [in productivity between U.S.A. and Europe] was due to its [America's] higher standards of capital formation and the use of more efficient techniques in production'.[4] An incidental fact of some interest is that differences in the rate of investment in new fixed capital were even greater than differences in income per head or in productivity; the U.S.A. level of investment, measured per head of population, being five times the level for Europe as a whole, and differences within Europe itself ranging from between $4 and $10 per head (in $ of 1938 purchasing power) in the poorest countries to between $30 to $50 in the richest.[5] In other words, there seems to be a tendency for countries with a rich heritage of capital equipment to get richer in capital at a faster rate than poorer ones, and for the gap between them accordingly to widen.

I think we may take it therefore that the largest single factor governing productivity in a country is its richness or poorness in

[1] *Economic Survey of Europe for 1948*, pp. 224–5.
[2] Ibid., p. 226.
[3] E.g. according to Dr Rostas the ratio of horse-power per worker in U.S.A. and the United Kingdom in the middle 1930's was about the same as the ratio of output per worker, namely around 2 : 1; *Comparative Productivity in British and American Industries*, p. 52; cp. also Colin Clark, *Conditions of Economic Progress*, p. 389.
[4] Ibid., p. 226.
[5] Ibid., pp. 47–55.

capital instruments of production—in its accumulated heritage of what Marx and the classics would have called 'stored-up labour', or 'dead labour', available as mechanical aids to 'living labour'. And I think that we shall not go far wrong if we treat capital accumulation, in the sense of a growth in the stock of capital instruments—a growth that is simultaneously qualitative and quantitative —as the crux of the process of economic development. In this mode of treatment technical change is regarded as being (in the main) internal and incidental to the process of capital accumulation, not a separate and external factor. I am aware that this way of looking at it does not embrace the whole of the matter. But I suggest that it is at least a very useful approximation, and an illuminating one in revealing facets of the problem of development which are commonly ignored.

One consequence of this emphasis which it may be of interest to this audience to mention concerns the traditional nineteenth-century division of the countries of the world into predominantly agricultural and predominantly industrial countries. This has been treated by the traditional nineteenth-century theory of international trade as a simple example of the international division of labour, and hence as something inherently natural and enduring. In fact it cannot be so treated, since agricultural countries are essentially those with a low quantity of capital per head and low productivity and conversely in the case of industrialised countries, in which industrialisation has been essentially a process of building up their stocks of capital equipment and thereby raising the productivity of their labour. Another consequence, more directly related to what I am going to talk about in this lecture, is that the growth of capitalism and the process of industrialisation are seen as part of one single process, since the growth of technique is *ipso facto* industrialisation as that term is customarily used. In what follows, therefore, I shall not try to explain why capital investment took the road of industrial development instead of remaining purely agricultural. This was the logical road for it to take, and in the circumstances was the only road open to it.

Having spoken of the correlation between a country's heritage of capital equipment and productivity, I want to qualify this by saying that I am far from wishing to imply that this connection is so close as to exclude other, and important, influences upon productivity. Not only do the technical possibilities available at any given period affect the relation between the rates of growth of capital accumulation and of productivity, but the relation between these may vary because capital is misdirected or equipment is wastefully used when brought into existence (e.g. under-utilised, as in a depression period), or its length of life abnormally foreshortened by premature obsolescence (a chronic product of uncertainty in a capitalist world). Yet again (and here we revert to the first of our three dynamic agencies), the rise in productivity may vary according to whether the full potentialities of division of labour are realised or not as the scale of production is extended (although it is probably true that indivisible specialised units of capital equipment rather than specialisation of labour provide the largest element in 'economies of large-scale operation' today). For example, excessive product-differentiation—the result of unequal income-distribution and its consequential bias towards variety in the interest of rich consumers, accentuated by the influence of monopolistic competition—may well be a leading factor in retarding the growth of productivity in modern capitalist societies, because such product-differentiation limits the extent to which advantages of specialisation can be exploited and prevents specialised mechanical equipment from being fully utilised or even introduced.

A word in parenthesis about population: at first sight it would appear surprising that population-increase should not have been included as a determining element in development; especially since thought and discussion among the classical economists was so largely obsessed with the causes and effects of population-growth. Some have, of course, so treated it, especially in recent times; but generally it has not been so regarded; and on reflection the reason for this is fairly plain. The main sense in which economic progress has been spoken of by economists is that of rising productivity of labour, as expression of increased mastery of man over nature, and of the possibility of sufficiency or abundance. This, at least, was the tradition set by Adam Smith when he enquired into the principal factor (or factors) upon which the augmentation of the productive powers of human labour depended. Population-growth, however, was regarded, at any rate in the Malthusian age, as a negative factor: as something which did nothing to augment productive power (save in so far as starvation was a stimulus to invention—which was doubtful) but instead brought into operation the tendency to diminishing returns. While it was true that 'with every mouth God sends a pair of hands', each additional pair of hands was regarded as adding proportionately less, rather than proportionately more, to the total produce. This, I suggest, was how the matter was traditionally regarded. How far, in fact, population may influence development indirectly through its effect either upon the labour supply or upon demand is a question upon which we shall touch later.

The central question to which I wish to draw your attention in this lecture refers to the dynamic impetus in a capitalist economy, where the decisions affecting development are in the hands of autonomous entrepreneurs, or firms, motivated by considerations of individual profit. I need hardly remind you that in such an economy development does not occur as the result of any thought-out and coordinated plan; it just happens—accidentally as it were—as the result of a large number of autonomous individual decisions each of them taken in ignorance of other and parallel decisions, on the basis of market data *plus* guesswork or 'expectations' as to future movements in that market data. In such circumstances the horizon of each decision-taker is straitly limited both in space and over time. On the face of it, such a system would seem likely to be conservative rather than adventurous, and any movement likely to be biased in the direction of the familiar rather than the novel and unfamiliar; small changes which involve little uncertainty being preferred to larger changes which hold a risk for the innovator of finding himself out-of-step with other sectors of the economic system. For (as Schumpeter was fond of emphasising) innovation essentially involves the rupture of a pre-existing equilibrium, which once established becomes a static routine—involves a deliberate refusal on the part of the innovating entrepreneur to adapt himself passively to the economic environment as he finds it.

To say this is to be in conflict, it is true, with what has been commonly presumed about the dynamic role of capitalism. But this common presumption may be the result of a century of propaganda, or it may derive from too much preoccupation with the period of the English industrial revolution and with American development, both of which should probably be treated as being, in this respect, 'special cases'. We shall see later that there is good reason to look upon them in this light: as representing exceptional transformations and rates of growth which find their explanations in circumstances that are to be regarded as abnormal and transitory rather than normal and enduring.

If then the view we have suggested be the correct one, we are at once confronted with this question: what factor or factors, were sufficient to give the initial impetus to so revolutionary a development as the rise of capitalism represented, and to maintain the impetus of that development for so long? Connected with this is a further question: are there factors in a capitalist economy which set a definite term to such a process of development? Does capitalist industry in its growth follow, as it were, a logistic curve (as some have suggested)? Does such a system contain, or generate within it, what Marx termed 'fetters' on development, which at a certain stage cause economic progress to slacken and to yield place to stagnation (absolute or relative)?

Let us look first at what economists have thought of the matter— of the way in which reality has been reflected in the half-illuminating, half-distorting, mirror of ideology. There is no doubt that the early economists regarded capital accumulation, and the developments which it generated, as a self-perpetuating process, provided that no external obstacles (such as State interference or restrictions on trade) were placed in its way. It was regarded as self-perpetuating because the capitalist entrepreneur, *sui generis*, was an accumulator, and from existing profits came the means for accumulation— that is, for future expansion. If any spur was needed to make him plough back rather than to hoard his gains, competition was that spur—the haunting fear of being ousted in the struggle if he did not continually improve his methods of production. Since the expansion of production by each furnished a market for the increased production of others, it was concluded (on the basis of 'Say's law') that an initiative towards expansion, if general to capitalist entrepreneurs as it was supposed to be, would be necessarily self-justifying. Each new round of investment and expansion realised the additional profits which were both its own justification and the source and impulse for renewed expansion. Once the mechanism had been wound up, in the sense of being provided with sufficiently attractive profit-opportunities, it would continue to run itself. This was of course subject to the proviso that subsistence for workers and the raw materials of industry were present in abundance—that their supply could be increased under conditions of constant cost. The early economists never had any fears of a deficient labour supply as an object of exploitation, so long as food was abundant and there were no restrictions on labour mobility; since according to Malthus population would always increase up to the limits of subsistence. It was the grand corollary of the Ricardian system that only the limitation of available land, and the operation of the law of diminishing returns (which redounded so powerfully to the interests of the landowners), was capable of putting a brake upon the process of capital accumulation and expansion. Only a rise of money wages consequent upon a rising cost of growing food (and with it rising rent) was capable of so lowering profits as to dry up both the source and the motive of accumulation, and substitute the melancholy hues of his 'long-run stationary state'[6] for the bright colours of that continuously progressive state of society— that 'cheerful and hearty state to all the different orders of the society' as Adam Smith had called it—which a regime of free trade and economic liberalism could open before capitalist society, at least until it had conquered the whole globe.

This optimism of the classical economists is well expressed in a passage from Malthus (in his *Essay on Population*) who was ready to paint an even rosier picture than Ricardo—provided that what he considered a proper balance between agriculture and industry was maintained:

> The countries which unite great landed resources with a prosperous state of commerce and manufactures, and in which the commer-

---

[6] Ricardo speaks of this as one in which 'the very low rate of profits will have arrested all accumulation, and almost the whole produce of the country, after paying the labourers, will be the property of the owners of land and the receivers of tithes and taxes': *Principles of Political Economy*, Chap. VI; *Works and Correspondence of Ricardo*, ed. Sraffa, Vol. I, pp. 120-1.

cial part of the population never essentially exceeds the agricultural part, is eminently secure from sudden reverses. Their increasing wealth seems to be out of reach of all common accidents; and there is no reason to say that they might not go on increasing riches and population for hundreds, nay, almost thousands, of years.[7]

But while this notion of a self-perpetuating impulse to expansion is plausible enough, once one has conceived of the process as being wound-up and started, it involves the incidental question as to how the process got started at all—a question which, by analogy at least, is of crucial importance for countries which today stand on the brink of an industrial revolution. Such a question is much less capable of a short and simple answer than our previous one; and it is one to which most economists have given little or no consideration—remarkably enough, since it concerns the whole historical and institutional basis of the capitalism which economists of the bourgeois school have taken for granted.

Time does not allow me to discuss the nature and significance of that process which Marx called 'primitive accumulation'. It must suffice to say that the essence of it was a *concentration* of ownership of property, which involved, as the other facet of the process, the dispossession of numerous small owners and the creation of a proletariat. Thereby, in the provision of a superabundant supply of the commodity labour-power, was created the condition *sine qua non* for the capital-investing process. In this respect Britain in the eighteenth century was more favourably placed than almost any other European country. Later, capitalism in America was enabled to expand (despite the lure of free land which kept wages higher than in Europe) by drawing upon the surplus populations of the more backward parts of Europe. This creation of a proletariat provided the *fons et origo* of capital investment in Britain and of capitalist profit. Eighteenth-century England also witnessed the growth of capitalist enclosed farming, which simultaneously swelled the ranks of the dispossessed and augmented the supply of corn so as to afford low corn prices and hence cheap labour (despite restriction of import and an expanding population)— save in exceptional scarcity years during the Napoleonic wars,

[7] 7th edition, p. 338.

such as 1800-1 and 1812-13, when it was the labourers who starved in obedience to 'Parson Malthus' and not the nascent capitalists who were burdened with the payment of higher money wages.

This was also a period when the market grew at a rate that was without precedent: not only that growth of the 'internal market' from growing division of labour between town and country of which Lenin spoke[8] in the case of Russia at the end of the nineteenth century, but also a growth of the export market: with the result that textile products in particular and also iron were apt to be in a chronic state of short supply. Moreover, the technical changes of this epoch were of a kind which extended the field of investment for new capital, so that investment in one direction was complementary to (not competitive with) investment in some other sector: steam-power and textile machinery, for example, creating the demand for a whole new industry of machine-making. At the same time (as I hardly need to remind this audience) colonial exploitation and loot were the basis of large individual fortunes, which, even if in the first instance they went into the purchase of country houses or of aristocratic titles or of government bonds, at second or third hand provided the liquid funds whereby the initial impetus of the industrial revolution could be financed. Moreover, it was the coincidence of such favourable factors at the same period and the influence of their combined operation which occasioned the remarkable rise in the tempo of development that characterised Britain's economy at the end of the eighteenth century.

The classical picture of a continuing process of expansion is, of course, undermined if there be anything in the internal logic of the process or any external circumstances which progressively weaken its impetus. This, as we have seen, was well appreciated by Ricardo; and (as Marx observed): 'what worries Ricardo is the fact that the rate of profit, the stimulating principle of capitalist production, the fundamental premise and driving force of accumulation, should be endangered by the development of production itself'; adding that this concern with a decline in profit showed 'his [Ricardo's] profound understanding of the conditions of capitalist production'.[9]

[8] In his *Development of Capitalism in Russia*, in *Selected Works of Lenin*, Vol. I.   [9] *Capital, III*, p. 304.

The significance of subsequent theories which have depicted a long-run tendency for the rate of profit to fall is precisely this (whether the fall be due, as Marx declared, to the changing composition of capital as accumulation proceeds, or, as underconsumptionists like Rosa Luxemburg and Hobson have declared, to a deficient expansion of final consumers' demand). If profit, for whatever reason, tends to fall as the process develops, then a vista of retardation and ultimate stagnation is opened. The Ricardian long-run stationary state comes back into the picture, but as something which is not solely dependent upon the onset of diminishing returns on land.

This is perhaps the place to make a brief digression, if you will allow me, to deal with two theoretical points. In doing this, I do not intend any serious analysis of the conditions under which a long-run tendency for profits to fall will operate, but simply wish to forestall possible misunderstandings.

The first misunderstanding relates to Ricardo's picture of a tendency for profits to fall owing to diminishing returns on land. It is sometimes supposed that this conclusion is immediately invalidated by introducing into the picture the so-called law of increasing returns in manufactures—a fact which Ricardo is supposed to have ignored—or alternatively progressive cost-reduction as a result of technical improvement. It was, however, crucial to the Ricardian theory of profit that only improvements in agriculture were capable of offsetting the tendency of profits to fall, and *not* improvements which increased labour productivity in manufactures. The latter resulted simply in an equivalent fall in the exchange value of manufactured products (relatively to products of agriculture) and had no influence upon profits as a *value-ratio* between labour and its product. While he did not deny the offsetting effect of agricultural improvements, these were treated as no more than an occasional offset to a persistent tendency to diminishing returns (persistent, i.e. so long as population was increasing): since, as Adam Smith had maintained, the division of labour had but a restricted application to agriculture. What Ricardo can with more reason be charged with neglecting (so far as concerned subsequent events in the nineteenth century) is the effect of transport development upon the cost of imported corn. But even this charge is not entirely justified, since the main practical corollary of his theoretical argument was that only a free and expanding import of corn could postpone the operation of this falling-profit tendency.

The same consideration applies to a common criticism that is levelled at Marx's falling-profit rate theory (which you will remember depended, not upon Ricardian diminishing returns, but on changing composition of capital, or the use of more capital— in value—per worker as capital accumulated). The question is commonly asked: why did he ignore or at least belittle (as he would appear to have done) the effect of technical change in raising the productivity of labour?[10] The answer is that he only considered this relevant to the determination of total profit if it affected the production of what in modern terminology would be called *wage-goods*, and thereby lowered wages (in value). Only then could it raise what he termed 'relative surplus value' by reducing the proportion of the labour force of society required to produce wage-goods or workers' subsistence. Without a change in this crucial ratio, total profit or surplus-value could not alter, whatever change in other, non-wage-goods might occur.[11] In conformity with the common opinion of classical political economy he doubtless regarded this application of technical change to cheapening foodstuffs as exceptional rather than the rule.

The second point which I wish to clear up relates to that distinction which some modern writers have emphasised between so-called 'capital-widening' and 'capital-deepening' as investment proceeds. Here I want to do no more than make explicit an assumption which seems to underlie that conception of capital accumulation-cum-technical change to which I have already alluded. This notion implies, as we have seen, that at any given time there is

[10] Mrs J. V. Robinson, for example, speaks of Marx's 'drastic inconsistency' in assuming that the profit-rate can fall in conditions of 'constant real wages': *Essay on Marxian Economics*, pp. 42–3. But this 'startling contradiction' (as she also calls it) disappears if technical change applies to non-wage-goods industries only.

[11] True, the profit-*rate*, as distinct from total profit, could also be affected by a change in value of 'the elements of constant capital': an influence which Marx, unlike Ricardo, explicitly allowed for, and which he seems to have regarded as modifying, but not strong enough to offset completely, the tendency for the profit-rate to fall.

generally little scope for investment in capital-widening (i.e. for expanding the stock of invested capital under constant technical conditions and preserving the *same* ratio of capital to labour), except to the extent that consumption-demand is expanding or some radical change of industrial structure is occurring, such as the creation of new (or virtually new) industries. As regards investment in capital-deepening, it is also usually implied that this will involve, in the absence of any radical change in the background of technical *knowledge*, a transition to technical forms which are initially less profitable (in relation to their cost) than the old— if only because otherwise entrepreneurs would previously have adopted them. Some such assumptions as these clearly underlay the view expressed by Keynes in his *General Theory*—a view which seemed novel and surprising to most economists at the time: 'I feel sure that the demand for capital is strictly limited in the sense that it would not be difficult to increase the stock of capital up to a point where its marginal efficiency had fallen to a very low figure.' A modern community,

> where population is not increasing rapidly [he considered] ought to be able to bring down the marginal efficiency of capital in equilibrium approximately to zero within a single generation; so that we should then attain the conditions of a quasi-stationary community where change and progress would result only from changes in technique, taste, population and institutions, with the products of capital selling at a price proportioned to the labour, etc., embodied in them.[12]

Whether such a tendency to declining profitability as investment proceeds will in fact operate, or whether it will be continuously, and not only intermittently, offset by changes in technical knowledge cannot, of course, be established by any process of *a priori* reasoning. The theoretical model one adopts may imply certain probabilities; but the real test must be the extent to which this model, when applied as an instrument of interpretation, succeeds in illuminating the actual march of events, and the ultimate appeal must be to economic history.

We might have expected doubt about the smoothness of capitalist development to arise as soon as attention was turned to the

[12] *General Theory*, pp. 220–1 and 375.

facts of the trade cycle: to the observed fact that capital accumulation did not move forward at a steady pace and on an even keel, but was periodically interrupted by the onset of crises and depressions, during which investment declined abruptly and excess capacity and unemployment emerged. Had not economists conveniently turned a blind eye to this phenomenon for so long, they would have early seen that it seriously damaged, even it it did not entirely invalidate, the picture of a self-generating impetus in capitalist development. If depression and stagnation periodically set in, what was to stop this stagnation from becoming chronic? If the momentum of development petered out at each downturn of the decennial cycle, what guarantee was there that the engine would ever get started up again? Marx's theory of the industrial reserve army, periodically recruited in the years of swelling unemployment, might serve to explain the empirical fact that recovery had succeeded depression to date—that the cycle itself contained a mechanism to replace the primitive accumulation of the early days of capitalism for cheapening labour-power and restoring profit as the source and motive of accumulation. But this gave no reason to suppose that the mechanism would always suffice, especially in an age when the population situation had changed and labour had become organised and more resistant to pressure. The more that thought returned to the subject, the more was doubt inevitably cast upon the enduring nature of capitalism's mission as an agency of development. The door was opened to the possibility that (as Mr J. R. Hicks has recently put it) 'perhaps the whole Industrial Revolution of the last two hundred years has been nothing else but a vast secular boom'.[13]

It is not the place here to discuss the causation of the trade cycle even if I were capable of saying anything new on the matter. I want only to draw attention to the link between this essentially short-term problem and the long-term problem of development in two main respects. Firstly, I want to suggest that the term 'crisis' may be more appropriate than the term 'cycle' to describe this crucial phenomenon of capitalist society; since 'crisis' implies a break or interruption in some more long-run movement, whereas cycle seems to imply an oscillation in which both turning-points—

[13] *Value and Capital*, p. 302.

the downturn and the upturn—are symmetrical and slump can be regarded as 'producing' or 'leading to' a subsequent recovery and boom, as much as the boom can be regarded as 'leading to' the slump. On the other hand, if one views the short-term phenomenon of fluctuation against the background of the long-term movement, the crisis-phase, or break in the long-term movement, and the subsequent resumption of investment and activity do not appear as necessarily symmetrical, and each may have to be explained quite differently. Secondly, I would suggest that there is much to support the view that the long-term development of capital accumulation continued up to the First World War (and in America up to 1929), despite the interruption of periodic crises, only because of the operation of special factors favourable to a shortening of the depression-phase and to a resumed momentum of investment activity once again—factors which were in their nature transitory, and in a sense external to the process of capital accumulation.[14] To review at all adequately the evidence for this contention would involve too large an excursion into modern economic history. All that I can do is to mention rather cursorily some of the factors which in the case of British capitalism powerfully sustained activity throughout the nineteenth century, and to refer you to a more detailed sketch of these factors which I have attempted elsewhere.

I have already mentioned, as a characteristic of the technical innovations of the Industrial Revolution, that technical developments continued to be complementary; investment in some technical novelty such as a steam weaving mill creating the opportunity for investment in some other direction. To this extent the Industrial Revolution can be said to have been a period when this cumulative

[14] Formally, in Mr Hicks' trade cycle model, they would be regarded, I presume, as 'exogenous' factors influencing the trend of 'autonomous invention' and hence setting a continually rising 'floor' to his cycle. What I am saying is, however, equivalent to the claim that the essentials of the problem of long-term development are better stated in terms of periodic breakdown and then resumption of a trend-movement than in terms of a self-perpetuating cycle. If I understand him rightly, Mr Hicks in his *Trade Cycle*, in stating that the cycle may be 'explosive' (and hence the 'floor' may have to be explained by a trend-movement in what he calls 'autonomous investment'), in effect admits that this is the case.

element, combined with an abundant reserve of labour, caused the demand for investment to expand as fast as the supply of capital increased. It was a situation in which the bourgeois optimism of Ricardo was justified. Some modern economists have claimed that this is always a characteristic of technical progress; deducing therefrom that a long-term tendency for capital accumulation to outrun the available investment-field is a myth. This, however, I think is a very dubious hypothesis except in a sense so general as to have little significance for the question in hand. At any rate, this complementarity is, I suggest, mainly characteristic, (1) of crucial periods of technical revolution which involve a quantitative and qualitative expansion of capital-goods production, (2) of geographical expansion. The first was to a large extent a unique consequence of the Industrial Revolution; although something of the same kind may have resulted from what has sometimes been called the second Industrial Revolution of the early part of the present century—the development of electricity and the internal combustion engine and also those developments, especially in America, which are known rather loosely as modern mass production. The second (geographical expansion) was specially characteristic of the railway age. Railways themselves were not only large absorbers both of capital and of the products of heavy industry throughout the middle decades of the nineteenth century in Britain and on the continent of Europe, and up to the First World War in America and in other continents, but they opened entirely new regions to economic development which had previously been outside the orbit of capitalist investment.

Perhaps I need hardly remind you that, so far as Britain was concerned, this favourable element in the situation combined with three others to sustain the momentum of capitalist investment in the century before the First World War: a rapid expansion of population, and hence of the available labour supply; favourable terms of trade with agricultural regions of the world, whereby food and raw materials could be cheaply obtained in exchange for products of British industry; and expanding opportunities for foreign investment. Significantly enough, it was a sudden freezing of the latter which precipitated 'the Great Depression' of the '70's: the first serious halt in the continued upward movement of the British economy's long-term curve. Significant also was the fact that it was the narrowed profit-margins of the depression years of the '70's and '80's and early '90's which gave birth alike to some of the first cartel-agreements and to the surge forward of British imperialism; while it was the revival of foreign investment, close on the heels of imperialist expansion, which supplied the momentum (at least the continuing momentum) of that 'Indian summer' of British Capitalism, the prosperity-phase of 1900-14. At the same time, this was a period when investment and technical improvement in British industry itself was lagging behind; this lagging being specially marked in the capital-goods industries; so that Britain was increasingly becoming what an American writer has called 'a consumption orientated economy'.[15] In the U.S.A. the epoch of geographical expansion extended into the present century—a period to which recent American discussion has referred as that of the expanding frontier. The American continent provided room within its own borders for what can be termed an 'internal colonialism', and for this reason the U.S.A. economy, in which capitalism was most mature and monopoly in industry and finance was to reach its highest stage of development, was relatively late in taking the stage as an imperialist power. Not until the turn of the century did she become a net exporter of industrial products and not until after the First World War did she start to go in for foreign investment on an extensive scale. Even when the period of the 'expanding frontier' had closed, continued momentum was given to technical change and industrial investment during the first three decades of the century, first of all by the creation of the new mass production industries (which we have mentioned), and secondly by capital export in the 1920's.

It is perhaps unnecessary for me to remind you how drastically over the past two decades the climate of opinion has altered in relation both to cyclical fluctuations and to the whole question of long-term trends. Gone is the old optimism, even in America where men talked in the '20's as though the economic millenium was only a matter of a decade or two. A diminishing number of American economists, and few, if any, outside America, would be found today to argue with any assurance that capitalism in its moribund

[15] Paul Baran in *American Perspective*, April 1949.

state of today was capable of being an agency *par excellence* of economic development and progress. Even those who dismiss the so-called stagnation thesis do so less by denying that stagnation tendencies exist than by asserting that there is no reason for supposing that the sort of buoyancy factors which sustained profit and investment in the past (new inventions, new industries and new worlds to conquer) may not continue to appear in the future. Even the most uncompromising defenders of the system have lost much of the old nineteenth-century (or pre-1930) dogmatism and assurance. Their speech and writing has a defensive note previously lacking from their utterances. Doctrines which at one time were voiced only in what Keynes called 'the underworld of heretics' have now become a commonplace of academic discussion and have even found their way into the staid pages of government reports.

This change in the climate of economic opinion since the great divide of the crisis of 1929-31 is a sufficiently familiar story. But it may not, perhaps, be entirely a waste of your time if I conclude this all-too-general and cursory survey with an attempt to summarise the main contrasts between the picture confronting us in the West today and the picture of a self-perpetuating process of development as the early economists saw it a century and more ago. These contrasts in the situation are quite fundamental; and I cannot myself feel any doubt that they effectively rob the classical picture of such realism as it may once have had.

Firstly, we have a complete change in the population situation. Instead of a natural increase of population at something like the Malthusian 'geometric ratio', the vista is opened, in countries of Western Europe and America, of a declining population. One by one, in each of the most advanced industrial countries the net reproduction rate in recent decades has fallen below unity, and is apparently falling even where it still remains above unity. Secondly, with the growth of the power of trade union organisation, the traditional mechanism for keeping labour cheap, the industrial reserve army, has lost much of its force—even if it can still operate effectively upon the wage levels of the smaller trades and the unorganised fringes of the larger. Thirdly, there is the influence of monopoly: an influence which varies from the sovereign power of the larger consolidations or holding companies which dominate a trade or a whole constellation of trades, through various looser forms of price- and output-restriction and price-leadership, to the imperfect competition or monopolistic competition of which recent economic literature has been so full. There can, I think, be little doubt that, although monopoly has raised the profitability of investment in the privileged and protected spheres, its influence upon investment generally has been restrictive; and I think there can also be little question that the modern tendency to meet any deficiency in demand by price-maintenance and output-restriction has accentuated excess capacity and unemployment, thereby deepening the downward spiral of collapse in an economic crisis. As such its net effect is the opposite of a 'buoyancy-factor'—namely, a drag or a fetter. Associated with it is that prevalent neo-Mercantilist 'fear of excess productive capacity' (echoing what Heckscher has termed the 'fear of goods' of the Mercantilist age) and the striving for export surpluses which has so generally characterised both governmental and business policies in recent times. Fourthly, the sphere available for colonial development, along traditional imperialist lines, has been drastically narrowed by the events of the past two decades. Possibilities for a renewal of the flow of capital export, on a scale adequate to make it a significant factor in the situation, seem remote—unless it be as a handmaid to war and the financing of corrupt and discredited regimes as outposts of empire. So far as Britain at least is concerned, the once favourable terms of trade which she enjoyed with agricultural areas of the world have now turned unfavourable.

It is, I suggest, a very significant fact that American economic opinion should have so largely come to accept in recent years a margin of five to ten million unemployed as a natural feature even of normal prosperity; and that one should find serious economic writers laying emphasis, as impetus to continued investment and economic activity, upon the maintenance of an exceptional (and therefore of course wasteful) rate of technical obsolescence, and upon inducing (by propaganda and advertisement) frequent fashion changes in consumers' tastes.[16] Already, however, there are signs

---

[16] For example: 'If growth-induced changes in the pattern of wants and production create a sufficiently rapid rate of obsolescence, there is no

of awareness that this is not enough; and it seems not unlikely that economic historians of the future will record that a war, or semi-war, regime, with its government expenditures and export surpluses and swollen demands upon industrial potential, proved to be the only means of sustaining the activity of an over-mature capitalist economy in the middle decades of the twentieth century.

---

problem.' David McC. Wright on 'Prospects for Capitalism' in *A Survey of Contemporary Economics*, ed. Howard S. Ellis, Philadelphia, 1948, p. 457.

Two

Some problems of industrialisation in agricultural countries

My intention in this lecture is to give a cursory review of some of the problems which face an agricultural country in carrying through a process of capital accumulation and industrialisation. In doing so I shall necessarily be generalising from what I know of European countries—especially from the experience of the U.S.S.R. during the last quarter of a century. I am aware that such generalisations may require modification when applied to countries of Asia, about which I have no special knowledge. I am even prepared for you to tell me that they have little or no application to the Indian situation. What follows must accordingly be taken with this limitation in mind. Nevertheless I still venture to believe that they have some relevance to the economic problems confronting you here, at least by way of analogy. Perhaps, even these analogies may turn out to be a commonplace among you, and be much more familiar to you than they are to us in the West.

You may remember that in my last lecture I suggested that the process of capital accumulation and the process of industrialisation were virtually identical, since the application of mechanical technique has been traditionally much more limited in agricultural production than in industry. Moreover, a rise in agricultural productivity is apt to be contingent upon a certain degree of development of industry: e.g. to supply agriculture with machinery, with fertilisers, with power and with transport facilities. For this reason, predominantly agricultural countries have generally (with a few exceptions) had a much lower level of productivity per head, and a lower average standard of life, than have industrial countries; and every shift in the proportion of the labour force engaged respectively in agriculture and in industry in favour of the latter generally has the effect of increasing the average level of *per capita* productivity. In other words, the essential reason for industrialisation is that it augments productivity per head, and hence opens the way for a higher standard of life than purely agricultural countries can generally expect to enjoy. Yet such a shift necessarily involves very substantial investments of capital, to the extent that methods of production in industry are contingent upon a larger amount of capital equipment per worker than production in agriculture.

It has been a fairly common assumption in the past among writers who have discussed the problems connected with this process that the essence of the problem is *financial*, in the sense that what limits the possibility of such a transition is the availability of financial resources as a basis for large-scale investment; and the problems of capital accumulation and investment have been viewed exclusively from this angle. Ultimately such resources can come only from the surplus of total production over necessary consumption; and in a poor country this margin will be a very narrow one. Moreover, full use may not be made even of the potential savings-fund which exists, because an undeveloped economy lacks the financial institutions and methods whereby these potential savings could be mobilised and canalised into industrial investment. According to this view (which I shall call the traditional view) the available and mobilisable 'savings fund' of the community is the crucial bottleneck which sets a limit to the possible rate of economic development. I believe I am right in saying that in the course of discussion about industrialisation in India the smallness of this margin between production and necessary consumption has been advanced as an essential reason why any large rate of investment and a rapid process of industrialisation would be impossible and if attempted would have serious inflationary consequences—in the absence, that is, of large-scale borrowing from abroad.

No one could reasonably deny that this picture corresponds to certain basic features of the situation. It is a truism to say that the larger the proportion of the labour force required to produce subsistence, the smaller will be the labour force available, *ceteris paribus*, for industrial construction. It is also not to be denied that under conditions of primitive capitalism a contributory factor retarding investment has often been a lack of liquid resources in the hands of potential entrepreneurs, with which to employ labour, and the absence of credit facilities to repair this lack. But to speak of development as being limited by the size of a basic savings 'fund' in the sense in which we have just spoken of it (or alternatively by the institutional mechanisms for mobilising such savings) only makes sense on the assumption that the margin between production and consumption can *only* be enlarged by lowering consumption and cannot be enlarged to any appreciable extent by enlarging total production. As soon as we drop this assumption and allow the possibility of an increase in total production, the limit upon development of which we have spoken loses its absolute character, and may even cease to have much meaning as a limiting factor at all. It will be one of the contentions which I shall recommend to your consideration in this lecture that the problem of industrialisation is essentially not a financial one, but a problem of *economic organisation*. If this contention be correct, the question is immediately raised (although I shall not have time to enlarge on it here) of a comparison between different forms of economic organisation as agencies of development: in particular between an unplanned capitalist economy and a system of socialist planning as forms of organisation adequate to carry through such an economic revolution as that which we have in mind.

Perhaps it is unnecessary for me to remind you that a common feature of countries at the stage of development which we are considering is the existence of a large and chronic rural overpopulation: of a population much larger than can be productively employed in agriculture. Investigation has shown that this surplus in a number of countries is quite surprisingly large. For example, it has been estimated that in the seven main countries of Eastern and South-eastern Europe (excluding the U.S.S.R.) the rural surplus population amounts to as much as a quarter of the agricultural population, or 16 million in all.[1] Other estimates speak of 'rather more than a third' of the agricultural man-power being 'superfluous' in countries such as Poland, Bulgaria, Rumania and Yugoslavia;[2] while in Slovakia this proportion rises to a half.[3] I am

[1] Doreen Warriner, *Revolution in Eastern Europe*, p. 176.
[2] H. Seton-Watson, *Eastern Europe between Two Wars, 1918 to 1941*, pp. 98–9; and Chatham House, *South-Eastern Europe*, p. 77.
[3] Doreen Warriner, op. cit., p. 176.

not acquainted with any comparable estimates for India; but there are all the indications of surplus rural population at least as large as that which has traditionally characterised Eastern Europe.[4] Where agricultural methods are primitive there is commonly a very big fluctuation between the 'peak' demand for labour at the busiest season of the year and the 'trough' of the slack season; and the population attached to the land is apt to exceed, not only the average, but even the 'peak' demand for labour.

From the existence of this actual or potential reserve of labour there follows a consequence which is very simple but at the same time crucial to any economic analysis of the problems of industrialisation. This is that the limiting factor upon economic development—limiting the rate at which construction can occur—is certainly not labour; and that to this extent the employment of labour in industrial production or constructional activity will not be competitive with the production of foodstuffs. Thus traditional notions about the rate of investment being determined in a fundamental sense by some pre-existing 'real fund of working capital' will not apply. It will not hold true that real investment in industry or transport or power-development can only take place to the extent that some prior act of saving has occurred—i.e. saving in the sense of a reduction in someone's claim upon foodstuffs and other consumer goods, so that an increased labour force in industry may consume instead. It is nowadays a commonplace that many traditional propositions in economic theory lose their basis in face of the existence of labour that is unused or unproductively employed. What I am now saying is no more than a particular application of that modern commonplace to the conditions of an agricultural country which has a surplus of labour on the land: surplus, i.e. above what can be absorbed with existing technical resources and with existing methods of production.

If it is not over-stressing the obvious, I will give a simple example of what I mean. Let us suppose that a programme of building a railroad or a series of power stations is launched in an agricultural country, and that previously agriculture has been the only form of productive activity. Then, if all the active labour of

[4] Cf. United Nations, *Economic Survey of Asia and the Far East, 1949*, p. 84.

the community had been previously employed productively upon the land, labour could only be transferred to construct the railway or the power stations at the expense of a fall in the output of agricultural products, and consequently a fall in consumption per head. In this sense 'saving', whether forced or voluntary, on the part of some section of the community would be a necessary condition of investment in constructional work. If, however, there had previously been a surplus of labour in agriculture, lacking employment on the land (or at least employed very unproductively), then the transfer of labour to building a railway or a power station would involve no reduction (or at most a negligible reduction) in agricultural output; and the capital construction could take place without any necessary fall in consumption per head. 'Hands' would move from the village to the new construction sites; with the hands there would also move mouths; and with less mouths to feed in the village the possibility would be created for food to move out of the village to supply the needs of the swollen army of construction workers, without any fall in consumption on the part of those remaining in the village. Of course, in practice workers may not readily move from village to construction work, or (as we shall see later on) the food supply may not be responsive to their movement. But that is another story, involving rather different problems and having different implications.

It is, moreover, worth noticing at this point that, not only will investment in industry in such circumstances be non-competitive with production in agriculture, but within a fairly short time (much shorter probably than has been commonly allowed) it may become actually complementary to it. This it will become in the degree to which the growth of industry can provide the means for improving the technique and the productivity of agriculture.

What I have just been saying has the effect, I suggest, of changing the whole setting for discussion of the economic problems of a process of industrialisation. It must, I think, put a radically different slant on our analysis of these problems from that which has been implicit in most economic analysis of them. And I think it may also be relevant to the interpretation which economists and economic historians give to industrial revolutions in the past as well as to those of the present and the future. But in stating strongly what I believe to be a consideration that is crucial to correct understanding and a correct approach to matters of practical policy, I have inevitably over-simplified it. And I want now to reintroduce some important qualifications.

In the first place, while there will be no scarcity of labour in general in the case which I have supposed (provided it can be moved to the right locations), there may well be shortage of *skilled* labour, and this may constitute a bottleneck on industrial development. The overcoming of this limit, however, will involve, not financial measures to mobilise savings, but the organisation of appropriate training schemes. From a long-run standpoint, indeed, one could say that nothing else but the development of industry itself could overcome this limit effectively, since it is only industrial experience and familiarity with the atmosphere of industrial technique that will breed a labour force capable of handling such technique.

Again, in the very early stages of industrialisation the limiting factor on development may be certain sorts of industrial equipment (such as power-station or blast-furnace equipment, locomotives or lorries or machine-tools) which are only obtainable by import from abroad. Short of foreign borrowing, this import can only be purchased by an increased export of agricultural products or of the products of light industries producing consumer goods (or alternatively by pruning other imports, which in our present context comes to the same thing). To this extent it is true that the consumption-fund of the country is reduced; and to this extent the traditional view of the matter embodies an aspect of the truth. However, if surplus labour is available, it is always possible that this can be turned to the production of things suitable for export (e.g. in light industries requiring little capital equipment, or in handicrafts); and in so far as this is so, the traditional view requires substantial modification even in this case. But apart from this possibility, the practical corollaries which are usually derived from the traditional view acquire a different complexion when one bears in mind that it is *specific* shortages—shortages of specific kinds of equipment—that are here in question, rather than shortage of productive resources in general.[5] For one thing, the financial

[5] The traditional argument has sometimes been put in the form that,

measures traditionally relied on may be much too unselective to attain their object in this type of situation. What is required in the case we are considering is not more imports *in general* but specific *sorts* of imports; and measures devised to increase saving and to secure economies in consumption in the home market may only serve indirectly to expand the export of the kinds of products which can find a market abroad; a large part of their effect being exhausted in pointlessly putting out of use economic resources specialised to the production of goods which are unsuitable for export.

Thirdly, it must be emphasised that even where the needs of industrial construction are met by drawing upon reserves of surplus labour in the countryside it does not necessarily follow that, as labour moves from village to town, the supply of food-stuffs made available by agriculture for the urban and industrial population will simultaneously increase. The appropriate financing of industrial investment will not suffice automatically to evoke an increase in this crucial supply of necessary subsistence. Now that there are less mouths to feed in the village, more of the villagers' own produce may be consumed by each of those remaining there. Those who remain may even be induced by the easing of their position to enjoy more leisure and to cultivate less intensively (in economists' jargon, their demand for income in terms of effort may prove to be so inelastic as to produce the situation of a backward-sloping supply-curve of agricultural output). In such a case, the increased wage-bill and expenditure of the industrial population coming up against an inelastic supply of *marketed* produce of agriculture will certainly have inflationary consequences so far as agricultural prices are concerned. This rise of agricultural prices might seem at first sight likely to bring its own cure by stimulating

---

although labour may be plentiful, capital in an undeveloped country is scarce; and hence 'saving' remains necessary to relieve the pressure on existing capital equipment. It is quite true that the practicable rate of investment may be limited by the amount of equipment in the capital-goods industries. But 'saving' may have no other *immediate* (or early) effect than to put out of use equipment specialised to producing consumer goods without at all augmenting the productive capacity of capital-goods industries.

a larger supply to be marketed. But if manufactured goods are not plentiful, on which agriculturists can spend their extra money income, the offer of a larger money income may merely reinforce the tendency to enjoy more leisure or for the villagers to consume more of their own crops.

Now if there is any factor to be singled out as the fundamental limiting factor upon the pace of development, then I suggest that it is this *marketable surplus* of agriculture: this rather than the total product, or the productivity, of agriculture in general. As we shall see in my third and closing lecture, this marketable surplus played a crucial role in the early stages of Soviet industrialisation. In terms of this marketable surplus as a determining bottleneck something resembling the traditional 'savings fund' theory could be reconstructed. This reconstructed theory, however, would have a significance quite different from the traditional one in at least one fundamental respect. The limiting factor, instead of being a natural and inevitable one—inevitable, i.e. in face of existing productive resources—is institutional in character, in the sense that the proportion of the crop that is marketed can differ with different types of social and economic organisation in the village (being different, e.g. under large-scale farming and under small specialised or mixed farming, under collective farms and under individual peasant holdings). The surmounting of this limit is accordingly a matter, not of providing appropriate financial policies and institutions, but of the appropriate organisation of the social and economic life of the village, of agricultural production and of commercial exchange between village and town.

One incidental point of some practical importance deserves to be mentioned here. The sort of investment programme to which I have been referring will involve in practice, not only an increase in the money income of the population as a result of more industrial employment, but in all probability also some increase in the spendable income of the population. So also may the supply of foodstuffs coming on the market rise, as we have seen; but if the marketed portion of the agricultural crop rises, then the money income of the agricultural population will be increased, as well as the income of those in industry (unless of course agricultural prices are reduced absolutely, and reduced by more than in proportion to the increase in the marketed supply). Hence the rural population will have more to spend on industrial consumers' goods (or alternatively upon agricultural implements). Moreover, the labour transferred to industry and constructional work will now be receiving wages which will almost certainly be higher than the income which they have recently been earning in the village, whether they have been working for their families or have been employed by some rich peasant or been unemployed and begging their bread. This rise of money income, in face of what for the time being will be an inelastic total supply of consumer goods, will tend to exert an upward pressure on prices, either of foodstuffs or of industrial consumer goods or of both (according to the state of their supply and the income-elasticity of demand for them). Later, however, as the industrial investment bears fruit in enhanced production, prices (at least of industrial products) should fall again. The important thing to notice is that this temporary inflationary pressure is *not* a symptom that 'forced saving' is necessary or is occurring; and it can happen even when on the average no fall in consumption per head is taking place (although of course it may well have distributional effects beneficial to some sectors and damaging to others). It is quite true that such inflationary pressure need not occur, or could be reduced, if the policy were adopted of matching the increased investment expenditure (and hence the increased spendable income of people) by the issue of savings bonds or by taxation. In a capitalist economy this would be an effective way of mopping-up some of the increased profits resulting from increased activity; although its effectiveness in our present context would be in proportion to the amount of those profits that would otherwise have been spent rather than saved. But in a socialist economy it would be a matter of tapping in this way the extra incomes of workers and peasants; and while something might be achieved in this direction, it is scarcely realistic to conceive of the whole of the extra income being drawn off in this way at a time when inducements are necessary for large-scale movements of labour and for increased supplies of foodstuffs and raw materials to be made available by the village for the towns. To say that it could be so drawn off would in fact be equivalent to saying that the higher level of industrial wages is (from the incentive angle) unnecessary. It seems to follow that *some* measure of inflationary pressure may have to be accepted as a temporary consequence of any large-scale development programme, i.e. as a temporary by-product of the investment itself in enhancing total money income, and not as the product of 'mistaken financial policy' (as is commonly supposed). At the same time, this *need* not mean that anyone is worse-off in the sense of their consumption being reduced (although in practice it may well happen that many are made worse-off if profiteering and speculation are not checked).

What I have been saying up to now implies that, although the practicable pace at which a programme of industrialisation can proceed without any reduction of the standard of life is appreciably greater than has been commonly supposed, it will be subject to certain crucial limitations. Connected with this question as to the practicable *rate* of investment is the controversial question of the *order* of development. To a large extent this latter question is the former in another guise. Should investment first of all be directed towards agriculture, extending and improving the 'food and raw material' base for subsequent economic advances in other fields? Or should investment in industry be given priority in order that its development may later extend the possibilities of agricultural improvement, as well as affording employment to the surplus rural population? And if investment in industry is to be given priority, should it be investment in the lighter consumer-goods industries or in heavy industry which produces capital goods? In practice, of course, it will always be *some* mixture of both. Development is likely to take place in most branches of industry, in varying degrees. But there will be an important question of priority—as to how resources available for development are to be distributed between these various sectors, and consequently which branch of industry comes first and develops fastest.

Decision upon such matters necessarily depends upon complex political and socio-economic factors,[6] and I shall not attempt here to do more than indicate some of the economic considerations

---

[6] For example, in the U.S.S.R. policy on this matter was influenced, *inter alia*, by the international situation and the war danger and internally by the *kulak* danger in the countryside—by the strength of this tendency and the danger of its perverting social development in the village.

which bear upon the question. In its purely economic aspect one can say that the problem is reducible essentially to this: that in all decisions about investment three dimensions are involved. What is usually termed the *rate* of investment involves a decision to devote a given quantity of resources to constructional work over a given period of time. This is a decision concerning the *amount* of stored-up labour to create in any given year or in any given quinquennium. But in choosing between the various alternative forms which this stored-up labour can take, one is also concerned with the question as to the length of time over which it is designed that this labour should be stored-up before it yields its eventual fruit in greater output of consumable goods. It is a question, if you like, of the *time-dimension* of the investment. Thus it is generally the case that a given investment in lighter industries will yield a speedier fruit than will investment in heavy industry (in building power stations or blast-furnaces and engineering works). The latter will be only a preliminary stage for an expansion of productive capacity in the consumer-goods industry, such as food industries or textiles, at some later date in the future. (Be it noted, I have said that this will *generally* be so. But in any given case the result must depend upon the shape of the total investment programme, in particular the extent to which it is dispersed over various constructional projects or concentrated upon a few only.) If the more quickly-yielding forms of investment are chosen, then of course the consumable income of the *near* future will tend to be larger to the extent that new clothing factories, etc., come into operation and begin to pour their products into the shops. On the other hand, the rate of *future* development will be restricted by the limited capacity of the industries producing machines and equipment, so that expansion in, say, the second quinquennium and the third quinquennium cannot be so great (leaving aside the question of import from abroad) as it could be if priority had been given in the first place to expanding the capacity of industries which produce capital goods. By contrast, if the constructional programme is initially geared so as to give priority to the latter—to building blast-furnaces and steel mills and engineering works—then the flow of consumer goods in the first few years will grow more slowly (and will be smaller than under the alternative scheme).

But future development in, say, the second quinquennium and after can be much more rapid, since the basis for producing machinery and capital equipment for industry in general has previously been enlarged. It is the choice of smaller-results-but-*quicker* against larger results eventually which are slower to accrue. It is analogous to the choice between adding a floor to an *existing* building—which will give you additional living space more quickly —and building new or enlarged foundations upon which a more extensive dwelling can later be constructed.

This was the crucial decision which faced Soviet planners and policy-makers in the 1920's, and formed the subject of vigorous discussion and controversy in those years. I need hardly explain perhaps that the issue was decided in favour of the more ambitious rate of development: giving top priority to the development of heavy industry and the power-base for future development, with the expansion of lighter consumer-goods industries being relegated (not entirely, but in the main) to the later and second stage of the building.

An incidental point of some importance which I would submit to your attention is that the choice between alternative economic policies of this kind has, I believe, to be treated by analogy with choice between alternative military strategies, in the sense that, not only will various elements of that policy be closely interdependent, but investment decisions once taken will condition what it is possible to do in the future—not of course for all time, but nevertheless over considerable stretches of time. Thus (as we have said) a decision to invest in consumer-goods industries during the first quinquennium will be a factor in determining the level of consumption, and simultaneously in limiting the possible level of investment activity in the second quinquennium and probably in the third as well. Conversely, if the contrary policy is followed, this will mean that a smaller proportion of the national income can be devoted to consumption ten or fifteen years hence, but will make it easier to maintain a high rate of investment in those future years—indeed not only easier, but obligatory to do so, if the steel and engineering capacity created in the earlier years is not to be under-utilised.

In the capitalist economies of the past the order of development has generally been the more gradual one; investment first being directed towards agricultural or extractive industries, then to lighter consumer-goods industries, especially textiles, and only at a later and more advanced stage towards heavy industry producing capital goods. Evidence of this is seen in the fact that the most highly developed capitalist countries like U.S.A. and Britain which have the richest inherited endowment of capital show the greatest development of capital-goods industries; while younger capitalist countries often have no heavy industry to speak of, or at any rate a heavy industry that is little developed compared with other sectors of the economy. It has been traditionally maintained that this is the normal and 'natural' order of development. Some go further than this in contending that it is contrary to the principle of the international division of labour for all parts of the world to develop heavy industry. The argument is sometimes put in the form that those parts of the world which have a high ratio of capital to labour should specialise on what are relatively capital-using or 'capital-intensive' industries; and that, conversely, countries with a high ratio of labour to capital should specialise on relatively labour-using industries. But this is a purely static argument. It starts from a *given* endowment of capital in each country; whereas the crucial question at issue in discussing policies of economic development concerns *change* in the capital-endowment of a country and how rapidly this capital-endowment should be changed. Evidently, the reason why 'younger' industrial countries in the past have tended to specialise in lighter industries and to be slow in developing more capital-intensive ones has been because investment in heavy industry is discouraged by the possibility of importing the products of heavy industry from older and more capitalistically developed countries. International trade has had the effect of 'freezing' an existing international pattern of industries and of factor-endowments, and so of arresting the development of the more backward countries at a certain stage; and against this conservative force the momentum of capital accumulation in the latter countries has been insufficient to carry them forward to a more advanced stage. Were it not for this, it would be quite natural to expect these 'younger' industrial countries (provided mineral and power resources were available) to enrich their own stock of capital equipment and to develop capital-intensive lines of production. If all countries are capable of enriching their heritage of capital instruments, then there is no reason why in the long-run international specialisation should be drawn along these traditional lines. To deny that specialisation should follow the traditional lines is not, however, to say that there should be no specialisation at all. There may be specialisation on specific products of heavy industry, as there can also be in the case of consumer goods or of agricultural crops. For example, the number of machine-tools today is so considerable as to make it uneconomic for any but a very large country to produce all of them simultaneously; and a number of countries may all have machine-tool industries and still leave plenty of room for each to specialise on certain types and for a considerable international exchange of these types to be conducted between them. It is a matter of the lines along which specialisation is drawn; and there is no reason at all why these should continue to be the traditional lines which in the past have divided the world into a few 'advanced' industrial areas and vast satellite 'colonial' areas.

Finally I want to allude to that complementary relationship, or interconnection, between different sectors of development which I mentioned in my first lecture as being of special importance at crucial stages of transition. I there suggested that this relationship might be an influence *sustaining* the momentum of the investment process in a capitalist economy. But let it be noted that I said 'sustaining', thus implying that the momentum was already there. I believe there is also another side to the matter; and if the momentum is not there in the first place, or is weak, this complementary relationship may actually become a retarding influence in a capitalist economy. Where other conditions are not sufficiently mature to supply independently a strong impetus towards investment, this may well be the major reason why the process of industrialisation is held back. In such circumstances it may well be an illusion to suppose that 'private enterprise' is particularly enterprising. I would even go so far as to suggest that it is a reason *par excellence* why a private enterprise economy is incapable of effecting major industrial transitions unless some exceptional combination of favourable circumstances gives it a quite unusual impetus towards expansion.

In a sense, of course, most economic decisions are interconnected —in the sense that an expansion of production in one direction may set in train a multiplier-effect of increased demand for expansion in other directions. This was an aspect of the truth upon which Say's Law seized. But what I am referring to here is that closer dependence of one decision upon another, where the one would be impossible or incomplete without the other. This case includes all cases of joint demand, whether this is a demand for several things in fixed proportions, or whether the proportions in which they are combined are capable of some (though not indefinite) variation. Thus the building of an industrial plant in a new location will be useless unless a railway is also built to that place: investment in the one necessarily implies for its completion investment in the other. It may also involve the provision of housing and communal facilities for workers if the necessary labour supply is to be attracted and retained. Moreover, it may be highly convenient even if not absolutely essential to have in the immediate neighbourhood factories which supply subsidiaries and components or which can utilise by-products. And the presence or absence of this convenience may make all the difference between investment in the initial product being economic or uneconomic. Modern industries (of which motors and aircraft are good examples) are apt to require a very large number of components: components which are generally produced by specialised firms or by plants in other industries; and the introduction of some industrial process may be dependent upon the existence of engineering firms capable of producing the necessary equipment. Again, a modern integrated heavy industry unit is a *congerie* of related processes (such as steel furnaces, coking plant and chemical works), containing a complex network of joint-demand and joint-supply relationships. An expansion of production in any one direction will in all such cases be contingent upon a simultaneous expansion in a number of others. This sort of interdependence has been familiarised among economists by the theory of external economies and its corollaries. What has been less noticed, and its significance even less appreciated, is that such relations of interdependence extend between different industries, and are not confined within the frontiers of a single industry or even of an industry and immediately contiguous industries.

One conclusion which the notion of external economies has made familiar to economists is that in a capitalist economy the decision to invest will be governed by calculation of the profits accruing to each firm, and hence by a calculation that excludes a considerable part of the effects of that investment. Such results (beneficial or otherwise) as accrue elsewhere in the economic system—outside the boundaries of that firm—will be ignored in the decision. When we put the problem in a dynamic setting, the fact that investment at one point on the economic front is dependent upon a simultaneous act of investment at other points may prevent that investment from being made at all, however economically justified it might prove to be if the whole series of related moves could be made in unison. When profit-expectation is abnormally optimistic, this may be no deterrent. But in the more normal case the uncertainty as to whether these parallel moves will be made, without which it cannot be justified in the outcome, may deter even the very boldest. At any rate, this uncertainty may prove a substantial additional cost, which greatly narrows the range of practicable investments and tilts the balance in favour of the cautious and against the ambitious path of development.

It is here, I believe, that (if I may end with a confession of faith) the quintessential superiority of economic planning is to be found as a mechanism of economic development, especially at those crucial and revolutionary turning-points of development where this kind of interdependence is a dominant element in the situation. By enlarging the unit of economic decision regarding investment from the single autonomous entrepreneur to the planned community treated as a whole, it enables these relationships of interdependence to be taken into account; and it makes possible for the first time a coordination *ex ante* of the various constituent decisions in a complex strategy of development, instead of the tardy (and, as experience has taught us, highly imperfect) coordination *ex post* which the traditional market-system provides.

This interrelationship, and hence the possibility of coordination of interconnected parts, applies not only over space (i.e. between economic decisions simultaneously taken in different industries and economic sectors), but also over time. This applies particularly to the technical form of an investment project. The most economic form for this to take will be affected by the probable rate of investment to be maintained in the future and by the probable direction and rate of technical innovation during the physical length of life of the plant in question. In an unplanned economy these are all unknowns. At best the entrepreneur can make an approximate guess by projecting past trends into the future. This is apt to have two opposite results according to the circumstances of the case. Where technical innovation is expected to be rapid, plant is scrapped long before its physical length of life is ended; and in America, where such 'premature obsolescence' is most startlingly in evidence, it is customary for firms to make allowance for this in advance by writing down the value of plant at a very high annual rate (with a consequent increase in the cost assigned to current operation). In yet other cases the existence of large amounts of capital sunk in older methods can act as an obstacle to the introduction of newer methods, and accordingly retard the rate of technical innovation. Both these results involve an economic waste. The best laid plan can never, of course, altogether abolish this uncertainty about future trends; if only because there must be a practicable time-horizon to any plan, if the plan is to be realistic and not just Utopia-spinning; and this time-horizon may even be narrower than the physical length of life of plant (or in a complex industrial unit the highest common multiple of the lives of the various plants composing the unit, which is then the relevant consideration). But planning can evidently reduce this uncertainty considerably; and to the extent that it is capable of so doing, it can economise on the amount of investment (i.e. the amount of sunk resources or stored-up labour) required over time to attain a given economic goal; thereby enabling that goal to be achieved both more speedily and more cheaply.

It is in this connection that I have elsewhere used the analogy of the famous pursuit-curve. Analogies should not be pressed too far. But I would like to conclude this lecture with the suggestion that, particularly in relation to the economic problems of un-industrialised countries, this particular analogy may succinctly embody a large element of truth concerning the essential role of economic planning in economic development.

This pursuit-curve can be represented by a homely illustration.

A dog starts running towards its master from a point (C) which is at right-angles to the path along which his master is bicycling (in the direction A–B). Being a creature of reflex-actions, the dog always runs towards his master in the direction of the point on A–B where its master at the moment is, so that his path in pursuit of his master is a curve. In fact, under these conditions he never *quite* reaches the bicycle, but only approaches it asymptotically. But if the dog were as rational as human beings like to think themselves to be, he would make a straight line towards the point on the path which calculation told him his master would shortly reach; and his path in pursuit of his master would then be the

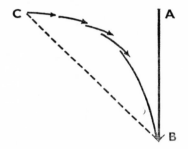

much shorter straight line C–B. The curved path C–B, I suggest, is analogous to the development-path which an unplanned economy is likely to follow in its (largely unconscious) movement towards a certain historical objective, while the straight line C–B is analogous to the path which a planned economy ideally would follow in pursuit of that same historical objective.

This analogy, however, is limited. It assumes, for one thing, that both economies pursue (if in different senses of the word 'pursuit') the same historical objective. As we have seen, they may do no such thing; and it might be more proper to say that the crucial difference between the development-path of these two types of economy is that the historical objective which it is practicable for one system to set itself is quite different from that which the other system can have (even 'unconsciously') on its agenda.

Three

Some reflections on the theory of investment planning and economic growth

This appeared as a contribution to *Problems of Economic Dynamics and Planning: Essays in Honour of Michal Kalecki*, Warszawa, 1964, and is reproduced here by kind permission of the publishers (Polish Scientific Publishers).

The economist Wicksteed once said that mathematical modes of statement served to 'precipitate the assumptions held in solution in the verbiage of our ordinary disquisitions'. What is less commonly recognised is that this virtue may have to be purchased at the price of a quite serious defect: namely that the more formalised is a theory, the more likely is it that corollaries derived from it will be vulnerable because of some implicit assumption concealed behind the formal structure rather than from logical flaws which are more easily detectable.

An example of this would seem to be an assumption implicit in most models of general market equilibrium in recent times (especially in the generalised type of model deriving from Walras), to the effect that the price of any commodity or productive factor which is in surplus supply will fall to zero.[1] A consequential corollary

---

[1] I.e. it will fall to zero if the excess of supply over demand persists despite an initial decline of price to some positive figure. If the latter promotes, e.g., demand-substitution of sufficient magnitude to take up the

which has done damage in recent decades to clarity of thought about the problems of underdeveloped economies with surplus labour is that there can be no conflict between the objectives of maximising what the classical economists called 'net product', or revenue, and of maximising 'gross product' or 'gross revenue'. Yet it may be remembered that David Ricardo thought otherwise, and that one of the differences between him and Adam Smith was the former's contention that 'Adam Smith constantly magnifies the advantages which a country derives from a large gross, rather than a large net income.'[2]

As soon as one scrutinises the above assumption as applied to labour, its absurdity immediately becomes evident. One does not need to be an adherent of a subsistence theory of wages (in any rigid sense, at least) to appreciate that wages must have some minimum level if work is to continue at all; since, unlike other categories of income, wages have the special character of an essential input to labour-power (as ores are essential inputs to metal production or textile fibres to cloth-making). Hence labour cannot be realistically treated as simply one among a series of n ultimate factors of production. Here classical political economy had more realistic sense in treating labour as unique from the standpoint of cost, and the defectiveness of modern formalism in its treatment of all factors of production and their prices as on a par becomes evident.

At a less formal level, when practical conclusions for policy have been in mind, the assumption of which we have spoken has sometimes been translated into the following proposition: that from the social point of view labour should be treated as having a zero social cost so long as there is surplus labour, and that optimal planning implies the assigning of a zero accounting-price to labour. But this proposition (which derives from the very contingent notion, so-

[2] The opening sentence of Chapter XXVI of *Principles of Political Economy and Taxation*: the chapter entitled *On Gross and Net Revenue* (Sraffa edition of *Works and Correspondence of David Ricardo*, Vol. I, p. 347).

excess supply, equilibrium will of course be reached at some positive price.

called 'opportunity cost') suffers from an analogous defect. In practice it is rarely if ever possible to increase the employment of labour without increasing total consumption. This is partly because an individual who is working a full working week has higher nutritional (and perhaps recreational) needs than one who is idle, and partly for incentive reasons. It is a familiar fact that in unindustrialised, or little-industrialised countries, wages in regular industrial employment are very substantially higher than the average standard of living in the village where labour is underemployed if not actually unemployed. It is also probably the case, under conditions of over-populated peasant agriculture, that the removal of a 'mouth' from the family unit (by migration from village to town) will leave total consumption by the family unaltered: it will merely mean that the remaining members of the family will relax their belts a little and take more from the common bowl now that population-pressure is eased. Such additional consumption consequent on an increase of industrial employment cannot be ignored as a social cost.

Failure to appreciate the distinction between maximising total product (including wage-earners' consumption) and maximising net product or surplus has led to a too hasty, and fallacious, identification of the conditions of so-called static equilibrium and the conditions for growth. To speak more specifically: it has enabled certain corollaries to be drawn from the Theory of Marginal Productivity and to be applied as imperatives for the process of economic development. These corollaries have affected the answers to two questions that are crucial to investment-planning policy: firstly the question of choice of methods of production, or of technique, about which there has been considerable discussion among Western economists over the past decade; secondly the question of the distribution of investment between sectors, in particular between production of capital goods and production of consumer goods (the famous Departments I and II of Marx). Analytically these two questions are distinct, though interrelated; but they have been commonly associated as conjoint questions in discussions of economic development and growth.

Traditionally it was assumed by economists in capitalist countries that the answers to both questions followed as direct corollaries from accepted economic theory. As regards choice of technique, this was held to be governed by the principle of comparative costs when factor-prices were determined in accordance with the theory of marginal productivity. According to the existing 'factor-endowment' (relative supplies of the factors of production) of a country, the relative marginal productivities of factors would determine factor-prices and hence influence factor-substitution and the choice of technique. At the same time it would determine the comparative costs of different products. Thus in a situation where capital was scarce and labour plentiful the marginal productivity and hence the price of capital would tend to be high, and equivalently the marginal productivity and price of labour would be low. This would encourage a substitution of labour for capital wherever possible by appropriate shifts both in the lines of industrial specialisation and in the methods of production used in any given industry. Lines of production tending naturally to employ a high ratio of labour to capital, (or with a low 'organic composition of capital', in Marx's terminology) would tend to be lower-cost lines than those where the contrary condition prevailed —namely a low ratio of labour to capital (or a high 'organic composition'). In so far as techniques in any given industry were capable of variation, the more labour-using (or 'labour-intensive') technique, which economises on capital, would tend, *ceteris paribus*, to come out as the lower-cost method of production.

On this basis was erected a veritable theory of a hierarchy of stages of development, each stage of development being characterised by a particular state of factor-endowment. At the lowest stage of development, where the economy of a country was characterised by abundance of labour and scarce capital, there seemed to be no possibility of doubt as to the most 'economic' policy to pursue regarding choice of technique and allocation of investment between industries. The principle of comparative cost dictated a concentration on industries that were labour-using and capital-economising and upon methods of production with a similar bias. In the degree that a country, in the course of development, accumulated capital, so that the ratio of capital to labour was appreciably raised, it could graduate towards more capital-intensive techniques and towards investment in industries involving a higher degree of mechanisation (which were usually identified, somewhat loosely, with 'heavy industries'). Here was both a simple and a direct corollary of economic theory as a guide to makers of economic policy. Many no doubt supposed that there could seldom have been a corollary of economic theory that was more certain and so beyond controversy. When a path in conflict with it was taken by Soviet development in the 1930's, economists in Western countries took for granted the uneconomic and probably self-defeating character of this attempt to leap over essential stages of growth. A development-policy of this kind which sacrificed economic rationality on the altar of national aggrandisement or military necessity could only increase the ultimate cost of growth. [3]

The Achilles heel of this plausible thesis consists in the purely static character of the analysis on which it rests and in its failure to appreciate that the needs of growth can, and do, conflict with the conditions whereby total production, or national income, and also employment are maximised at any given date. There is also the further consideration (on which we shall not dwell here) that the doctrine of comparative costs, if it is to sustain those free trade implications which have been deduced from it since Ricardo's day, must depend on another implicit assumption: namely that changes in the amount of trade undertaken by a country do not exert any appreciable influence on the terms of trade (which is equivalent to assuming that the relevant demand-elasticities are very high). It is a familiar fact that in the case of underdeveloped countries this assumption is least of all justified.

In the discussions of recent years among economists in England and America it has been the view that investment-policy should be judged primarily in terms of its effect on the rate of growth that has formed the main ground of criticism of traditional doctrine (or at least of its corollaries). If the effect of investment-policy on growth is adopted as the guiding criterion, substantially different conclusions are reached from those drawn from the comparative-cost-*cum*-marginal-productivity doctrine. In particular, the desirability is indicated of a higher degree of capital-intensity of investment

---

[3] Mr Peter Wiles in a recent work, *The Political Economy of Communism*, Oxford, 1962, persists in maintaining that any departure from what he calls 'balanced growth' is pointless and uneconomic.

than traditional doctrine prescribes and also the advantage of allocating as large a proportion of investment as possible to the capital-goods sector in order to broaden the basis for future investment. This discussion is probably familiar already to most readers, and no more than a summary of the argument and of its main implications will be attempted here.

Analysis of the effects of particular policies on growth will, of course, depend on what is regarded as being the main investment-determinant (or determinants), since the rate of growth is very largely (though not, of course, exclusively) dependent on the rate of investment that an economy can achieve. The older notion that such a determinant is to be sought in some kind of 'savings fund' can certainly not be maintained in conditions of surplus labour; and the notion of an independently given 'savings-ratio' as setting a ceiling upon investment is manifestly inapplicable to conditions of a planned economy where the chief components of such a ratio are among the dependent variables of planning policy. But this does not mean that there is no economic 'ceiling' on investment short of a rate of investment that immediately absorbs all unused resources into production (so that the condition of a labour reserve for industrial expansion that we have posited as characteristic of countries at early stages of development disappears). It means merely that we have to look for such limiting factors among the 'real' or basic features of an economy, connected with its conditions of production or its productive structure.

There are two limiting factors which experience has shown to be particularly relevant to underdeveloped economies. Firstly, there is the supply of wage-goods available to meet the consumption-needs of workers employed in the investment sector of the economy (meaning by this a sector that includes both the work of building and construction and the manufacture of constructional materials and equipment used and installed in the new construction-projects). In turn this supply of available wage-goods will depend upon the surplus of production over consumption in the wage-goods industries.[4] Secondly, there is the productive

---

[4] These will include agriculture, so that in a predominantly peasant country this surplus will largely depend upon the productivity of peasant agriculture relatively to peasant consumption.

capacity of the industries producing capital goods of all kinds (Marx's Department I)—a productive capacity consisting in the size of the installed capital equipment of this group of industries.[5]

As bottlenecks these two factors may well be jointly operative rather than alternatives: they may be always present in the background of every historical situation. Yet it seems likely that in any given situation one of them will be more important than the other; possibly the former of them at early stages of development in underdeveloped countries and the latter at later stages when industrial construction has got well under way and a substantial industrial base has been constructed. At any rate there is no need to argue about their relative priority. This may well vary in different cases as well as changing at different stages of development; and although the practical consequence of emphasising each of them is rather different, there is in this respect no conflict between their respective implications, which can be regarded as constituent elements of any planning policy designed to maximise growth.

At first sight it might seem as though the surplus of wage-goods over the self-consumption of them by their producers bears an analogy with the savings-ratio mentioned above which forms the crux of many theories of growth, in particular those of the Harrod–Domar type. In a sense such an analogy can be found; but it is mainly a formal analogy, since the savings-ratio as customarily conceived is compounded of (and dependent upon) the savings-propensities (or their inverse, the consumption-propensities) of individuals. Viewed concretely in the context we have here indicated, it has an important difference; and attention is at once focused upon a particular way in which the surplus-ratio may be raised, namely by raising labour-productivity. This is, indeed, the crux of the case for choosing more capital-intensive techniques than the traditional theory allows—a case that has been argued in

---

[5] I leave it as an open question whether this should include the production of raw materials ('objects of labour') or be confined to the production of metals and machinery ('instruments of labour'), each of the two main sectors being treated as vertically integrated back to the production of their several raw materials. For many purposes the latter seems to be the more convenient.

the past decade by the present writer and by Professor Amartya Kumar Sen.[6]

It does not follow, because labour-intensive techniques are deleterious to the growth-potential (by keeping labour-productivity low), that capital-intensity can with advantage be raised *indefinitely*, since more capital-intensive equipment will tend to be more costly to produce, and at some point this rise in cost will offset (in its effect on the use of a given investment-potential to promote growth) the favourable effect of a rise in productivity of those using this equipment, and hence in the surplus-ratio. There comes an optimum point in the choice of more capital-intensive methods: a point that will tend to come sooner, *ceteris paribus*, the lower is the initial level of real wages, and conversely. In a simplified two-sector model used by the present writer some years ago this point was formally defined by saying that, if p_c and p_i stand for the productivity of labour in the consumer-goods (or wage-goods) sector and the investment sector (producing capital goods) respectively, there will tend to be a certain relationship between a rising value of p_c and falling values of p_i ($1/p_i$ being the cost of capital goods). If we write L_c and L_i for the labour force of the two sectors and

$$\frac{s}{w} \left(= \frac{p_c - w}{w} \right)$$

for the ratio of surplus product to wages (= consumption) in the consumption-goods sector, the output of capital goods can be seen to depend upon the size of $L_i p_i$, and L_i in turn upon $L_c \cdot s/w$. The condition for maximising $L_i p_i$, and hence the rate of growth of the economy, is that a relation between p_c and p_i should normally be chosen (as one moves along the range of relevant alternatives in

[6] M. Dobb in *Economie Appliquée*, 1954, Vol. VII, No. 3; in *Review of Economic Studies*, 1955–6, Vol. XXIV, No. 1; and in *An Essay on Economic Growth and Planning*, London, 1960. A. K. Sen in *Quarterly Journal of Economics*, November 1957, and in *Choice of Techniques*, Oxford, 1960. Cf. also W. Galenson and H. Leibenstein in *Quarterly Journal of Economics*, August 1955, where, however, it is implied in places that there is advantage in choosing an indefinitely high capital-intensity: this as will be seen above is not so.

the direction of more costly techniques) such that the following condition is fulfilled:

$$\frac{-dp_i}{p_i} = \frac{dp_c}{p_c} \cdot \frac{s+w}{s}.$$

It may be noted that it is only in the unreal case where $w = 0$ that this would be identical with the point where the total output of consumer goods is maximised[7] (and the capital–output ratio minimised) according to the prescriptions of the traditional theory. Total consumption in the immediate future will be smaller, therefore, if investment is governed by this criterion than if less capital-intensive methods had been chosen; so also will employment be smaller. To this extent there is a conflict of objectives. But the conflict is no more than a short-period one. A policy that maximises the rate of increase in investment will *ipso facto* maximise the rate of increase both of total employment and of the output of consumption goods; and in the longer period (which may not be so very long in time) will make the absolute level as well as the increase of employment and consumption greater than if the more cautious and gradual path of development had been taken. For this reason it seems preferable to express the issue in terms of a difference between the short-period and the long-period effects of different investment-policies, rather than as a conflict of objectives as has sometimes been done (e.g. the objective of maximising employment or consumption *versus* the objective of maximising growth). Such a conflict, as we have said, only applies within a certain time-horizon; and beyond it what maximises investment and its rate of increase will also maximise employment and consumption.

It should perhaps be emphasised that what has been said about choice of technique applies on condition that consumption per head (i.e. w in the notation adopted) does not rise proportionately with the rise of productivity consequent on choosing a more expensive technique. In a capitalist economy (and *a fortiori*, perhaps, in a peasant economy) there is no guarantee that this will not occur, since the higher productivity will accrue as higher individual

[7] That is, identical with the point where the proportionate rise of p_c is *equal* to the proportional fall of p_i.

incomes (in particular higher profits) which may result in higher consumption-standards and in proportionately higher individual consumption. In countries with a peasant agriculture it is a familiar problem (and itself constituting a barrier to development) that improved agricultural productivity (or alternatively price- or tax-concessions in favour of agriculture) may have little, if any, effect on the marketed surplus of agricultural foodstuffs, but instead exhaust its effect largely in augmenting the self-consumption of peasant producers, or alternatively encouraging them to enjoy more leisure. This is one of the reasons why a high growth-rate policy such as we have described can be expected to be char- acteristic of planned socialist economies (or at least of economies with a large State sector) and not of free market economies.

Regarding the second of the two limiting factors of which we have spoken, somewhat analogous considerations apply: namely that while a policy of assigning priority to investment in the capital-goods sector will cause consumption to grow relatively slowly in the immediate future, by augmenting the investment- potentiality of future years it will eventually enable consumption to increase more rapidly, both absolutely and proportionately, than it could have done if the capital-goods sector at earlier dates had grown more slowly. If, of course, the existing level of consumption per head of the labour force has to be regarded as constant (e.g. for efficiency or incentive reasons), then the allocation of invest- ment between the two main sectors is determined for us, within very narrow limits, and there is little or no choice in the matter. Output-capacity in the consumption-goods industries must expand in step with total employment; hence the capital-goods sector cannot expand faster than the consumption-goods sector, unless expansion of the former is accompanied by a shift towards more labour-saving techniques. Expressed in the notation employed above, growth must be so balanced as to observe the equality $L_i = L_c . s/w$: that is, employment in the investment sector can grow no faster than does the surplus production of the wage-goods sector, and (apart from a raising of productivity by rationalised organisation or improved technique) investment must be allocated so as to keep the growth-rates of the two sectors uniform.

But although real wages are subject to a minimum level and even above this level may be causally related to working efficiency, the existing wage-level may have some flexibility at least over limited periods of time. In this case[8] it will be possible to expand the investment sector more rapidly than the rest of the economy; which will have the effect of increasing the relative investment-potential, and hence the rate at which the system can grow at future dates. It should be noted that, although this will mean (unless technical innovation is sufficiently rapid) that consumption will grow more slowly than employment, this is not inconsistent with a continuing rise in total consumption and even in consumption *per capita* of the population (since the proportion of the whole population employed in industry is rising). Total consumption will, as we have said, increase more slowly in the immediate future than if investment-priority had been given to the consumption-goods industries instead of to capital-goods industries; but after a certain date in the future total consumption under the high-growth-rate policy will rise above what it would have been under a policy initially more favourable to consumption.

It will have been noted that the simplified model of which we have been speaking is essentially a model in terms of labour and its product, in which capital does not figure separately as a quantity, or as a factor of production: merely capital goods that are products of labour at some previous stage of production and which play the role of aids to labour influencing labour's productivity. The problem of choosing the type of capital good, and the appropriate distribution of labour between the sectors, that promoted maximum growth could have been expressed as a minimum problem in terms of cost—minimising the social cost of maintaining a given rate of growth. In any economy where calculation is in value terms, it will be in this form that the problem will be immediately expressed, at any rate to those taking decisions 'decentrally' at lower levels, such as administrators of particular industries or managers of enterprises. Some interest accordingly attaches to the question as to how our principle applies when

---

[8] Also if technical innovation is sufficiently rapid; or again if the supply of consumer goods and/or capital goods can be augmented by improved terms of trade with other countries or with an agricultural hinterland of the developing economy.

expressed in this way. What kind of price-structure is conducive to the taking of the right kind of decision?

At first sight it might seem that, from the nature of our model, the principle must now appear as one of minimising labour-input to produce a given quantum of output. But this cannot be so in any *simpliste* interpretation of minimising labour cost; since such a principle can only be applied subject to a certain investment-constraint—that labour is so distributed and methods of production so chosen as to maximise investment (measured in terms of labour-inputs). Otherwise, the principle of minimising expenditure of labour would lead to the use of the most productive known techniques however expensive and capital-intensive, so long as increase in capital-intensity yielded *any* addition, however small, to net productivity (in the notation of our example used above, it would imply choosing the highest possible value of p_c when this is interpreted net of the cost of maintenance or replacement of equipment). It follows that cost must be so interpreted as to make some allowance for such an investment constraint (for which purpose, incidentally, capital goods currently produced will need to be priced and aggregated into a total). Such an allowance seems only possible if the use of capital goods is in some way debited with the contribution which it can make to the appearance of a surplus product.

Professor V. V. Novozhilov of Leningrad has suggested a method of pricing that makes an allowance of this kind; and there is some interest, accordingly, in considering how the operation of his method (and the use of 'minimum cost' so interpreted) is related to the principle we have enunciated. To do this was the object (in part) of an article by the present writer in the journal *Kyklos* in 1961 (Vol. XIV, Fasc. 2, pp. 135–50); and the remainder of the present paper will consist of a reproduction of the analysis in the concluding part of that article.

Professor V. V. Novozhilov's proposal is as follows.[9] A ratio

[9] Cf. *Ismerenie Zatrat i ikh Resultatov v Sotsialisticheskom Khoziaistvie* (Comparison of Expenditures and their Results in a Socialist Economy) in *Primenenie Matematiki v Ekonomicheskikh Issledovaniakh* (The Use of Mathematics in Economic Investigations), ed. V. S. Nemchinov, Moscow, 1959, pp. 42–213.

which he terms the 'marginal effectiveness of investment' is calculated thus. A given quantity of investment funds is allocated according to a uniform ratio at the margin of all uses and in such a way that, when possible investment projects and their variants have been arranged in an order of their effectiveness, all projects yielding an effectiveness-ratio higher than the ratio selected as standard are given priority. When the whole investment fund has been allocated in this way without surplus or deficiency, there will be a given minimum effectiveness-ratio at the margin of allocation. This will constitute for the time-being the standard ratio. The ratio in question is defined as that of the reduction of operating cost (or prime cost) resulting from a given increase of investment to the absolute amount of this investment. Thus, where C_1 and C_2 stand for the prime costs respectively in two projects of different technical types, and K_1 and K_2 for the initial capital cost, the effectiveness-ratio will be

$$\frac{C_1 - C_2}{K_2 - K_1}.$$

Writing the above ratio as r, Professor Novozhilov then proceeds to show that if rK is added to C to represent the social cost of a product (which he calls *narodnokhoziaistvennaia sebestoimost*, or national-economic cost), this will render the cost of a product lowest when produced by the technique, or method of production, that yields an effectiveness-ratio of r. It is to be noted that rK as a magnitude will be independent of the units in which K and C are expressed (i.e. the relative valuation of capital goods and the elements of prime costs); since the larger is K relatively to C, the smaller will be r, and conversely.[10]

Thus, suppose that there are three technical variants under consideration such that:

$$K_1 < K_2 < K_3 < K_4 \text{ and } C_1 > C_2 > C_3 > C_4,$$

and

$$\frac{C_1 - C_2}{K_2 - K_1} > \frac{C_2 - C_3}{K_3 - K_2} > \frac{C_3 - C_4}{K_4 - K_3}$$

Let

$$\frac{C_2 - C_3}{K_3 - K_2} = r;$$

[10] V. V. Novozhilov, loc. cit., pp. 112–15.

then it will follow that

$$rK_3 + C_3 < rK_4 + C_4; \text{ also} \leqslant rK_2 + C_2 \text{ and} < rK_1 + C_1.$$

It follows that if one adopts this principle as the basis of social costing (whether for the purpose of accounting prices only or of fixing actual prices) and alternative methods of production are chosen according to which of them yields the least cost, the result will be the maximum economy of social labour, in the qualified sense of which we have spoken (qualified, i.e., by an investment constraint). The inclusion of rK as an element in cost, in addition to C, is a recognition of the latter constraint and is itself a reflection of it in the costing-process.

At first sight this may seem to bear no close relation to the criterion for maximising growth discussed above. Reflection, however, will show, I think, that there is such a connection. Let us first try to express this connection in formal terms in this way. We have said above that in our model a condition for maximising growth[11] is that

$$\frac{-dp_i}{p_i} = \frac{dp_c}{p_c} \cdot \frac{s + w}{s}$$

$$\left(\text{or alternatively that } \frac{dp_c}{p_c} = \frac{-dp_i}{p_i} \cdot \frac{s}{s + w}\right).$$

It can also be shown that the magnitude $(s + w)/s$ is a measure of the proportional increase in surplus resulting from a proportional rise in p_c: i.e.

$$\frac{dp_c}{p_c} \cdot \frac{s + w}{s} = \frac{ds}{s}.$$

Now Professor Novozhilov's rK (which we have seen is, as a composite magnitude, independent of the relative valuation of K and C) when expressed as a ratio to C if C consists exclusively of wages (or alternatively as a ratio to that proportion of C which consists of wages) can be shown to be a measure of the relationship in our model between the proportional change of p_c and the proportional

[11] In what we have called elsewhere a 'normal' case where the p's at different (vertical) stages of production are approximately uniform.

change of p_i.[12] This relationship we have just seen is $s/s + w$ when growth is being maximised. Accordingly, if we write as a the proportion of prime cost that consists of wages, $rK/aC = s/s + w$, since r we have seen is derived by allocating investment so as to have the maximum effect in raising the productivity of labour.[13] For any economic unit (e.g. an industrial enterprise) to which rK is debited as a cost as well as C, that method of producing a given output which minimises $rK + C$ will be the most profitable (or involve the smallest loss), at whatever level the selling-price may be, *provided* that selling-prices are proportional to the Novozhilov cost-price. But if *only* C is debited to it as an actual cost, that method of production will only be the most profitable if the selling-price is so fixed as to make profit above C when expressed as a ratio to $aC = s/w$: i.e. to make it greater than rK/aC by $s + w/w$.[14]

In commonsense terms the point of this may be expressed in this way. We are comparing the reduced wage-cost of producing a given output with the increased investment-cost of making this reduction; and rK is a measure of this relation. In other words, it measures the economy of labour resulting from more investment against the additional expenditure of labour in the investment

[12] Since r is equivalent to dp_c/dp_i and rK can be expressed as

$$\frac{dp_c}{dp_i/p_i}.$$

This when divided by p_c (which in this context would be the equivalent of C if C consisted exclusively of wages) becomes

$$\frac{dp_c/p_c}{dp_i/p_i}.$$

[13] This is subject to a crucial proviso, however: that the output-plan is appropriately fixed. If output is not fixed in a manner consistent with maximising growth, the above equality may not hold, since the allocation of investment is relative to a given pattern of output, and accordingly r may have different values for different output-patterns.

[14] Since $$s/w = \frac{s/s + w}{w/s + w}.$$

So far as consumer goods are concerned, prices will only be equilibrium-prices (ignoring direct taxes on wages or saving out of wages) if they are at this average level (cf. the writer's *Essay*, pp. 91–2, 95–6). It may also be noted that, if selling-prices are proportional to $rK + C$ but diverge therefrom, total profit as a ratio to K will not be uniform in all industries.

sector that is involved thereby. With a given investment-potential for the economy as a whole, the use of more investment in one direction involves reduced investment, and hence a reduced contribution to growth, in some other direction. This reduced contribution to growth in another direction is the addition to surplus that the investment could there have yielded (assuming that surplus is a crucial investment-determinant). If rK is to be an adequate measure of the social cost of using more investment, it must be a measure of the marginal contribution being made in the economy as a whole to the increase in labour-productivity. It follows that for relative prices to be an adequate reflection of social cost, whether they are prices of consumer goods or of capital goods, they must at each stage of production be proportional to C plus rK.[15]

It has often been supposed that a quantity such as rK can be used to determine the rate of investment itself as well as its optimum allocation. But this is not so. Professor Novozhilov's rK can only be derived on the basis of prior postulation of the amount of total investment (measured, for example, in a given aggregate output of the capital-goods sector). Since in the real world planners can never make the volume of investment what they will (but can only influence its rate of change), one need not be unduly worried or surprised that theory should be unable to postulate on *a priori* grounds some optimum rate of investment. If in the real world investment is subject to definite determinants, theory is only being realistic (and is not being arbitrary) in starting from the postulate of a given volume of investment, and then investigating the limits within which, and the means by which, this quantum of investment can be changed over time.

It remains, in conclusion, to make one general observation about the implications of the approach we have outlined for practical problems of economic development. One thing that follows is that what matters from the standpoint of actual policy is not so much what the rate of investment happens to be at some initial date: this

[15] K will here represent, of course, the value of the capital goods used in the particular production-process in question, not some generalised K averaged out over production as a whole. The value of r will be derived, however, from a generalised *social* effectiveness-ratio applying to the economy at large.

will be largely determined by past history, at least so far as the 'ceiling' on it is concerned. What matters most is how that volume of investment is utilised and the difference made by the mode of utilisation to the *rate at which that rate of investment can change.* Investment-allocation must accordingly be thought of, not in terms of equations defining a static equilibrium, but in terms of this rate of change. To take some pre-existing 'savings-ratio' and extrapolate it into the future (as is implicitly done in so many 'Western' discussions of the limiting factors upon development) tends to give an unduly conservative bias. Any such ratio, based on today's situation or yesterday's, is not the rigidly limiting factor that it is commonly supposed to be, because it can itself be changed by the course of development, if development is planned to that end. Economically backward countries may not be able to 'pull themselves up by their own bootstraps': if, for example, they altogether lack the means of producing machinery themselves, they must inevitably import machinery, at any rate for a time: if they possess a purely subsistence agriculture that yields little or no surplus, they must even import food. But their dependence for development on outside aid is much less, and their ability to develop out of their own resources is much greater, given correct policies, than economists have traditionally allowed. True, such more optimistic perspectives will not emerge from the free opera-tion of market forces, but presuppose planning both as a mechanism of coordination and as a means of imposing a correct order of priorities; and planning if it is to be comprehensive in turn pre-supposes social ownership of the means of production.

Four

The question of 'Investment-priority for heavy industry'

This was written at the beginning of 1965 as a contribution to a projected volume of essays in honour of the
late Paul Baran, to be edited by Professor Bernard
Haley and to be published by the Stanford University
Press. The project was unfortunately abandoned a year
later, so that this article is published here for the first
time.

So-called investment-priority for heavy industry has come to be
regarded, in discussing policies of development, as a leading characteristic of Soviet industrialisation. This and the coupling of rapid
industrialisation with collectivisation of agriculture are generally
treated as composing the hallmark of the specifically Soviet mode
of development. As such it has been counterposed to the traditional
process which Professor Rostow christened 'textiles first'; and as
a deviation from the traditional method it has been commonly
denounced in the past by economists in Western Europe and
America as an uneconomic and humanly wasteful way of attaining
its postulated goal. In underdeveloped countries, faced with the
problem of either launching or sustaining the momentum of an
industrial revolution, its economic *rationale* has been more frequently appreciated; and in the last ten or fifteen years discussion
has shifted to the general applicability of this method to underdeveloped countries and whether or not it can be regarded as a
general condition for achieving a high rate of growth. Certainly in
Paul Baran's treatment of economic development and its problems

in his influential work, *The Political Economy of Growth* (New York: Monthly Review Press, 1957), this 'heterodox' principle is virtually treated as an axiom of rapid economic growth. This is how the matter is epitomised:

> Large investment in producers' goods industries is tantamount to high rates of growth sustained during the entire planning period, and correspondingly a program directed towards economic development *via* consumers' goods industries implies automatically not only smaller initial investment but also much lower rates of ensuing growth. (Ibid., p. 284.)

Firstly to say something of the historical background of this precept. There are two reasons in particular why this is a peculiarly Marxian notion (at least in the sense of something that comes naturally to mind to one using Marxian categories of thought). In the first place it is a fairly obvious application of Marx's famous two-departmental schema in the second volume of *Das Kapital*. Secondly, Lenin had advanced the view, in the course of his controversy with the Narodniks, that Capitalism had developed the production of means of production faster than that of means of consumption: that this had, indeed, been an essential part of Capitalism's 'historic mission'—'production for the sake of production'.[1] If this had been done by Capitalism, then it surely seemed to follow for any Marxist that this must *a fortiori* be the aim of a socialist economy, especially in the situation in which the Soviet Union found herself in the 1920's. In the economic controversies of that decade about how to build socialism in a backward country that was predominantly agricultural and had a weakly-developed heavy industry, this way of presenting the problem had already become familiar. Theorists of the Right-wing, like Shanin of the Commissariat of Finance, had explicitly talked about a necessary sequence of development, consisting first of agriculture, secondly of light industry mainly in response to the demands of the village market, and thirdly and lastly of heavy industry as and when the growth of agriculture and light industry

---

[1] *The Development of Capitalism*, Moscow, Foreign Languages Publishing House, 1956, pp. 31–4.

had brought in their train a sufficient expansion in the demand for capital goods. On the other hand, the so-called 'Left Opposition' of the time consistently complained of the relative backwardness of heavy industry (which in the process of reconstruction after the war and civil war had recovered its prewar position considerably less well than other branches of industry). When critics of Preobrazhensky's policy of laying the main burden of financing industrialisation upon the peasantry argued that such a policy, by narrowing the peasant market for industrial products, must inevitably retard the growth of industry, Preobrazhensky retorted that the lead in the process of industrialisation would be taken by heavy industry which would supply a demand generated in the process of its own expansion—serve a market internal to itself. When the First Five-Year Plan eventually came to be formulated, the notion of investment in heavy industry as *leading* the process of development, instead of passively following it, was firmly established as the fulcrum of economic strategy.

Actually it was the economic writer G. A. Feldman of Gosplan, long-neglected but now comparatively well-known (since rediscovered by Domar), who really formalised the notion that investment-priority for the capital-goods sector was a pre-condition for attaining a high rate of growth. His analysis was based on Marx's famous two-departmental schema of expanded reproduction; but in order to suit them to the purpose in hand, he appropriately adapted these so as to include in the capital-goods sector only the production of what catered for the needs of growth (i.e. represented net *additions* to capital); leaving in the consumers'-goods sector all stages of production (including raw materials and replacement of equipment) necessary to produce 'the consumer goods necessary for satisfying an existing level of needs'.[2] On the size of the former sector (which he designated the u-sector), measured in terms of productive capacity, the size of total investment, and hence *growth* in productive capacity, at any date depended. It is to be noted, *inter alia*, that his method of presentation was *not* in terms of the customary antithesis between growth and consumption, but in terms of the necessary condition for achieving a given and desired growth-rate of consumption in future years. To every desired

[2] *Planovoe Khoziaistvo*, 1928, No. 11; 1929, No. 12, pp. 100–19.

(constant) growth-rate of consumption in the future as a planning objective there corresponded a certain relative size of the capital-goods sector and hence a certain proportionate allocation of investment to the capital-goods sector at all intervening dates. The higher the desired future growth-rate, the larger, *ceteris paribus*, the proportionate allocation devoted to expanding the capital-goods sector must be.[3] In the course of propounding this, he used an equation formally identical with the Harrod growth-equation, the difference being that it was expressed in terms of productive capacity and supply: namely, the growth-rate was equal to the productive capacity of the capital-goods sector as a proportion of total productive capacity multiplied by the 'effectiveness of capital' (the inverse of the capital–output ratio).[4] The rate of *increase* in the growth-rate depended on the rate of increase in the proportionate size of the capital-goods sector, and hence on the proportionate allocation of current investment between the two sectors.

In other words, he was postulating a linkage over time between investment, of different kinds, at different dates: between the possibility of enlarging productive equipment in (say) the clothing industry at any date subsequent to some future year t_n and enlargement of productive capacity in the machine-making industry itself at some previous date, t_o. It was concerned, at a macroscopic (and simplified two-sector) level, with an input-output relationship extended over time, with inputs and outputs severally dated to allow for the time-lags involved in an actual development process in which capital construction and enlargement of productive capacity are involved. It was concerned, in other words, with the allocation-pattern between investments that differed as regards the time-destination of the final output-flow to which they would give rise.

The proposition that, *ceteris paribus*, the future potential growth-rate of output will be higher the larger is the proportion of current investment devoted to enlarging the productive capacity of capital-goods industries, has always seemed to the present writer suf-

---

[3] The relative sizes of the two sectors (which he wrote as K_u/K_p) he called 'prime indicators of the level of industrialisation'. An increase in rate of growth of national income required a rise in this level.

[4] *Planovoe Khoziaistvo*, 1929, No. 12, p. 116.

ficiently obvious, once stated, to admit of little if any dispute.[5] Of course it implies a certain view of what constitute crucial limiting factors in a process of development; and choice regarding invest-ment-allocation in the relevant sense will be subject to certain constraints—in particular, the minimum level of real wages and the annual rate at which this is required to rise (e.g. for social or efficiency reasons) in the immediate future. Moreover, the proposi-tion may be said to imply a way of looking at things that is unusual for many, if not most, 'Western' economists—namely of viewing supply-conditions as preceding in time the satisfaction of a given demand or end-use, and hence consumption and investment at any date as being causally dependent on previous investment-decisions at earlier dates.[6] But to deny that there is any connection at all between future growth-potential and present investment-allocation is to deny that any realistic meaning can be given to a differentia-tion of investments according to a dating of the output-stream to which they eventually give rise. None the less there are some who have questioned this, and even denounced the whole notion as an illusion.[7] To examine the question again, with some of its implica-tions, may not, accordingly, be altogether otiose.

[5] Cf. the writer's *Essay on Economic Growth and Planning*, London, Routledge, 1960, pp. 66–8.

[6] The more usual method is for economic theory to treat the investment-potential at any date as governed by a so-called 'savings-ratio' pertaining to the income-expenditure balance of the economy at that date. Things are mainly demand-determined according to this view and not supply-determined.

[7] For example Prof. Peter Wiles, in his *Political Economy of Communism*, Oxford, Blackwell, 1962, pp. 291–300, argues that 'no ultimate benefit results' from shifting the proportionate distribution of investment be-tween sectors, and that one cannot do anything by such shifting that could not be achieved by what he terms 'balanced growth' (i.e. by an equi-proportional expansion of productive capacity in all sectors). (The present writer has commented on this argument in a review in *The Economic Journal*, September 1963, pp. 490-1.) Another example is Mr M. FG. Scott in *Oxford Economic Papers*, February 1962, pp. 103–7, who denies that there is 'special virtue in "basic" materials or machines'. On the other hand, Prof. Leif Johansen (in an unpublished paper pre-sented to a Symposium on Econometric Analysis for Planning, organised by the Colston Research Society in Bristol, 6th–10th April, 1964) defends the use of a two-sector model of this type for planning problems and

What for brevity can be called the Feldman-proposition admittedly depends on the assumption that the output-capacity of industries such as metals and machine-making constitute in some sense a principal bottleneck upon construction and development. They may not be the only such bottleneck—all essential inputs can become bottlenecks at various times if they are in short supply relatively to other inputs. But the former must be in some sense the main bottleneck or for some reason the most enduring one. Countries with underdeveloped industry are apt to be particularly deficient in heavy industry (as was the U.S.S.R. in the '20's), if only because those industries which develop first are likely to be those catering for an immediate demand in the home market or for export; and traditionally metals, machine-making and constructional trades have only grown under the stimulus (if not of export, which is unlikely) of a rapid increase in the former type of industry. In such circumstances what can be produced by the capital-goods sector of industry is highly likely to be the crucial limiting factor on what a scheme of planned development in that country can achieve.

This is not to deny that there may be situations to which the Feldman-proposition will not apply. In a completely free trade world, with high demand-elasticities, it would make little difference to development whether a country could make structural steel and machinery itself or produce other commodities (even primary commodities) with a sufficient market abroad, since by exporting the latter it could procure the means to import the steel and machinery on which development depended. Perhaps some free trade model of this kind is what sceptics and critics of the notion of investment-priority for heavy industry have at the back of their minds. But this type of situation is, of course, very far from that which prevailed in the U.S.S.R. in the '20's and '30's; and it is recognised fairly widely today that many, if not most, underdeveloped countries of the world have their export-capacities limited fairly straitly by low demand-elasticities.

---

compares the type of development that allocates investment to the capital-goods sector with the aim of maximising consumption later to the 'turnpike theorem'.

Again it is true that if real wages are at some minimum level which cannot be lowered for social, efficiency or incentive reasons, it will be impossible to expand the capital-goods sector, measured in terms of employment in it, any faster than the productive capacity of the sector of consumer goods is expanded (at least of consumer goods that constitute 'wage-goods'). This will remain true, at any rate, in the absence of technical change (or alternatively rationalisation or reorganisation and fuller use of productive capacity) adequate to exert a strongly labour-saving influence, or alternatively lowering (and not raising) the capital–output ratio—a matter to which we shall return. This is an example of the constraints within which the Feldman-principle necessarily operates, as we mentioned earlier: in this case there would be no area of choice within which the pattern of investment-allocation could be varied.

One thing that can be seen to follow directly from the case we have just mentioned is that the immediate tendency of a Feldman-type of development will be to expand employment faster than consumers'-goods output, *ceteris paribus*, with a consequential tendency to a decline of real wage-rates. This is not the same thing as a fall of total consumption or even of consumption *per capita*. It is quite possible for both total consumption and consumption *per capita* of the population as a whole to *rise* while real wages fall, since industrial employment will be increasing, and if this increase is fed by transfer from previously unemployed or under-employed labour or from peasant agriculture, this generally involves a transfer from a low level of consumption to an appreciably higher one.[8] This I have heard described by a Polish economist as a process of 'redistribution of income within the working class', whereby the newly employed gain in part at the expense of the older generation of industrial workers. Manifestly a policy of

[8] If Miss Janet Chapman's estimates are to be relied on, this is what was happening in the U.S.S.R. in the prewar decade. According to her, *per capita* household purchases rose by 61 per cent between 1928 and 1937 (when measured at 1928 prices—but by only 10 per cent when measured at 1937 prices), while real wages fell by between 17 and 42 per cent (according as they are measured in 1928 or in 1937 prices). Janet G. Chapman, *Real Wages in Soviet Russia since 1928*, Harvard, 1963, pp. 158, 169–70.

accelerated growth of this kind can only be pursued for a period; it cannot be a continuing and long-term policy, since the tendency for employment to outrun the output of wage-goods will sooner or later bring the system against the constraint that we have mentioned, in the shape of a minimum 'floor' to real wages, which itself constitutes a 'ceiling' on the proportionate allocation of investment in favour of capital-goods production. In addition to this there is the consideration that, as the capital-goods sector grows in size, the proportion of annual net investment directed towards it will need to be progressively increased in order to boost the growth-rate further. As Feldman was at pains to point out, as the size of the capital-goods sector grows relatively to the consumers'-goods sector (K_u/K_p in his notation) the effect of any further increase of relative size upon the growth-rate of consumption rapidly decreases (approaching a ceiling growth-rate given by the 'effectiveness of capital', or the output–capital ratio, in the capital-goods sector). At some stage in development it is inevitable that the degree of investment-priority in favour of this sector will have to be relaxed. It can be a policy for a period or phase of development only (as Feldman himself fully realised).

In the course of this later stage of relaxation there are two possibilities. Firstly, the proportions in which investment is allocated between the sectors may be stabilised at its existing level. For a time the capital-goods sector will continue to grow the more rapidly,[9] although at a slackening rate: i.e. grow more rapidly than total output, and *a fortiori* more rapidly than the output of consumer goods. The growth-rate of the latter, however, will now be accelerating, and eventually all three growth-rates (of capital goods, of total output and of consumption) must be equalised. From then on there will be 'balanced growth' at a level somewhat higher than that reached at the end of the preceding stage: a level determined by the size of the capital-goods sector relatively to the economy as a whole.

Secondly, in the interests of raising consumption more rapidly

[9] This is on the assumption that investment allocation had previously been such as to cause the relative size of the capital-goods sector to grow:

$$\text{i.e.} \quad \frac{dK_u}{dK_p} > \frac{K_u}{K_p}.$$

than in the first case, allocation-preference in favour of capital-goods production may be reduced, and the distribution of invest-ment made more favourable to consumption. When this occurs, the rate of increase of consumption will rise above the average growth-rate of total output, but the latter will itself tend to fall, *ceteris paribus*.

Growth in these three types of situation (the first period of accelerated growth, and the two variants of the second period in which investment-priority for capital goods is terminated or reduced) can be depicted as follows. Here growth-rates are repre-sented by the *slopes* of the relevant curves and the horizontal axis to each diagram represents time. *K* stands for the production of capital goods, *C* for consumers' goods and *G* for the average growth of total output.

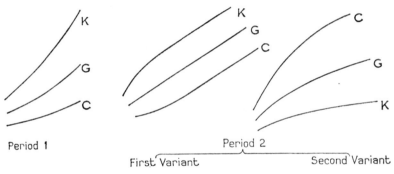

Period 1   Period 2

First Variant   Second Variant

Our first period roughly corresponds to what was happening to the Soviet economy in the dozen years before the Second World War, and in varying degrees to what was happening in countries of Eastern Europe in the ten years after the war. During the past decade it would look as though the Soviet economy had been in process of transition to the first variant of the second period, since there has been a much closer approximation in the growth-rates of the two sectors, while the over-all growth-rate has been lower than formerly and has even shown a tendency (in the last quin-quennium) to fall.[10] In principle investment-priority to heavy

[10] In the Seven-Year Plan for 1958–65, as originally projected, an output-increase of 85 per cent in Group A was provided for and 62–5 per cent

industry is still adhered to (and emphasised recently by the special weight attached to developing the chemical industry, with an eye to raising agricultural yields). But there have been some hints of a trend of opinion in the direction of the second variant of our Period 2, which might well prevail if spending on defence industries could be relaxed with a *détente* in the Cold War. Even so, it is unlikely to be pursued for more than a temporary interval, since the sharp rise in consumption which it would immediately facilitate would be purchased at the expense of a fall in the overall growth-rate—except in so far as this was counteracted by an acceleration of technical progress. The more likely objective over the next two decades (in the absence of war) would seem to be something approximating to our first variant.

An incidental difficulty in this connection perhaps deserves mention. The Soviet distinction between the so-called A Sector and the B Sector and Marx's original two-departmental schema have alike certain disadvantages when one is trying to relate the kind of analysis we have been making to concrete data concerning growth. One way of interpreting Marx's two departments or sectors—and for most purposes I think the most convenient way—is to treat each of them as being vertically integrated back to their own raw materials, grown from or extracted from the earth.[11] This involves, in turn, treating the products of Department I as consisting

---

[11] This was the interpretation employed by the present writer in his *Essay on Economic Growth and Planning*, Chapter V, cf. esp. p. 66. This was also Feldman's interpretation; who even included in B the repair of current wear and tear of productive equipment used in B.

---

in Group B (or an average annual rate of increase of 9·3 and 7·3 per cent respectively). For 1958–63 the actual annual averages achieved were respectively 10·8 and 7·1. For the decade 1949–59 as a whole the annual percentage growth of net material product has been calculated as being 10·5 but 11·3 for the first half of the decade and 9·5 for the second half. *Some Factors in Economic Growth in Europe during the 1950's*, U.N., E.C.E., Geneva, 1964, Chapter II, p. 15. Cf. also A. Arzumanian in *Pravda*, 24th–25th February, 1964, who, after saying that in the past decade the output of capital goods had grown faster than that of consumer goods by only 20 per cent (compared with a 70 per cent excess of the former in 1929–40), declared: 'Life sets us the task of bringing the rate of growth of Departments 1 and 2 still closer together.'

exclusively of machines and equipment: that is, of constituents of fixed capital and *not* of the raw material constituents of circulating capital. This is not, of course, quite the way in which Marx treated the distinction, since his 'constant capital' bought by Department II from Department I included raw materials. Similarly the Soviet A and B classification includes under the former the manufacture of raw materials and components used by the consumers'-goods industries. Indeed, early stages of manufacture of consumers' goods are sometimes included in Sector A, unless there is vertical integration in the industry. The precise frontier between the two has to be decided in many cases by administrative practice. (In *principle* there seems to be no way of deciding at what stage a raw material such as cotton ceases to be a raw material input and becomes part of the production-process of a final consumers' good—when it becomes combed and carded cotton, or when it is spun yarn or when it has become woven but unfinished cloth?) By reason of this difficulty, and as an alternative to the assumption of vertical integration backwards, some have preferred to operate with a three-sector model, one of the three consisting of raw material production for the other two. This does not banish completely the arbitrary element in the drawing of frontiers, but certainly reduces it. Some element of arbitrariness must even remain (as regards nomenclatures and classification) when one treats all such questions in terms of an input–output matrix of products and their components, with as many industries, or production-processes, as there are separate products. But whereas such a method of treatment overcomes the crudeness of aggregation necessarily involved in two-sector or three-sector models, and is more directly operational than the latter, its very complexity obscures the type of relationship in growth with which we have been here concerned.

By reason of this difficulty and of the way in which A and B industries are defined in the Soviet classification, the comparative growth-rates of A and B industries may not necessarily bear the interpretation that was given to them above. In particular, one would be wise to observe caution in deducing from the figures of comparative growth since 1955 any very firm conclusions as to which of the three phases of growth the Soviet economy can be said to be now in. None the less, to the extent that group A is weighted predominantly by metals production and machine-making, the conclusions that were tentatively deduced above have a strong likelihood of being true.

So far we have said little about the capital-output ratio, and have tacitly ignored the possible effects of changes of this ratio over time and of differences in it between sectors. Obviously, the size of this ratio (or rather of its inverse) in capital-goods industries places an important upper limit upon the rate of growth achievable by raising the capital-goods sector to a certain relative size (as we have seen that Feldman took pains to emphasise). Moreover, it is on the basis of an alleged tendency of this ratio to rise over time that the higher rate of increase of capital goods than of consumers' goods has sometimes been supported. Manifestly something should be said about this before we close.

To refer, firstly, to differences in this ratio between the sectors: obviously to the extent that it is different its weighted average for the economy as a whole will be affected by any change in the relative size of the sectors. Let us suppose that the capital–output ratio is *higher* in the capital-goods sectors (and the 'effectiveness of capital' lower). Then the Feldman-proposition will be qualified to the extent that, as this sector is enlarged, the consequential lowering of the effectiveness of capital will exert an offsetting effect to the rise in the investment-ratio, so far as raising the growth-rate is concerned. There will accordingly be a ceiling beyond which no further raising of the investment-ratio can exert a positive effect upon the growth-rate (and will, indeed, tend to lower it). For any likely differences in capital–output ratio this ceiling, however, will be a fairly high one,[12] and may well be higher than the ceiling imposed on the operation of the Feldman-proposition by the other considerations we have mentioned.

To refer, secondly, to changes in the capital–output ratio over time: it is not, I think, open to question that to support a given

---

[12] If this is not intuitively obvious, an arithmetical example or two will suffice to show that unless the difference in the capital–output ratio is of an order of magnitude greater than 10 : 1, this ceiling will not be reached at an investment-ratio (i.e. ratio of net investment to total output) lower than some 60 per cent.

growth-rate of output, when the capital–output ratio rises, there will need to be a larger proportion of investment devoted to enlarging the equipment of the capital-goods sector (if that growth-rate can be supported at all). On occasions, however, this necessity has been deduced from a tendency for the capital–*labour* ratio to rise.[13] A rise in the amount of capital equipment per worker will also raise the capital–output ratio if the former is not offset by an equivalent increase in labour-productivity (as a result, e.g. of improved productive equipment). It is quite possible, however, that technical innovation may have sufficient influence to cause labour-productivity to increase in equal (or greater) proportion to any increase in the ratio of capital equipment to labour. It also has to be borne in mind that every increase in productivity in the manufacture of capital goods themselves, by cheapening the production of these goods, will tend, *ceteris paribus*, to *lower* both the capital (in value)–labour ratio and the capital–output ratio.

As regards the actual situation, there is a good deal of statistical evidence to suggest that the capital–output ratio may have fallen in countries of Western Europe and North America over the past three or four decades.[14] There is also evidence that a falling tendency was characteristic of Soviet industry up to the last few years of the past decade.[15] True, in the last few years it has shown signs of rising (i.e. the *marginal* capital–output ratio has been).[16]

[13] This is implied in Lenin's reference (op. cit., p. 31) to the tendency under Capitalism for production of means of production to increase faster than means of consumption; since he bases this on the tendency of 'constant capital [to] grow faster than variable capital' (and hence faster than workers' consumption *plus* the consumed part of surplus value).

[14] Arzumanian in the above-quoted article in *Pravda* himself cited figures from U.S. manufacturing industry to illustrate this. He dates the change from the '20's.

[15] Cf. Y. Kvasha and V. Krasovskii in *Voprosi Ekonomiki*, 1959, No. 8, p. 8, who give figures of ·60 in 1940 and ·49 in 1956 as the ratio of *fixed capital* to gross production of Soviet industry. The same authors in *Voprosi Ekonomiki*, 1962, No. 9, p. 57, cite ·69 for 1940, ·57 for 1956 and ·57 for 1960 (the latter set of figures is probably affected by revaluations in the Census of Fixed Capital). Between 1928 and 1940, however, the ratio seems to have been rising.

[16] Cf. a recent discussion, opened by Khachaturov, reported in *Voprosi Ekonomiki*, 1964, No. 7, p. 153, in which it was stated (in Khachaturov's

Soviet economists, however, speak of this rise (whether rightly or wrongly) as due to temporary factors to be overcome: they certainly do not seem to view it as the start of a long-term trend. The kind of temporary factor referred to is the lengthening of the construction-period of new projects, thereby increasing the time-lag between the incurring of investment expenditure and the increased output which it occasions. Another possible influence mentioned by Khachaturov in a recent discussion of the question is that up to 1958 the emphasis was predominantly upon technical re-equipment of existing plants and more intensive use of plant and equipment rather than on building completely new plants, whereas since 1958 the emphasis has tended to shift towards the latter.[17] It *could* be, of course, the (again temporary) result of buying more durability with more solid or finished construction, just as it could also be the result of an overcrowding of the investment programme, which generally has the result of construction-delays and falling-behind-schedule. A switch from building hydro-electric to thermal power stations, recently much talked of, would, however, tend in the opposite direction—as indeed should methods of rationalised construction-site activity and accelerated construction. Another factor capable of influencing any average ratio of this kind is structural shifts which alter the relative weighting of industries with a high ratio of capital to output compared to those with a low ratio. But such shifts are as likely to move the average in one direction as in the other.

There is one feature of the changing situation in the Soviet Union and in some others of the planned economies that might be held likely to produce a permanently rising trend. This is the approach to a situation of labour-shortage (if this has not already been reached), despite an increasing population. When a country is relatively underdeveloped and mainly agricultural, it is apt to be characterised by surplus labour, on which a process of industrialisation can feed in its early stages. Increased industrial output can

[17] *Voprosi Ekonomiki*, 1964, No. 7, p. 153.

report) that from 1958 to 1963 fixed capital in industry had risen by 50 per cent and gross production by 45 per cent; meanwhile total capital (fixed *and* circulating) had risen by 56 per cent and national income 'only by 36 per cent'.

then march in step with increased employment by a simple process that economists have sometimes called 'widening' the capital structure. When surplus labour is no longer available, growth of output can no longer come from the employment of more labour; it must come from increased productivity of an existing labour-force (or, at least, of one that is increasing much more slowly than formerly). In such circumstances, 'widening' must give place to 'deepening'; which means changing and improving technique in a more capital-intensive direction—raising the amount or the effectiveness of capital equipment per worker. There are signs that this has been happening now for some time in the Soviet economy: for example, the output increases of the recent quinquennia have come predominantly from higher productivity rather than from extended employment. A transition from the earlier phase of development to this later one would seem in most countries to have represented something of a climacteric, involving novel problems and requiring new adaptations. It is possible that one of these new problems may be a tendency for the capital–output ratio to rise, with resulting repercussions upon growth-policy.

We have seen, however, that while an increase in capital equipment per worker *may* have this effect,[18] it *need* not do so. The result depends on the nature of technical progress and on innovation in methods of production and in methods of organising production. It is quite possible (and in the contemporary world apparently quite common) for technical innovation to be capital-saving as well as labour-saving: in other words, to increase labour-productivity without an equivalent increase of capital expenditure. We may conclude, therefore, that there is little ground for building a case for 'investment-priority for heavy industry' upon a forecast of a probable trend in the capital–output ratio.

What could perhaps be said is that in a stage of development where surplus labour has been absorbed and labour-shortage instead has supervened the capital–output ratio will tend to be

[18] On the static assumption, so commonly made, of constant technical knowledge, with technical change having the form of movement along a 'production-function' or 'isoquant', a change in the direction of higher capital-intensity would have this effect. But this is to abstract from progress in technical knowledge and innovation.

higher than *would otherwise have been the case.* Maintaining the growth-rate accordingly presents a more serious problem. But to rest policy-prescriptions upon such a statement would be to lay rather a severe strain on a *ceteris paribus* clause; and it could surely carry little persuasion as a reason for further enlarging the relative size of the capital-goods sector if the latter were already within sight of its ceiling.

Indeed, approach to a situation of labour-shortage might well prove to be a reinforcing reason for making the transition from the first to the second of the development-periods distinguished above, and even for opting in favour of the second variant of the second period, with its temporary gain in the growth-rate of consumption at the expense of the investment sector.[19] When the economy has no longer a reserve of labour to draw upon, its growth will be limited by the rate of population increase (i.e. of the working population) and the rate of increase of labour-productivity due to technical change. The output of capital-goods industries, to the extent that it is no longer needed for providing equipment for new additions to the labour-force, will go to replace old equipment (in both sectors) with new equipment of latest technical type, including equipment of higher capital-intensity and higher productivity.[20] Thus the economy would be purchasing higher productivity, and hence growth, with the larger initial investment-cost associated with higher capital-intensity.[21] As opportunities for

[19] In the Stoleru-theorem (cf. L. G. Stoleru, 'An Optimal Policy for Growth', *Econometrica*, April 1965, pp. 321 seq., which appeared after the present article was first written), in the *later* years of the period during which unemployment is being absorbed, production of capital goods is reduced both absolutely and relatively. This is because only one technique is assumed to exist (and technical progress assumed absent), so that once full employment is reached growth is restricted to the rate of increase of (working) population. Hence in the immediately preceding years the size of the capital-goods sector has to be adjusted downwards to what is required to maintain this growth-rate.

[20] In other words, there will be movement *along* any given production-function (or isoquant) in the direction of higher capital-intensity *as well as* movement from one production function (expressive of older technical opportunities) to a new one in the course of technical progress.

[21] This would be a once-for-all boost to the growth-rate while transition to more productive equipment was being made (although the higher *level*

doing so approached exhaustion (probably some time before this), and the ratio of additional productivity gain to higher investment-cost grew smaller, there would be an inducement to reduce the relative size of the capital-goods sector in favour of the consumer-goods sector in the interests of a higher level and rate of increase of consumption, even at the expense of a slackened (and slackening) over-all growth-rate (as shown above in the second variant of our second phase).

---

of productivity achieved would be, of course, permanent). For the enhanced growth-rate to be sustained, a *continuing* resort to more productive techniques would be necessary; and this continuing resort would probably become progressively more costly in terms of investment.

Five

Planning and Soviet economy : eight articles

One

The discussions of the 'twenties on planning and economic growth

Reprinted from *Soviet Studies*, October 1965 (Vol. XVII, No. 2), by kind permission of the editors and publishers of that journal.

That extraordinarily interesting and fertile debate in the 1920's about the possible roads of Soviet development was singularly neglected by English economists at the time. It did not seem to fit into their categories of thought, still set in a very Victorian mould, from which only a few were emerging. To do economists justice, one has to remember that the Soviet debate had a very alien sound to their ears, even when they were aware of it. Much of it was conducted in polemical tones and in a strange jargon. For the 'Western' economist it was rather shocking to listen to nonsense (even 'wicked nonsense') about finding ways of transition to socialism and about such things as class conflict and 'breaking out of capitalist encirclement'. Like most polemics from any century, this one was impatient of the finer touches that academic discourse is apt to regard as the hallmark of professional sophistication, and often tended to lack the precision of formulation which any Ph.D. candidate is supposed to wear. Even when the debate had an academic flavour, it was overlaid with Marxian terminology and with tiresomely unfamiliar concepts like departments of social reproduction, constant and variable capital and surplus product.

The climate of thought has now changed on both sides of the Atlantic, even in the most exclusive seats of learning. Study of growth, balanced or unbalanced, development and dynamic equilibria are all the rage; and it is academically fashionable to conduct empirical studies of 'underdevelopment'. In this more realistic context the relevance of those forty-year-old debates is beginning to be appreciated; they are going through the process of being 're-discovered' (even if sometimes rather condescendingly) and the extent of their originality is being recognised. The collection of articles from this period, which we owe to Professor Spulber,[1] is a witness to this recognition; as is also the welcome announcement of a translation, by Mr Brian Pearce, of Preobrazhensky's famous contribution to the debate, his *Novaya ekonomika*.[2] The Spulber collection should be of great use for all students of the period, as well as for students of development who are discerning enough to acquaint themselves with the classic case-study of a policy discussion about industrialisation in a socialist context. This volume ranges widely and includes, not only the main representatives of the central debate about methods and roads to industrialisation, Shanin, Bazarov, Preobrazhensky, Bukharin (his famous Notes of an Economist) and even one of Stalin's first (and still fairly moderate) attacks on the Right, but also Groman, Strumilin and Krzhizhanovsky on the early plans, even rather surprisingly a 1927 critique by the celebrated Kondratiev, and three articles (or rather extracts from) by that pioneer-builder of growth-models G. A. Feldman, who deserves to be much better known (despite Domar's rediscovery of him) than he is both within and without his own country. Many will be surprised to find the extent to which mathematical modes of formulation were prevalent in planning circles, and especially in the Gosplan organ, at that time.

Unfortunately we do not get all the voices in one controversy grouped together consecutively, as the selections are not classified according to the subject-matter of argument, but on a more formal plan. The three parts into which the book is divided are: I. Macro-Economic Models; IIA. Economic Growth: Strategies of Development; IIB. Economic Growth: Pace and Efficiency; III. Planning Theories and Methods. Perhaps any other classification would have presented equal difficulties. But the result is that a reader trying

[1] *Foundations of Soviet Strategy for Economic Growth: Selected Soviet Essays, 1924–1930*, edited by Nicolas Spulber, Bloomington, Indiana University Press, 1964.
[2] E. Preobrazhensky, *The New Economics*, trs. Brian Pearce, Oxford University Press, 1965.

to follow through a particular issue, such as the major one between the so-called 'Left Opposition' and the Centre-plus-Right (with its sequel Stalin versus the Bukharinite Right), is a bit baffled and uncertain how to proceed. Even the three parts of the Feldman-thesis are separated and distributed among the three parts of the collection, even though two of them were labelled in the original as two instalments of a 'Theory of Growth Rates of National Income' and the third (published a year later in 1929) is in effect a continuation of the same theme although appearing under the separate title of 'An Analytical Method of Building Perspective Plans' (all three were reports for the long-term planning section of Gosplan, working on the so-called *Genplan*—destined to be attacked and buried for 'mathematical formalism' and lack of realism). There are editorial notes to each of the four parts to afford some guidance to a reader uncertain of his way about; but these, unfortunately, are rather less helpful than one might have expected (they seem to do much less than justice, for example, to the striking nature of the ideas advanced by Preobrazhensky and by Feldman). Is it ungrateful to say that these editorial aids convey too little sense of historical awareness of the peculiar situations of this unique decade, and read rather flatly in their exciting context?

What does emerge from several of the contributions presented here and is of particular interest is that a number of concepts and techniques which have become the object of renewed attention in the late '50's and the '60's were already being considered then. This is true of the notion of the effectiveness of investment (defined as the increment of output divided by the increment of capital), which is central to Feldman's analysis and is the subject of two articles translated here, by Goldberg and Rozental respectively. Moreover, as the editor in his first Note points out, 'taking the schema [of Marx] as starting point, P. I. Popov and L. Litoshenko devised a pioneering input-output type of balance', which they did in contributions to a symposium of 1926 entitled respectively 'A Balance of the National Economy as a Whole' and 'Methods of Constructing a National Economic Balance'. Important in this connection was also an article by Barengolts, which was 'the first to suggest the use of input coefficients in Soviet planning'. It is good to have the originality of these pioneers in a quite new line of country recognised and brought to our notice. It is also of interest to see here the article which Wassily Leontief (of subsequent input-output fame) contributed to *Planovoe Khoziaistvo* in 1925 on the appearance of the first official 'Balance of the National Economy'. His article opens with the statement:

> Among various problems which must be solved by contemporary Russian statistics, that of representing in numbers the total turnover of economic life is perhaps the most interesting as well as the most complex. As a result of many years' work by the Central Statistical Administration, the *Balance of the Economy of the U.S.S.R. in 1923-4* has appeared. The principal feature of this balance, in comparison with such economic statistical investigations as the American and the English censuses, is the attempt to represent in numbers not only the production but also the distribution of the social product, so as to obtain a general picture of the entire process of reproduction in the form of a *Tableau Économique.*

(Popov had himself introduced the comparison with Quesnay's *Tableau.*) From this balance derives 'the methodological principle of exclusively material accounting' (i.e. accounting for material goods only). The article is notable for emphasising the distinction between (*a*) net product or 'value added', (*b*) what he calls 'real product' (net product *plus* original inputs or costs) and (*c*) gross turnover, and the dependence of the latter on 'the number of [separated] partial stages of a connected process of production'. He further insists that it is the gross turnover that is 'more suitable for balance accounting', since 'the more deeply and widely individual relationships are included, the more clearly the organic structure of the economic whole appears'. From this seminal idea, simple and unarresting as it may appear when one first meets it, the whole system of input–output analysis evidently derives.

But the system of balances was a planning technique and its interest is mainly for specialists. The heated discussion around Preobrazhensky's thesis on 'primitive socialist accumulation' (which he defined as 'accumulation of material resources in the hands of the State—primarily from sources lying outside the State economy') involved issues of historical strategy at the dawn of the socialist epoch, and is therefore of dominating interest (or should be) for all historians of the twentieth century as well as of interest to all economists concerned with the theory of growth. The background of this discussion was the weak development of Russian industry, still incompletely recovered from the disorganisation of the civil war years, and the political and economic isolation of revolutionary Russia from the rest of the world. It had been the hope and expectation of the Bolsheviks that the Soviet revolution would be the beacon light for the more industrially advanced countries of central and western Europe. The armies of counter-revolution had eventually been beaten back, after two and a half exhausting and terrible years; but the failure of the German revolution, and its eventual eclipse after 1923, was a heavy blow to early Bolshevik hopes. Unless defeat were to be accepted, a reorientation of previous revolutionary thinking seemed necessary. Although born of an essential pessimism as to the possibility of building socialism in a country of backward industry, without aid from the West,[3] Preobrazhensky's theory represented an attempt to chart the historical situation that in these circumstances confronted the Soviet revolution. The historical analogy which he drew with the dawn of capitalist accumulation was an arresting one, and his framing of the problem of a 'transfer' of the resources for building up industry from the sector of petty production in Marxian categories of class relations and law of value greatly enhanced its contemporary appeal. 'The notion that a socialist economy can develop on its own without touching the resources of the *petite bourgeoisie*, including peasant economy', he denounced as reactionary *petit bourgeois* utopianism: to which he added that 'it behoves the socialist state to take more, not less, from small-scale producers than capitalism took'. But the whole conception, especially its underlined corollaries, could hardly fail to be explosive in the highly delicate situation in which the Soviet State found itself in the early and middle '20's, poised as it was on the summit of a political pyramid of which the base consisted of some 25 million peasant households, primitively

[3] Cf. the last sentence of the first excerpt from Preobrazhensky in this collection (p. 173)—a relatively late article on 'Equilibrium in the U.S.S.R.': 'All these contradictions show how closely our development towards socialism is connected with the necessity of making a breach in our socialist solitude; not only for political but also for economic reasons we must be aided in the future by the material resources of other socialist countries.'

equipped, many of them no more than subsistence farmers, and in the aggregate supplying less than one-sixth of their crop for the market. Lenin's whole October policy had rested on the class-alliance between a numerically weak industrial proletariat and the peasant masses, in opposition to propertied reaction: an alliance that had remained sufficiently strong when 'land to the peasants' was the order of the day, but became more tenuous when, after the dispossession of landlords and upper bourgeoisie, reconstruction of economic life on the basis of NEP and the transition to socialism dominated the agenda. The precarious coracle of State could be very easily rocked to a dangerous extent. The notion that building socialism must have exploitation of the peasantry as its main buttress was to invite a *La Vendée*. It was inevitable that this should be officially repudiated. In the middle '20's the situation was such that it would have been, surely, to court disaster to lay the crucial worker–peasant alliance under serious strain, even if in return for a faster growth of industry.

Similarly the corollary that price-policy should be used as a main instrument for 'transferring' resources from peasant agriculture to State industry, coming as it did on the heels of the 'scissors crisis', inevitably appeared as an attack on the official policy of closing the price-scissors (as was, indeed, its intention) and as a defence of 'the monopolist position of State industry' on the market. It would have been difficult, if not impossible, to combine the doctrine with any notion of the peasant–worker alliance as centre-piece of political and economic strategy for the coming period, however much lip-service had been paid to this crucial *smytchka*. *Per contra* the doctrine was admirably fitted to form the standard of an opposition engaged in criticising what were regarded as conservative policies induced by determination to preserve that alliance at all costs (or rather, as the opposition alleged, by a policy of including the kulak in that alliance, and hence engendering a 'kulak-deviation' with consequential danger of a 'kulak-degeneration' of the regime). At any rate, it was as such a standard that the daringly provocative theory of Preobrazhensky came to be regarded.

One thing that has been insufficiently appreciated is that the criticism of Preobrazhensky did not deny that this notion of 'transfers of resources from peasant agriculture to State industry' had any relevance at all to the problem of building socialism in a backward country: what was disputed was the emphasis laid on these transfers as central pivot and in particular the policy implications which the theory was made to yield. This was true at any rate of Bukharin's criticism; and at the theoretical level Bukharin was the chief spokesman for the official standpoint at that time in the polemic against the Left. This is important if we are concerned with the question, as some now seem to be, of how much foresight one can credit to Preobrazhensky in the light of subsequent history. It is not something that will be clear to a reader of this collection; and for this reason one is inclined to regret that some writing of Bukharin more germane to this discussion (e.g. extracts from his *Kritika ekonomicheskoi platformy oppozitsii* of 1926) was not included. It is good to have an extract from *Zametki ekonomista*; but this belongs to a different context, when Right-wing views had become the main target of attack, when the Centre (as represented by Stalin) were on the point of uniting with some of the former Left in a campaign for eliminating the kulak and for carrying through the 'maximal variant' of the First Five-Year Plan.

Thus Bukharin said in 1926 (in a speech to Party officials in Leningrad on 28th July):

> Our State industry cannot obtain the means for its expansion solely from the labour of the working class within this State industry itself, and it must necessarily draw upon the non-industrial reservoir for the means to support and expand industry. . . . The peasantry must take its share in helping the State to build up a socialist system of industry. . . . It would be entirely wrong to say that industry should develop solely upon what is produced within this industry itself. . . . The whole question is: how much can we take away from the peasantry, to what extent and by what methods can we accomplish the 'pumping-over process', what are the *limits* of the pumping over? . . . Comrades of the opposition are in favour of an immoderate amount of pumping-over, and are desirous of putting so severe a pressure upon the peasantry that in our opinion the result would be economically irrational and politically impermissible. We do not in the least hold the standpoint that we are against this pumping-over, but our calculations are more sober; we confine ourselves to measures economically and politically adapted to their purpose.

He then goes on to say that by first encouraging agriculture, in order that industry could later build on its progress, as official policy was doing, there might be 'a slower rate of advance this year, but compensated later by a rapid rise in the curve of development. But if we adopt the policy of the opposition, we fly to a high summit of capital investment during the first year, only to fall the more inevitably, and probably with a very abrupt drop.'

Two years before, speaking directly of Preobrazhensky's proposals, he had said: 'it would be nonsense on our part to renounce the advantages of our monopoly position'; none the less it was vitally necessary to avoid 'diminishing the powers of absorption of the home market', on the contrary to 'increase these powers'. 'This is the most important point. The next is that we must utilise every advantage gained so that it may lead to an extension of the field of production and a cheapening of production, to the reduction of cost-prices and consequently to ever cheaper prices in successive cycles of production.'[4]

There was another strand of Preobrazhensky's theory, which was distinct from the 'peasant-exploitation' issue, even if not unrelated to it, and which had a bearing on the particular form of the argument used by Bukharin against him in the passage just quoted. In the contribution of Shanin translated in the Spulber collection (an article in *Bolshevik* in 1926) it is clear that the writer (in common with Sokolnikov and others of the Right at the time) is envisaging a very 'orthodox' type of development: namely, a concentration in the first stage on expanding primary production for export (*plus* agricultural processing industries), even at the expense of a temporary *de*celeration of industrial development, and only at a later stage developing industry by means of resources that increased export capacity has made available.

Since under our conditions [Shanin writes], agriculture as a rule requires less capital than industry, preference should be given to agriculture. The development of agriculture to the full extent of what the world market can absorb ought to have been the basic directive. The possibility of achieving an upsurge in the national economy through agricultural exports, i.e. of achieving it in the cheapest possible way, is our economy's biggest asset. . . . In our circumstances investment of capital in agriculture is more profitable than investment

[4] *Pravda*, 12th December 1924.

in industry. The organic composition of capital is considerably smaller in agriculture, and labour requirements are considerably greater. . . . Ultimately the absolute growth of industry will be greater than with the type of industry that is based on immediate diversion of resources under maximum forced draught.[5]

The classical doctrine of comparative costs could scarcely have had a more forthright champion. (Preobrazhensky by contrast was advocating 'socialist protectionism'.) Politically it was open to the objection that it would make socialist industrialisation precariously dependent on the world market of capitalism.

In an article of a year before (1925) Shanin had spoken of a 'disproportion', consisting in the fact that

industry's fixed capital is developing too fast and that the industrial branches which are developing are not those which could satisfy consumers' goods demand. . . . We must definitely realise that the heavy industries can be developed only on the basis of extensive preliminary development of light industry (or importation of consumers' goods). . . . Development of consumers' goods production and of our country's export branches is our central object.[6]

Manifestly such a policy was diametrically opposed to any notion of 'pumping over' a surplus product from agriculture to finance investment in industry: the latter would retard the expansion of agriculture, at any rate of its marketable surplus, and also (as some argued) defeat its own ends by narrowing the peasant market for industrial products and thereby throttle industrial expansion.

To this Preobrazhensky had an answer. This was that the growth

---

[5] Spulber ed., op. cit., pp. 214, 219–20. (The concluding word of this passage has been rendered here as 'draught' in place of 'draft' in the Spulber translation.)

[6] Ibid., pp. 206, 208–9. Bazarov also spoke of the need 'in carrying out industrialisation' to 'follow a strict system with regard both to the types of new enterprises and the priority to be awarded to them. . . . First to be constructed must be the industries producing consumers' goods and those kinds of producers' goods for which something like a mass demand already exists. In all other industries, so long as they have not acquired a broad enough base within the U.S.S.R., it would be preferable to purchase essential products abroad or grant concessions to foreign capitalists' (ibid., pp. 221–2).

of industry would create its own market internal to itself—in expanding it would absorb more industrial products as inputs to feed its own expansion, by a circular process of outputs becoming inputs for 'productive consumption'. This retort was a perfectly valid one—provided that in the process of industrialisation heavy industry (or, more strictly, capital-goods industry) could be conceived of as *leading* the process (instead of following it). Thus there emerged a self-consistent 'polar opposite' to the 'orthodox sequence' of agriculture first, then light industry and lastly (and only as required by the first two) capital-goods industry, which Shanin and others of the Right were expounding. It was indeed this '*un*orthodox sequence' that was to characterise the process of industrialisation in the '30's, with its 'investment priority for heavy industry'. And it is at this point that Feldman comes into the debate, with his formal analysis and growth equations derived from the Marxian 'schema of reproduction'; his crucial equation expressing the growth-rate as a product of the proportionate size of the capital-goods sector (*net* of capital goods produced for replacement), measured in terms of productive capacity, multiplied by the 'effectiveness of capital'. In his own notation this crucial equation was written as:[7]

$$D' = S \cdot \frac{D_u}{D}$$

where S stands for the effectiveness of capital (or ratio of output to capital), D_u for the output of the sector producing *new* capital goods (i.e. *net* of production for replacement, which was included in the other sector), D for total output (and D', of course, for the rate of increment of output, or the growth-rate of the economy as a whole).

A by-product of the campaign against the Bukharinite Right, which rose to a climax in the course of 1929, was a polemic against certain Gosplan economists, who had been associated with the advocacy of methods designed to import realism into planning and to purge it of 'subjectivism', and who were to become the unfortunate incidental casualties of the larger battle. No doubt in the changed political climate, where innovation and high growth-rates

[7] *Planovoe Khoziaistvo*, 1929, No. 12, p. 116.

and the virtue of 'storming heaven' were the order of the day, their influence was a conservative one. Constant appeals to past experience and a *penchant* for extrapolating trends and 'equilibrium relationships' into the future deflated the new optimistic, dynamic mood. The result was none the less unfortunate: that they should have been involved in a rather sterile antithesis between the so-called 'genetic' method of planning and the 'teleological', and been denounced as cautious (if not worse) empiricists and determinists who treated future possibilities as manacled slaves of what the past had witnessed. Two of the chief economists in question were Groman and Bazarov. Groman had been largely responsible for the methodology of the series of annual Control Figures from 1925–6 onwards and of the perspective plans drafted in Gosplan to date; and he deserves credit for these distinguished pioneer contributions to planning techniques, however much he might have been held to be a deserving subject of later criticism for underestimating the possibilities of a high growth-rate policy in the post-1928 situation. Bazarov had been so ill-advised as to defend in 1925 the notion of a 'descending curve of growth' as applied to the postwar 'restoration process' (he seems to have regarded this as a general feature of any 'restoration process'). In 1930, when a lot of what had been written with reference to earlier situations was raked over again, this thesis was not merely held against him but was given the damning label of 'a wrecking theory' of planning. The theory (if it still applied) should no doubt have been made the subject of reasoned debate. But history works otherwise than this; and in the highly-charged atmosphere of 1929–30 (as happens, *mutatis mutandis*, in wartime) accusations of wrecking were recklessly thrown about. In the Spulber-edited volume extracts are reproduced from two of the articles in the same number of *Planovoe Khoziaistvo* (October–November 1930) where the names of Groman and Bazarov are coupled together (even linked with Kondratiev) and denounced in this sense. One of the articles was by an R. Boyarsky[8]—an intelligent but unpleasant piece of work, spiced with charges of 'theoretical sabotage', and a curious foretaste of the degraded style of polemic of the period to come, when the tumbril so often

[8] This subsequently turned out to be a mistake of the Spulber-edition for *A*. Boyarsky.

marched with the public denunciation. Feldman and Kovalevsky, one might have thought, would have been spared, since they leaned in the opposite direction. They, it seems, met criticism for being over-optimistic and deriving long-term trends from abstract models. Optimistic they may have been (although this can scarcely be said of the three Feldman articles), but so was the general mood of the time.

Professor Spulber has had the idea of accompanying his useful collection with a booklet[9] of his own by way of introduction to the discussion and to the period. This, like the editorial notes to the larger volume, is conscientiously and painstakingly done, and may well perform a service as a kind of well-informed Baedeker or primer for those seeking to find their way about over this terrain for the first time. The useful core of the booklet consists of Chapters 3, 4 and 5, headed respectively 'Strategies of Economic Development', 'Efficiency and the Rate of Growth' and 'Principles and Procedures of Planning', even if they do not entirely fulfil the promise of their titles. In addition, Chapter 2 contains a clear, brief summary of the essentials of the Feldman model—'an exploration in which he anticipated some aspects of modern income growth analysis, for example Professors Harrod and Domar's "warranted or equilibrium rate of growth" '. One cannot help adding, however, that, by comparison with the companion collection, the booklet disappoints. From a specialist standpoint it is rather lightweight; and for those knowing anything of the period it is neither deep enough nor extensive enough to tell them much that is new. It may strike some, I think, as being a rather colourless rendering of an exciting period; without much evidence, perhaps, of the inspiration needed if the author were to bring its theme alive and to lend it historical perspective. This is a pity, since we are dealing with a pioneering decade that constituted an historical landmark of our century: a decade rich in novelty and in drama, deserving of something much better from both the economist and the historian.

One question which it raises, however, we should perhaps refer to in conclusion. Professor Spulber takes for granted what is admittedly a widely held view in 'the West', that Stalin's policy at the end

[9] Nicolas Spulber, *Soviet Strategy for Economic Growth*, Indiana University Press, Bloomington, 1964.

of the decade simply took over the policy of Preobrazhensky and the Left, embodying it in the strategy of the First Five-Year Plan. How far is this a true judgment? What is certainly true is that the new policy shared a number of common positions with the Left in its opposition to the Bukharinite Right: in particular in opposition to the latter's conception of a 'gradualist' development, with the growth of industry essentially bounded by the advance of peasant agriculture. Moreover, Preobrazhensky and others of the Left (though by no means all, and not Trotsky himself) themselves spoke at the time of Stalin having adopted a 'Left course' close to their own position. The offensive against the kulak, the emphasis on heavy industry and rejection of the Shanin sequence of development were cases in point. We have seen, however, that everything here depends on exactly what the question is that we are answering. If it is concerned with Preobrazhensky's thesis that in the initial stages of industrialisation the surplus product of agriculture must provide a major source of the real funds necessary for industrial investment, then there can be no serious doubt that the commonly accepted answer is right. This proposition was fully borne out by subsequent events. But this proposition was not denied even by Bukharin: disagreement, as we have seen, was about the relative weight to be assigned to it as a source, compared to other sources internal to industry. If the question is the more practical and political one as to whether the policy of extracting this surplus product from agriculture (by taxation and price-policy) should be given precedence over the policy of cementing the worker–peasant alliance and restoring agricultural production, then it is impossible to give an answer to this question without *dating* it. Which should have been given priority in 1925? Obviously there need be no inconsistency in returning one answer in 1924–5 and a different one in 1928–9. (No one can seriously pretend that Preobrazhensky was simply propounding a timeless abstract theory without relevance to current application and immediate policy; as the 'professional revolutionary' that he once described himself to Keynes as being, he was the last person to do anything of this kind.) An economic fact which changed the whole climate of the NEP between 1925 and 1928 was the serious lag of the marketable surplus, especially of grain, behind the restoration of agricultural production. What transformed both the policy advanced by the 'Centre' in 1928 and its estimate of what was now possible was the new willingness to face up to collectivisation as solution of the agricultural *impasse* and faith in its practicability (which has to be credited to Stalin). This was a lynchpin of the new policy which had been absent from the conception of 'super-industrialisers' in previous years—a conception which (like the Right, though yielding a contrasting answer) still projected the problem as being one of how to reconcile industrialisation with an overwhelmingly small-scale peasant agriculture. Once the latter assumption could be dropped from the argument, both problem and solution could be redefined; and a principal result of doing so was, of course, to release the 'Centre' from its previous reluctant tethering to the Right-wing conception of the 'precedence of agriculture and of its development over industry'.

Two

The revival of theoretical discussion among Soviet economists

This article appeared in *Science and Society*, Fall 1960 (Vol. XXIV, No. 4), and is reproduced by kind permission of the editors of that journal. It has also been reproduced in *The Soviet Economy*, ed. Harry G. Shaffer (New York, 1963).

To convey the true shadings of a discussion is difficult if not impossible unless one is part of it. Not only will its finer nuances be missed, but also essential links, particularly policy implications, and unseen antagonists taken for granted by participants even when not openly stated. Only some rare act of intuition will enable an interpreter at a distance to grasp these non-apparent links, let alone the subtler shades. This has always been the trouble with the so-called 'Soviet experts' in the West with their guessing-games and confident interpolations, whether they are part of the intelligence brigade of the Cold War or independent and unstipended amateurs.

This might seem to some a very good reason for not embarking on the present article. At any rate, the reader has been warned to read what follows with proper circumspection and without inflated expectations.

One thing, at least, seems quite certain: after a fairly long period of dormancy, there has been in the last few years quite a remarkable revival (one is tempted to use the word *renaissance*) of economic discussion and theoretical activity in the Soviet Union, as well as in some other of the socialist countries, and signs of a new and more creative approach to the problems of a socialist economy.

1 *The period of quiescence*

After the animated debates of the 1920's, it seemed as though a pall had descended over economic discussion during the next two decades. At first one was inclined to consider this to be not unnatural in view of intense preoccupation with practice in the 'heroic' prewar decade and the decade of the war and its aftermath — preoccupation with details of policy within a fairly narrow time-horizon and with issues that were politico-social in character so far as the general objectives of policy were concerned. One was inclined to assume that more strictly economic questions of planning were the subject of intra-departmental discussion which seldom emerged into print, but the products of which one would be able some day to discern.

There were some straws in the wind, however, that caused one to think there might be more to explain than this. On the one hand, there were recurrent complaints about the low level of economic theory, the prevalence of 'narrow practicalism' and purely descriptive writing, and the failure to generalise the experience of a socialist economy—complaints that became more emphatic after the war.[1] On the other hand, when occasional *ex cathedra* pronouncements on matters of economic theory were made, the subsequent commentaries on them, alike in the U.S.S.R. and other socialist countries, were surprisingly empty of content and bore an exceptionally abstract, even scholastic, character. One may instance the question of the law of value and its continuing 'influence' under socialism; about which we were told little more than that this law was used 'consciously' in planning; that this did not mean that price-relations coincided with value-relations, but that in a manner unexplained they 'deviated from values' in the interest of the objectives of the plan—though in such a way as to leave 'total prices equal to total values'. Such generalisations were apparently accepted as the sufficient essence of wisdom. At any rate, no more than this showed above the surface to form even the prolegomena to a Political Economy of Socialism. Thirty to forty years after the revolution, this was a little strange, to say the least, despite the interruptions of two major wars.

[1] Cf. pp. 334 of the writer's *Soviet Economic Development since 1917*, 1st edition.

During the past quinquennium it has become fairly evident that there were several other factors in the situation to explain the grave theoretical lag in advancing towards a new Political Economy of Socialism. Firstly, there was, apparently, a prevalent assumption that anything in the way of an original departure in theoretical generalisation could only come 'from the top' (an obvious product of the 'personality cult' of the period). This was not an atmosphere in which younger or lesser men were disposed to 'stick their necks out' and risk a novel hypothesis—however much they might be prodded by official pronouncements deploring the 'low level of theoretical work'. Secondly, there seems to have been something of a 'Chinese wall' between political economy (with the academic economists concerned in its teaching and cultivation) and the problems and techniques of economic planning. A hint of this separation was contained in Stalin's surprising statement to the effect that political economy is concerned exclusively with 'the laws of development of men's relations of production' and that 'to foist upon political economy problems of economic policy is to kill it as a science'.[2] Price policy, it seems, fell within the province of planners and of economic practitioners in industrial Ministries, but not of 'political economists' proper. Such a glaring divorce of theory from practice could hardly fail to breed scholasticism and dogmatism—a dogmatism probably reinforced by the fact that much of the inspiration and even the personnel of political economy at *vishaia shkola* level tended to be from agit-prop departments, the horizon of scholarship for which was too often 'talmudism' (as Stalin himself dubbed it). Thirdly (and obviously connected with what we have just said), it now transpires that a dominant view was that political economy was primarily (if not exclusively) concerned with the study of the *qualitative* aspects and *differentia* of economic and social phenomena. This emphasis (resulting in a kind of economic sociology) is well exemplified in the Soviet *Political Economy Textbook* of a few years ago, and may serve to explain the scarcely-concealed dissatisfaction with it on the part of many Marxists both within and without the Soviet Union. Attention to the *quantitative* aspect of economic relations was liable to be denounced as 'formalism', and 'bourgeois

[2] *Economic Problems of Socialism in the U.S.S.R.*, Moscow, 1952, p. 81.

formalism' to boot. As Academician V. Nemchinov writes in a recent issue of *Voprosi Ekonomiki* (1960, No. 6, pp. 13 f.):

> Quantitative analysis of economic phenomena stands at the present time as one of the bottlenecks of Soviet economic science. The reason for this consists not only in the sharp raising of the level of demands upon Soviet economic science, but also in a definite under-estimation by a section of economists of the necessity for scientific analysis of the quantitative side of economic processes in socialist economy. . . . Some economists began incorrectly to regard econo-mic science, and particularly political economy, as a science only of qualitative economic laws, leaving out of sight the huge significance of theoretical methods of analysis of the quantitative aspect of economic laws of development of socialist society. In the recent past our economists even denied the possibility of a theoretical approach to the quantitative side of the laws [*zakonomernost*] of development of socialist society. . . . It is impossible for the political economy of socialism to limit itself merely to qualitative analysis. Economic science . . . in conditions of socialism can and must become an exact science.

2 *The economic effectiveness of investment*

In the circumstances it is, indeed, quite surprising that discussion about the problem of 'calculating the economic effectiveness of investment' should have occupied Soviet economists as early as it did (from the late '40's) and should have had the outcome that it has. Probably some of the credit for this should go to the veteran economist Strumilin, who opened up the question in his much-quoted article on 'The Time Factor in Planning Capital Invest-ment', published in the *Izvestia* of the Academy just after the end of the war.[3] But it seems likely that a more important part of the explanation is that the question arose from the demands of practice itself, and hence had the strong backing, if not of Gosplan, of engineering-economists in the industrial *glavki*. Perhaps the fact that long-term planning came to be placed on the agenda after the war had something to do with it. At any rate, if what we have said

---

[3] *Izvestia Akademii Nauk U.S.S.R.*, Economics and Law Series, 1946, No. 3; also translated in *International Economic Papers*, No. 1.

is true, both the initiative and the continuing impetus came from outside, rather than from inside, academic political economy—came from the research staffs of Ministries and of specialised industrial institutes who had the actual handling of problems of choice between technical variants. The formulation of operational criteria, such as the recoupment-period and ratio of effectiveness, was largely the work, apparently, of transport-economists and their opposite numbers in electricity-generation and construction; and it is noteworthy that Professor T. S. Khachaturov, who deserves so much of the credit for carrying forward this discussion to a successful issue, was a transport specialist and author of a well-known textbook on transport problems. If opposition to this raising of (or way of raising) the issue came, as one supposes, from the dogmatists (who smelled a 'rate-of-interest heresy' in it), then it was a clash between the *doctrinaires* and the practical men, with the latter having quite a few notable cards stacked in their favour.

The main issue in this debate can be explained in non-technical terms quite simply. Most industrial construction, whether it be a power-plant or a clothing factory or an engineering works, is capable of being planned according to several so-called 'technical variants'. Once planned investment has been allocated between various industries (and even before this stage is reached) this presents itself as the crucial problem of investment planning (or project-making as it is usually called in Soviet literature). These technical variants will differ:

> (*a*) in their initial cost of construction;
> (*b*) in the results which they will subsequently yield when in operation—results which may be alternatively regarded as an increase in productivity of labour or as a decreased expenditure of labour (or prime cost) required to produce a given output.

In any given case, (*b*) can be expressed as a ratio to (*a*); and different variants or projects can be arranged in an order according to the size of this ratio in each case. It will not follow, of course, that a higher labour-productivity in operation (e.g. when a new machine is installed and in use) will always be associated with a higher initial (investment) cost. When it is not, there is no doubt which of the alternatives to use: for practical purposes only one of them, that which yields the higher productivity, will ever come upon the planning agenda, the others being rejected from the start as inferior. But a real problem of choice will arise in the case of any pair of alternatives in which higher productivity is associated with higher investment-cost.

For example, by expending large additional sums on the construction of an expensive hydro-electric plant much cheaper electricity[4] can be produced eventually than if cheaper (and possibly smaller) coal-burning power-plants are constructed. How to decide which to construct? If one had enough steel and equipment, etc., at any one time to place no ceiling on the total construction the economy could undertake (or the size of its general investment plan), there would be no problem—hydro-electric stations would win every time. But in actuality this is never so—some ceiling is necessarily imposed by the existing size and productive capacity of the capital-goods industries (Marx's Department I). Hence a limit has to be placed at some point on the additional investment-cost that it is worthwhile to incur in order to achieve a given result.

The Soviet ratio of effectiveness is one way of imposing such a limit. A standard ratio is set which any project must fulfil if it is to qualify for inclusion in the plan; anything that fails to fulfil this minimum requirement being rejected. The effectiveness coefficient or ratio is usually expressed as the ratio of the difference in operating cost (or prime cost) to the difference in initial investment-cost (e.g. of a hydro-electric plant compared with a coal-burning one of equivalent capacity). Essentially the same ratio is sometimes expressed in a different form (the one being simply the inverse of the other) as a so-called 'period of recoupment' of the original investment—the number of years within which the original investment-cost will be recovered, or recouped, by the annual saving of operating cost.

In comparing investment projects there are also questions of differing periods of construction (e.g. a hydro-electric plant usually takes longer to construct; so will a railway line which, to reduce

---

[4] Provided that there is not a big seasonal variation in the flow of water, preventing full-capacity utilisation from being maintained throughout the year.

gradients or detours goes in for a lot of tunnelling and embankments) and different durabilities of a plant or equipment once installed. If a more durable plant costs more to build, *how much* additional cost is worthwhile to achieve a given lengthening of life? Then, again, there is the kind of alternative where constructing the *complete* project now (whether building, power-plant or railway) is cheaper in the long run but involves the larger expenditure here and now; whereas developing it in stages, doing part now and then finishing the remaining part later, will place less strain on present resources but at the cost of a larger total expenditure over time. An effectiveness-ratio can be used to decide this type of question also by providing a discount-factor by means of which future expenditures or costs are reduced to terms of present values, to enable a comparison in terms of the latter to be made and hence a choice of the alternative that comes out more advantageous or cheaper.

There was evidently a good deal of opposition in the early stages to the use of this sort of device. This opposition was first of all in principle to the use of such an 'un-Marxist' notion. Had not Marx exposed the 'myth of compound interest' as a metaphysical notion?, one writer asked; was this not the bourgeois notion of a specific 'productivity of capital' in disguise? Investment, it was also argued, could never be decided on economic grounds alone, still less according to mechanical rules: 'political' considerations which could not be quantified were always an element in planning decisions. Others claimed that such a device was too selective, and as used tended to ignore a lot of the side-effects of an investment project—what were called 'supplementary investments' such as those involved in housing the additional labour force or even in re-equipping other industries so as to release the labour required for the new plant in question. (Mstislavsky tried out a complex and unusable construction in terms of the total of supplementary investments that would be needed elsewhere to replace the additional labour employed.)[5] Yet other critics concentrated on subordinate issues of interpretation: whether it was proper to use as a standard ratio one express-

[5] This and one or two other contributions to the 1949 discussion are summarised in Charles Bettelheim's interesting work, *Studies in the Theory of Planning*, Bombay and London, 1959, pp. 155 f.

ing the average or the marginal effectiveness in a particular industry; whether such a standard ratio should differ as between industries and sectors, or alternatively be uniform for the whole economy; whether the use of such a rule would retard technical progress.[6]

The debate, however, was to go in favour of the advocates of such ratios. In 1954 there was an interim summing-up of the question in the journal *Voprosi Ekonomiki*, which declared in principle in favour of the 'comparability of investment expenditures and their resulting economies' and the use of such calculations in industry intra-branch investment-decisions. No agreement was reached, however, as to the proper basis for fixing a standard or minimum effectiveness-ratio. In 1956 there was issued a 'temporary standard method' for calculating effectiveness of investment; and

[6] One thing that has always been puzzling about Strumilin's article mentioned above is that he seemed to be opposed to the use of such ratios, while at the same time stressing the crucial importance of the *problem* that such ratios were designed to handle. It now seems clear that his main criticism was directed against their application in a situation where prices were 'arbitrary' (in the sense of diverging from 'values'), and that he was looking for something more fundamental in which to express such a relation, i.e. in terms of labour and labour-productivity.

There was, however, another criticism that he made and which he has continued to repeat more recently: namely, that one should not measure the results of investment merely in terms of the saving in *wages*, but should measure the resulting saving of labour in terms of the *full value* (wages *plus* surplus, or $v + s$ in Marx's notation). Hence effectiveness-ratios, he thought, were unduly biased against the introduction of new technique. Actually there is a very simple answer to Strumilin on this point. Firstly, whether one measures the 'saving of labour' at wages only or at 'full value' will make no difference to the *comparative* effectiveness of alternative technical variants. Secondly, with a given size of the investment plan, no more investment could be undertaken than there were capital goods provided; hence a mere numerical change in the ratio as calculated could not affect the *real* volume or nature of investment projects (as Vaag and Zakharov, in an article we cite later, point out very aptly in relation to an analogous objection to the raising of capital-goods prices from their present low level). All that would happen if Strumilin's proposal were adopted would be that the *standard* effectiveness-ratio would have to be set equivalently higher so as to bring the aggregate cost of all the separate construction-projects into line with the total investment-plan.

in June 1958 there was convened in Moscow an All-Union Scientific-Technical Conference on Problems of Determining the Economic Effectiveness of Capital Investment and New Techniques, with Professor T. S. Khachaturov delivering the chief report[7] (followed by Strumilin). Just previously to this, towards the end of 1957, a special Scientific Council had been instituted by the Academy of Sciences to direct and coordinate research work on this problem—a problem now promoted to being 'one of the most important problems in the building of communism'. Meanwhile a resolution of the Twenty-First Party Congress emphasised 'the outstanding significance of the most effective direction of capital investment, providing for the least expenditure of means in cultivating productive power'; and Mr Khrushchev was to stress the need 'for calculation of the time factor', in connection with the comparative advantages of hydro-electric and coal-burning power-plants. Finally, in 1960, there was issued, by joint agreement of the Economics Institute of the Academy and the Scientific Research Institute of Gosplan, a definitive 'Standard Method' (*Tipovaia Metodika*), which was summarised in the Gosplan journal *Planovoe Khoziaistvo*, 1960, No. 3, p. 56, and also published separately as *Tipovaia Metodika Opredelenia Ekonomicheskoi Effectivnosti Kapitalnikh Vlozheni* (Moscow, 1960).

There were here enunciated standard rules for fixing effectiveness-ratios in industry, construction and transport; and (making a

[7] Khachaturov had been made a Corresponding Member of the Academy and, early in 1957, became one of the editors of *Voprosi Ekonomiki* (which for a time seemed to have been in opposition to the Khachaturov school in this matter). Among others, Kantorovich, the mathematician, Nemchinov and Novozhilov (whom we shall mention again below) took part in the discussion at this conference.

Curiously, however, Khachaturov expressed himself in favour, not of a uniform ratio, but of a ratio that differed in different sectors and industrial branches—and for reasons that do not seem convincing to the present writer, apart, perhaps, from a reference to different rates of technical progress, which may be intended to imply a reference to different rates of obsolescence and the need to adjust ratios to them. (See his article, 'Problems of the Economic Effectiveness of Capital Investment' in *Voprosi Ekonomiki*, 1957, No. 2, p. 118.) This compromise (if this is what it represented) is embodied in the final proposals that have emerged, although definite limits are set to the inter-branch variation.

concession to the view that there should be some inter-branch variation in this ratio instead of uniformity) the statement advocated the setting up by each industrial branch of standard coefficients of 'not less than ·15 to ·3', with transport and electrical power as exceptions where as low as ·1 (or a recoupment-period of ten years) was suggested.[8]

3 Prices and the law of value

As soon as the use of such ratios is regarded in the setting of the most efficient use of economic resources in the economy as a whole, it becomes obvious that the whole question of price-policy is inevitably raised. Any comparison of investment cost with subsequent economies in operating cost is a comparison in price terms; and the result is likely to be different according to the relative prices of the various commodities entering into the comparison. For example, suppose that one is comparing construction projects involving different constructional materials, say the use in one case of cement, in another of stone and in a third case of timber. Evidently it will make all the difference to the comparative effectiveness-ratio of these projects whether cement is dear and timber cheap, or conversely cement is the cheapest building material and compared with it stone and timber are expensive. In Poland a complaint of critics of the old pre-1956 price-policy was that the setting of an abnormally low price for coal prejudiced the comparison between coal-burning and hydro-electric power stations—and this at a time when coal was scarce and urgently needed for export. The debate on price-policy which was opened in

[8] Following its publication, however, two writers in *Voprosi Ekonomiki* (L. Vaag and S. Zakharov, 'On Calculating What is the Most Economical' [*Ekonomichnost*], 1960, No. 7, p. 103) complained that, despite this measure of agreement as to practice, there was still insufficient theoretical clarity on the reasons for it and called for further discussion of the theoretical issues involved. The article emphasises the connection between calculating economic effectiveness and pricing according to the principle of prices of production, and is largely concerned with a carefully argued reply to theoretical objections made by critics of effectiveness-ratios, including that of Strumilin mentioned in an earlier footnote above.

the middle '50's was accordingly the heir to the discussion of effectiveness-ratios in investment-planning.[9]

The door was opened, if as yet only slightly, to a discussion of price-policy by Stalin's much-quoted declaration, in one of his last published statements, to the effect that the law of value, even if it 'has no regulating function in our socialist production', 'nevertheless influences production, and this fact cannot be ignored when directing production'; 'consumer goods, which are needed to compensate the labour power expended in the process of production, are produced and realised in our country as commodities coming under the operation of the law of value'.[10] Discussion started cautiously, and to begin with remained at an abstract level, concerning itself with such questions as whether the operation of the law of value depended upon the 'existence of two forms of property' (State property and collective farm property), and hence upon commodity-relations in the exchange between industry and agriculture, or upon the 'specific character of social labour under socialism' (payment of wages according to work, and the existence of a retail market where these wages were spent).

In December 1956, however, the sluice-gates were opened. A full-dress discussion was organised under the auspices of the Institute of Economics of the Academy, and attended both by economics teachers in the University and also by members of the research departments of Gosplan and of the Ministries of Finance and of Trade and of the Central Statistical Department. The note preceding the published summary of the discussion in *Voprosi Ekonomiki* said:

> As is well known, in this sphere there are many unsettled questions. A number of positions taken up in our literature until now and widely adopted need more precise working out, and some of them appropriate emendation. . . . Reform of price-policy has great economic significance since directly linked with it is an improvement in the forms of economic accounting, planning of prime costs and the

[9] Cf. Khachaturov's remark that deviation of prices from values may cause 'untrue expression of actual effectiveness', *Planovoe Khoziaistvo*, 1959, No. 8, p. 80.
[10] Op. cit., p. 23.

profitability of production, questions of calculating the effectiveness of capital investment and of introducing new techniques, etc.[11]

This was followed by a further discussion six months later (with Ostrovitianov as chief *rapporteur*).

The main report at the first discussion, 'On the Law of Value and Questions of Price-Formation in U.S.S.R.', was given by Kronrod who advanced the thesis that prices ought to be brought into greater conformity with values;[12] the particular corollary of this upon which emphasis was laid being the prices of means of production (Group A products). These were in most cases sold below values. The wholesale transfer-price at which they passed between State enterprises was based on prime cost *plus* a small profit-margin, but *without* turnover tax and hence without any proportional share in the 'surplus product' of society. The alleged result was to encourage wasteful use of capital goods and insufficient incentive to economise in the use of fuel and power and raw materials and machinery. This standpoint was supported by Strumilin among others. Some speakers criticised the existing reign of what they termed 'arbitrary' prices (Malishev spoke of 'subjectivism in price-formation'). These prices were arbitrary in the sense that they were fixed, not according to any general economic principle, but in order to achieve this or that particular administrative objective of the moment; the implication being that this was the sole ground of most of those 'deviations of prices from values' of which so much had been heard. Academician Nemchinov called on economists to recognise their 'obligation to create a theory of planned prices'.

Once this general issue had been raised, numerous subsidiary issues, of varying degrees of importance, came to the fore. There was the question raised by Strumilin in an article in *Promishlen-naia-Ekonomicheskaia Gazeta*[13] whether in extractive industries

[11] *Voprosi Ekonomiki*, 1957, No. 2, p. 71.
[12] Kronrod introduced his report with the statement that it was the peculiarities of labour under socialism that lay at the base of commodity-exchange and the law of value; since with these peculiarities of labour was linked the need for material incentives to labour, and this 'necessitated the exchange of products on the principle of compensating for the expenditure of labour, i.e. economic exchange'; *Voprosi Ekonomiki*, 1957, No. 2, pp. 71-2, 79-82.   [13] 7th April 1957.

the wholesale selling price should not be based on cost (or value) under the least favourable natural conditions, rather than on an averaging of the different costs of various differently-situated enterprises. (This was a question which also occupied Polish economists about the same time in the form of the familiar marginal *versus* average cost principle.) More fundamental, and in many ways more interesting, was the discussion between advocates of different interpretations of the 'value' principle as basis for price-reform: those who interpreted this as meaning literally that prices should be made proportional to values and those who interpreted it as meaning proportional to 'prices of production' (in the sense of Marx's Volume III of *Capital*).

Manifestly, if the 'surplus product' of society was to be distributed over all commodities in some uniform proportion, there were three main ways in which this could be done. Firstly, the 'surplus product' could be distributed over different products and industries so that it bore a uniform proportion to the wage-bill of each industry (in Marxian terminology, with s standing for surplus and v for variable capital, this would be roughly equivalent to making s/v uniformly equal in all lines of production). Secondly, the surplus production could be so distributed as to make it uniformly proportional to the prime cost (*sebestoimost*) of production (i.e. so as to make $s/$ (used-up $c + v$) uniformly equal in all industries). In practice this would mean building-up the selling-price from the prime cost by adding to the latter everywhere a proportional mark-up (e.g. by means of a uniform rate of turnover tax). Thirdly, the surplus product could be so distributed as to make it proportional to the amount of capital (both constant and variable, fixed and circulating) normally employed in that industry. This was Marx's 'prices of production' (equals cost-price *plus* a share of total surplus, made proportional, *not* to this cost-price itself, but to the total stock of $C + V$ employed).[14]

In the 1956 debate the third interpretation was sponsored in particular by Bachurin (of the Ministry of Finance) and by Malishev (of Gosplan); later by others including Z. V. Atlas, a

[14] Cf. the articles by S. Turetsky and by Bronislaw Minc in *Voprosi Ekonomiki*, 1957, No. 5, p. 62, and 1958, No. 1, p. 96.

well-known writer on monetary questions.[15] A link was immediately established, by implication, with the effectiveness-ratio discussion, because the main practical argument employed by this school of thought was that both criteria and incentives for the economic employment and usage of capital goods would be disturbed *unless* prices of capital goods were constructed in this way. Said Bachurin:

> Distribution of net income [surplus product] proportionately to expenditure of living labour . . . will be unfavourable to branches [of industry] with a large specific weight of expenditure of stored-up labour. . . . Prices built on this principle would not stimulate technical progress, since net income would be greater where manual labour had the larger specific weight.[16]

Malishev pointed out that to base prices directly on values, as Kronrod had proposed, would cause the profitability of various branches of production to differ widely, causing it to be lower 'the higher the technical level of the branch', thus discouraging technical progress.

> In our conditions [he said], the basis of price-formation must be the more developed, enriched, concrete form of value, prices of production, with a different social content from what this has under capitalism. . . . Profitability must be determined, not in relation to prime cost or to the wage-bill, but in relation to the value of all basic and turnover funds [fixed and circulating capital] of an enterprise. This gives the possibility of more fully calculating the effectiveness of capital investment.[17]

The arguments on the other side were that prices of production are a value-form belonging to capitalism which could have no place under socialism: they depended on the existence of

[15] 'On Profitability of Socialist Enterprises' in *Voprosi Ekonomiki*, 1958, No. 7, esp. pp. 123–5. In a postscript-note to a book of last year to which we shall refer below Academician Nemchinov listed as advocates of the 'prices of production' standpoint the following: I. Malishev, L. A. Vaag, V. D. Belkin, Z. V. Atlas, V. A. Sobol, M. V. Kolganov.
[16] The last sentence is from his contribution to the second discussion in May 1957, reported in *Voprosi Ekonomiki*, 1957, No. 8, p. 91.
[17] *Voprosi Ekonomiki*, 1957, No. 2, p. 73, and No. 3, pp. 99–105.

competition with its tendency to a uniform profit-rate, and the latter had no function outside those conditions of market competition from which it arose. To impose an equal profit-rate on industries would, indeed, conceal real expenditures of social labour and stand in contradiction to the principle of maximum economy of social labour. Some, indeed, seem to have thought that it would somehow stand in contradiction to giving priority in development to the capital-goods sector of industry. Another rather curious objection was that prices of production restricted the expansion of more technically advanced industries by raising the price of things produced under conditions of high organic composition of capital (the direct contrary to Malishev's argument that such prices would alone make these 'advanced' techniques profitable).

It does not appear that any general agreement was reached on the major issues of the debate, much less so, at any rate, than in Poland where a substantial measure of agreement was arrived at and embodied in the so-called 'New Economic Model' of 1957, drawn up by the State Economic Council under Professor Oskar Lange's chairmanship, and adopted in principle by the Council of Ministers. In the U.S.S.R. there was a magisterial summing-up by Ostrovitianov in *Kommunist*; but this confined itself to the more abstract issues. There was also a kind of interim summing-up by *Voprosi Ekonomiki*, giving the views of its editors, in the form of replies to a variety of correspondents, and an article by Kulikov with which the editors expressed substantial agreement.[18] But these pronouncements do not seem to have closed discussion, unlike previous occasions when *ex cathedra* pronouncements wrote *finis* to publicly expressed disagreements. (Perhaps historians looking back on these years may even point to this as the most significant change of all.) Although the existing price-system had and continues to have stout defenders (for example Maisenberg and Turetsky, both of whom spoke in a conservative sense in the 1956–7 discussion),[19] one has the impression that they may be now rather on the defensive, and that the idea that prices ought to bear

---

[18] *Voprosi Ekonomiki*, 1958, No. 2 and No. 8.
[19] Cf. S. Turetsky, loc. cit.; also his interesting book *Ocherki Planovogo Tsenobrazovaniya*, in the first chapter of which he defends the existing system (while admitting some of its imperfections) against the price-

a closer relation to values than they do, and 'deviations' therefrom require specific justification,[20] has made quite a strong impact. So far no more than minor changes seem to have been made in administrative practice as regards pricing, though the tendency of these has been towards greater flexibility. In the case of consumer goods, some lessons have been learned from the experience of the price-reductions of the 1950's as to the need for adjusting particular retail prices to varying demand conditions.[21] The attention of planners and administrators has evidently been preoccupied with the sweeping measures of regional decentralisation adopted in 1957, one consequence of which may well be a greater tendency to experimentation by particular regional Economic Councils *Sovnarkhoze*. The greater measure of decentralisation of decisions (about output-plans, about supplies, and even about investment and about price-fixing) is likely to give increased importance to questions of price-policy; so that the next round in the price-discussion may, like that on effectiveness of investment, be immediately provoked by 'the demands of practical life' rather than by *a priori* considerations. At any rate, the advocates of price-reform, especially the price-of-productionists, continue to sustain their argument, and with some confidence.[22]

[20] One such justification could well be the raising of price to encourage economy in the use of some temporarily scarce commodity. Both the effectiveness and the need for such a price-change will depend, however, on the strictness or otherwise of the system of supply-allocation.

[21] Turetsky, op. cit., pp. 411–14. In one of the last articles of the late Prof. Bliumin (I. Bliumin and V. Shliapentok, 'On the Econometric School in Bourgeois Political Economy' in *Voprosi Ekonomiki*, 1958, No. 11, pp. 79–93), the 'practical usefulness' of the concept of demand-elasticity (both price- and income-elasticity) in the study of market conditions was explicitly recognised; the work of Prof. H. Schultz in the United States on demand-studies being singled out for approval (pp. 88–9). Emphasis was laid in the article on the need to distinguish 'problems of political economy' from 'technico-economic problems'.

[22] Cf. the recent article by Vaag and Zakharov cited above. A new and connected discussion now taking place is on 'differential rent in conditions of socialism'.

reformers—without, however, mentioning any names. It may be noted that a forthcoming book on the subject by Malishev has also been announced.

4 Mathematical economics

The third main direction in which economic thought and discussion have shown a welcome revival in the last few years is the development of mathematical economics and an increasing interest, if a critical interest, in developments in this direction in the West during the past two decades. Partly, but by no means entirely, this has a simple technological explanation: the increasing employment of electronic computers in industry and planning, and an admitted neglect previously of the study of 'cybernetics', has emphasised the need for developing programming-techniques for handling economic material in this way. At first there was a good deal of prejudice against the introduction of any of these methods, which were regarded as a 'Trojan horse' of bourgeois concepts imported into Soviet economic thought and practice. The term 'mathematical economics' had always been used to denote the kind of general equilibrium theory derived from Walras and Pareto, and hence in essence a justification of competitive equilibrium in a market economy in subjective terms. What truck could Marxism have with this kind of thing?

For some little time, however, there has evidently been an influential group, particularly among statisticians, who saw the grave limitations and defects of so parochial a view. Russian mathematics was pre-eminent: why should the social sciences alone be barred from enrichment from this source? Some mathematicians (such as Kantorovitch of whom we shall speak in a moment) had already made some contribution to techniques of economic and social accounting, but were in danger of being ignored because of the prevailing prejudice. Apart from the technical needs of the new computing machines, what seems to have sapped previous distrust and prejudice is the demonstration by mathematical economists and statisticians that two of the principal techniques in question had their roots in Soviet reality and not in the bourgeois world as had been supposed. Firstly, it was emphasised that the input-output method, associated with the name of Wassily Leontief, was in fact derived from the 'method of material balances' developed by Soviet planners in the '20's (about which Leontief had indeed written an article in *Planovoe Khoziaistvo*, the Gosplan organ, in

December 1925). This has been repeatedly underlined in articles by Nemchinov and others during the past few years. Secondly, the technique known in the West as 'linear programming' was, it now appears, developed by the Leningrad mathematician Kantorovitch, and published by the University of Leningrad in 1939 under the title of *Matematicheskie Metodi Organisatsii i Planirovania Proizvodstvo* (*Mathematical Methods of Organising and Planning Production*).[23] This was several years before the public appearance of the American inventors of the method.

True, it looks as though little attention was paid to Kantorovitch's discovery at the time (perhaps the fact that Leningrad was under siege within two-and-a-half years of its publication had at least something to do with this); and although the presentation of input-output data in a matrix (or chessboard as it was called) was common in planning, the algebraic refinements of matrix techniques and iterative methods do not seem to have been developed. They were even discouraged officially in the '30's, Kuibishev when in charge of Gosplan condemning the 'statistical-arithmetical deviation in planning'.[24] However, in both respects it is clear that this lag is now (roughly since 1956) being overcome. One writer in 1957 tells us that 'in recent times the question of elaborating the chess-board balance has been raised repeatedly, in particular at the All-Union Conference of Statistics in June 1957'.[25] Linear programming techniques have been applied not only in transport but also in a number of individual industrial plants and even farms in the Leningrad region.[26] A new work by Kantorovitch was published last year by the Academy, entitled *Ekonomicheskii Raschot Nailuchshego Ispol'zovania Resursov* (*Economic Calculation of the Best Utilisation of Resources*). An article by him, explaining his calculation in terms of what he calls 'indirect' as well as 'direct'

[23] The method was called by him that of 'decisive multipliers'.

[24] Cited approvingly by G. Sorokin of Gosplan in *Planovoe Khoziaistvo*, 1956, No. 1, p. 43, in the course of a criticism of planning by 'abstract models'.

[25] V. Belkin in *Voprosi Ekonomiki*, 1957, No. 12, p. 147.

[26] Another interesting example was that a Working Brigade of the Cheliabinsk Polytechnical Institute together with workers of the local tractor factory used linear programming methods 'with positive results', A. Aganbegian in *Planovoe Khoziaistvo*, 1960, No. 2, pp. 54 seq.

expenditures of labour, was even published in *Voprosi Ekonomiki*, usually cautious in such matters.[27] His critic in a later number of that journal fully recognised the value of Kantorovitch's method when applied to the handling of particular scarcities (i.e. scarcities of particular productive resources) in a short-period situation; what he disputed was its validity in a dynamic setting (and hence as a general basis for pricing) when the task of socialist planning consisted essentially of changing and liquidating previous scarcities, for which purpose he considered that calculation in terms of actual or 'direct' labour-expenditure was appropriate.[28]

Indeed, quite a number of articles on econometric topics have recently appeared in the journals.[29] In addition to the Laboratory of Computing Machines and Methods of the U.S.S.R. Academy, a special institute attached to the Siberian branch of the Academy in Novosibirsk has been set up to study economic applications of electronic computer-techniques, and has worked in close association with the regional economic council. A new department of mathematical economics is to be formed this year in the Economics Faculty at Leningrad (and similarly in Moscow at the State University) and extra-mural lectures on linear programming and other mathematical techniques are being organised for engineers and workers in industry. At the same time the Leningrad Institute of Mathematics is working in conjunction with the

[27] 'On Calculating Productive Expenditures' in *Voprosi Ekonomiki*, 1960, No. 1. However, a note was appended to the effect that 'the editors differ from a number of points of view in this article and propose to submit these to critical examination in a forthcoming number of this journal'.
[28] A. Katz, *Voprosi Ekonomiki*, 1960, No. 5, pp. 117 f. In general Nemchinov seems to agree with this criticism.
[29] One of the earliest of them, in *Voprosi Ekonomiki*, 1957, No. 12, about input–output matrices was by V. D. Belkin of the new Laboratory of Computing Machines and Systems of the Academy; Bliumin's survey of Econometrics in 1958 we have already mentioned; the following year came A. Boyarsky, 'On Econometrics and the Use of Mathematics in Economic Analysis' in *Planovoe Khoziaistvo*, 1959, No. 7, which was a review of the subject from Walras, through the Cobb-Douglas theorem and Leontief, to Kantorovitch and the Theory of Games; A. Aganbegian in *Planovoe Khoziaistvo*, 1960, No. 2, dealt mainly with linear programming; and in *Voprosi Ekonomiki*, the most recent articles by Kantorovitch and Nemchinov have been already mentioned.

Leningrad *Sovnarkhoz* which is itself setting up a computer section. In April 1960 in Moscow a scientific conference on the use of mathematical methods in economics and planning was called jointly by the Economics-Philosophy-Law Section of the Academy and the Academy's Siberian branch. This heard as many as fifty-six papers read (in plenary session and in six specialised sections) with more than ninety persons taking part in discussion.[30] A further conference is mooted for the autumn of 1961, and also this year the setting up in the Academy of an inter-departmental scientific council for the study of mathematical methods in economics and planning. Already at the end of 1959 there had been held in Warsaw a conference of all the socialist countries on questions of elaborating the balance of the national economy, in the course of which the question of input–output tables and work being done on them received particular attention.[31] And in his recent *Voprosi Ekonomiki* article Academician Nemchinov called for the publication of a special journal devoted to mathematical economics. How far the specific input–output techniques associated with Leontief are being used by Gosplan itself is not quite clear. Probably their precise use and application are still matters of some controversy; one of the incidental difficulties apparently being that statistical information is not always available to Gosplan at present in the requisite form.

This is how Nemchinov sums up the attitude to input–output analysis, etc., in his most recent article:

> Rejecting bourgeois conceptions of the American economist V. Leontief, we can successfully utilise the 'input–output' method of analysis, or, more strictly, the method of analysis of inter-branch productive relations, especially as this method without doubt arose under the direct and immediate influence of the first Soviet balance of the national economy built by the U.S.S.R. Central Statistical Department in 1923–4. We must not shun, still less fear, the term 'econometric investigation', properly understood, of course, and properly utilised in the conditions of socialist economy. It is essential to study

[30] *Planovoe Khoziaistvo*, 1960, No. 5, pp. 88–90. Nemchinov gave the main report. The conference was extensively reported in *Voprosi Ekonomiki*, 1960, No. 8, pp. 100–28.

[31] *Planovoe Khoziaistvo*, 1960, No. 5, pp. 92–6.

critically investigations in the region of foreign econometrics and mathematical economics, and all that is useful and valuable in accounting and mathematical instruments, suitable for the analysis of economic relations, must be utilised in the practice of our planned economy.[32]

Indicative of these new developments was the publication last year of a collective work edited by Academician Nemchinov entitled *The Use of Mathematics in Economic Investigations*. In addition to two contributions by Kantorovitch, there is a set of elementary lectures on linear programming delivered by a Hungarian economist in Budapest, chapters on the applications of linear programming, especially to transport problems, and the translation of an article by Professor Oskar Lange (written originally for the Indian statistical journal *Sankhya* and embodied in his *Textbook on Econometrics*) in which he compares Leontief's input–output method with Marx's schema of expanded reproduction. Of particular interest to the present writer is a long contribution, running to nearly 200 pages, by Professor V. V. Novozhilov, one of the Leningrad group of pioneers of the linear programming approach.[33] What is specially interesting about his contribution is his linking up of the effectiveness of investment coefficient with the question of prices. In this connection he suggests a new cost-category which he calls 'national economy cost', to include, in addition to prime cost (*sebestoimost*), a quantity designed to measure the effectiveness of investment in the economy as a whole. He shows that a cost-price constructed in this way will show the method of production that yields the standard ratio of effectiveness as the least-cost method—i.e. it will ensure that a thing produced under this method of production will show a lower cost than the same product when produced under any alternative technical method.[34]

[32] *Voprosi Ekonomiki*, 1960, No. 6, p. 19. For adherence to the more traditional emphasis in East Germany, however, see *Wirtschaftswissenschaft*, 8, Jahrgang, 7. Sonderheft; also, I. Dvorkin in *Voprosi Ekonomiki*, 1960, No. 8.

[33] See his early articles of 1939 and 1946 published in translation in *International Economic Papers*, No. 6.

[34] Specifically what Novozhilov suggests is that, if r stands for the standard effectiveness-ratio (as defined earlier in the present article), K for the capital-cost involved, and C for the prime cost, then what he calls

This he claims is an application of the only correct principle of calculation for a socialist economy, that of minimising labour expenditures (through minimising expenditures of labour *subject to a given output of capital goods*, governed by the existing size of Department I industries).

It is of interest to note in this connection that, in a postscript-note to the volume, the editor, while drawing attention to the analogy between Novozhilov's 'national economic cost' and 'price of production', emphasises that it has certain qualitative differences which make it a superior version of a 'transformed form of value' relevant to socialist society: in particular, that it can be treated as an accounting-price category only, and does not imply 'market autonomism' as its background; moreover that it does not necessarily depend on the use of a rigidly uniform effectiveness-ratio for all sectors and branches. It is, further, interesting (and may possibly be significant in connection with future changes in the system of actual prices) that as an accounting-price for use in investment-decisions Novozhilov's proposal has been embodied in the recent 'Standard Methods of Determining the Economic Effectiveness of Capital Investment'.[35]

5 'Copying the West' or 'towards a political economy of socialism'?

The reaction of most economists in the West to these developments is that they represent simply a belated importation of previously

[35] It is advocated for use at the enterprise-level as a special 'coefficient of profitability' of investment. Whenever several variants are to be compared, the formula '$C + E.K$ = minimum' is recommended, where E is the standard coefficient of effectiveness for the branch: *Planovoe Khoziaistvo*, 1960, No. 3, pp. 56 f. See also Khachaturov's reference to 'including in current expenses of production a percentage of original expenditures, equal to the established coefficient of effectiveness of that branch', *Voprosi Ekonomiki*, 1957, No. 2, p. 120.

'national economic cost' should be calculated in each case as $rK + C$. This solution can be shown to be essentially the same as that proposed by the present writer in his *Essay on Economic Growth and Planning*, Chapter VI, where it is suggested that if (in the so-called 'normal' case) price is so fixed as to include a proportional share of surplus product in addition to wage-cost, that technique will be most profitable to use which maximises growth (maximising growth with a *given* labour force being, of course, the same as minimising the labour needed to produce a given output).

neglected notions of 'bourgeois economics', and that while this can be welcomed as a rational step it is hardly an intellectual innovation to admire. This view is based, I believe, on a crucial misconception: a misconception that rests on an underestimate of the ideological element in thought. By this I mean, not simply the intrusion of ethical ideas and so-called 'value judgments' into our thinking, but the fact that ideas have significance as part of a complex 'picture of the real world', and this picture is inevitably influenced by the perspective in which we view the world and the presuppositions which we inherit as part of our mode of thought and belief. In the social sciences at any rate it is not at all a simple matter to separate a purely formal notion from the whole framework of thought, with its tangle of implicit definitions and assumptions, in which it has been traditionally embodied. Such a notion cannot, therefore, be as easily transferred from one context to another as the simplifiers and eclectics think: that is, it cannot be easily transferred without importing along with it a whole number of associated ideas, of a more institutional or historically relative kind, that have become inextricably entwined with it. Take, for instance, the notion of 'elasticity'—a purely quantitative ratio borrowed from mathematics. What could be more purely a non-ideological, non-'superstructural' 'tool'? But does it not at once imply some entity, called a 'demand curve', *of which* it is a measure —an entity about whose nature there may be much controversy and whose very 'existence' could be called in question? Moreover, in contemporary economic thought that entity is connected with a whole conceptual system of 'indifference curves' or 'behaviour lines', from which it has been derived, together with a series of assumptions about individual consumers' behaviour or thought-processes which these abstract notions were created to express. And what is true of an elasticity is true, *mutatis mutandis*, of the notion of an interest-rate, however much we may regard it, abstractly, as a 'pure ratio' connecting entities having different datings in time.

In other words, it is only by an astringent process of critical analysis that one can separate out notions from their historical-ideological content and from other institutionally-relative notions with which they are associated, and hence be in a position to discover what meaning (if any) and relevance the former may have when transferred to a qualitatively different social context. In the absence of such a critical examination it may well be a sound instinct to oppose such a 'transfer', by reason of the large amount of dross that an ounce of gold may bear with it. Yet to oppose is, at the same time, an admission of intellectual poverty—of the immaturity of one's own critical thought.

Partly no doubt it is true to regard what has been happening recently in the U.S.S.R. (and in some of the contiguous countries) as an emerging from the shades of dogmatism, which cramped enquiry and discussion for too long. But this is no more than part of it, possibly a minor aspect. More important, and certainly more encouraging, about this new stage in theory and discussion is the extent to which it betokens a new maturity of Marxist thought—a maturity when it can use its tools of criticism, no longer only negatively but also positively, so as to make constructive use, within its own conceptual framework, of ideas and techniques that it once feared, and at the same time foster creative thought and discussion to the end of 'generalising the experience of socialist economy' and building a Political Economy of Socialism.

Three

A comment on the discussion about price-policy

Reprinted from *Soviet Studies*, October 1957 (Vol. IX, No. 2), by kind permission of the editors and publishers of that journal.

Anyone acquainted with Marxist discussion of such questions will appreciate that 'the law of value' is regarded as applying essentially to a market- or exchange-economy; and the debate as to how far production is (or should be) 'influenced', or alternatively 'regulated', by the law of value is a debate about the degree of influence exerted by the market (and by prices as indices of exchange-relations) upon production. In the new debate (as was pointed out in the last number of *Soviet Studies*) the sufficiency of Stalin's formulation in *Economic Problems of Socialism in the U.S.S.R.* is questioned, to the effect that the law of value continues to exercise an influence because of the survival of market-relations between the two main sectors of Soviet economy, state industry and the collective farm peasantry. Instead it is now maintained that it does so because of the persistence of exchange-relations between State industry and the consumer (i.e. of the retail market for consumer goods). Thus the influence of the law of value is made to depend, not upon an incidental (and in a sense 'external') feature, but on an essential feature of socialism (regarded as 'the first or lower stage of communism'): namely, its wage-system, with the corollary that if wage-differentials continue to play a role as a production-incentive, wage-earners must be able to spend their wages freely on a retail market. Curiously enough, this is referred to in Stalin's booklet as a reason (p. 23: 'consumer goods, which are needed to compensate the labour-power expended in the process of production, are produced and realised in our country as commodities coming under the operation of the law of value ... precisely here ... the law of value exercises its influence on production'). But subsequently this reason is forgotten apparently and is assigned no more than a quite secondary role.

It is of some interest to note that a similar discussion took place a year ago among Polish economists,[1] and also towards the end of the year among economists in East Germany.[2]

In this discussion it seems to me that three questions need to be clearly distinguished.

1. Should central planning of economic decisions be replaced by a mechanism whereby economic decisions are taken automatically by economically autonomous units ('enterprises') on the basis of market prices? In the Soviet discussion no proposal of this kind has been canvassed (nor has it, to my knowledge, in the Polish and German discussions; although opponents of change have denounced tendencies to substitute 'market autonomism' for planning); but any decentralisation must represent *some* move in this direction to the extent that it shifts more of the responsibility for economic decisions down to the level of the individual enterprise. In Yugoslavia in recent years a substantial degree of 'market autonomism' applies to consumer-goods industries.

2. Granted that economic decisions are centrally planned, should such decisions, at least so far as they relate to the production of consumer goods, be guided by economic indices based on market prices? This applies particularly to decisions about investment designed to expand the output-capacities of different lines of production by various amounts. And is it a corollary of doing so that the prices of producer goods (machinery, fuel and power, raw materials) should be adjusted according to some consistent principle?

3. The question of providing an inducement to managers of

[1] See especially article by Professor W. Brus, 'On the role of the Law of Value in a Socialist Economy', and other papers at a Congress of Polish Economists and discussion of them, in *Ekonomista*, 1956, No. 5; also articles in *Gospodarka Planowa*.
[2] See the special number of *Wirtschaftswissenschaft* devoted to 'Ökonomische Theorie und Politik in der Übergangsperiode', February 1957.

enterprises, in carrying out the targets assigned to them, to produce things in 'correct' amounts and proportions by fixing 'correct' prices both for their output and for all constituents of their input. This will be the more important the more discretion is left to managers. However centralised the planning may be, there is bound to be a considerable margin of discretion *de facto* about the precise assortment and detailed specification of products, as well as the methods of production; and the recent tendency of greater decentralisation has evidently been to extend this discretion. It is noteworthy that a recurring complaint over a number of years has been the failure of industries to fulfil their so-called 'assortment plans', i.e. the range of variety assigned to them. (This was also a matter of complaint in the Polish discussion.) Repeated attempts seem to have been made to correct this by administrative measures and stricter planning. If it persisted so long notwithstanding, this must have been presumably because the structure of relative prices was such as to provide a chronic inducement to produce the 'wrong' assortment (profitability to the enterprise being in conflict with the objectives of the plan).

With regard to this last point, it might seem that the problem was a purely empirical one and that no issue of principle was involved. In each particular case the planners can make prices what they need these to be in order to promote fulfilment of the plan. Prices (like taxes or subsidies) become an arbitrary planning instrument, and as such they have been used in the past. (This was denounced by one participant in the discussion as 'subjectivism' in price-policy and 'the rule of the arbitrary').[3] If too much of one constituent of input is being used (e.g. a scarce fuel or transport long-hauls), prices can be raised to encourage economy and substitution; if too little of some line of textile cloth is being produced, its selling price (*optovaia tsena*) and hence the profit-margin to be enjoyed on its production can be raised. If there is a tendency to hold unduly large stocks of materials or goods-in-process, then an interest-charge can be made for bank-credits with which enterprises hold stocks above the stipulated 'normative'. This view of prices as arbitrary planning instruments, adapted *ad hoc* to meet

[3] I. Malishev in *Voprosi Ekonomiki*, 1957, No. 3, p. 97.

particular supply-demand situations, clearly becomes inadequate the wider the area of discretion that is allowed to the management of enterprises (if, for instance, output targets for only one-third of the products and product-varieties are stipulated in the central plan, then for two-thirds of them no planned targets exist to the fulfilment of which prices can be geared). There are also more general objections that can be made to so empirical an attitude; chief of these being that it provides no answer to the question as to whether, when the price of a scarce input is raised to encourage economy in its use, this is to be regarded as the permanent solution, or whether alternatively efforts should be made in subsequent plans to expand the supply of the input that is in temporarily short-supply. If the latter answer is given, then it may well be preferable to ration the scarce supply temporarily instead of varying its price.

What the new discussion is concerned with is some principle that will define 'normal' price-relationships and enable some uniformity of treatment to be established in such cases.

A large part of the Soviet discussion has been occupied with the price-relationship between consumer goods (Sector B) and producer goods (Sector A)—this rather than the structure of relative prices *within* each group. (The Polish discussion, on the other hand, was concerned with both questions, and particularly stressed the need to adapt the pattern of output of consumer goods to the pattern of consumers' demand.) In particular it is said that the prices of producer goods are 'too low' relatively to the prices of consumer goods and should be raised, e.g. by levying turnover tax on the former as well as on the latter, and at similar rates.

Under the existing system, as is well-known, turnover tax is levied as a rule (there are some exceptions)[4] only on consumer goods, and levied between the producer and the retail market. The wholesale (*optovie*) prices at which products leave the factory are based on 'planned costs' which include the cost of wages and

---

[4] Some examples of these are given by Sh. Turetsky in *Voprosi Ekonomiki* 1957, No. 5, p. 62. They include cases of materials in short supply and also products of extractive industries (e.g. fuels) where the tax is used to deal with the difference between 'average costs' and costs of the least favourably situated sources of supply (rather like the proposal of the Ridley Committee for the British Coal Industry).

salaries and raw material, *plus* an amortisation charge (but not an interest-charge) on plant and equipment. Thus, the selling-price on which industrial enterprises operate, whether they belong to Sector A or Sector B, is based virtually on prime cost. The *rationale* of this system (which was defended in the discussion by Turetsky and Maisenberg) consists in the following very simple relationship. Ignoring for the moment what Strumilin calls 'social consumption' (incomes of non-productive workers in the health and education services and defence and salaries of administrative workers above the level of industrial enterprises), and remembering that in a 'closed system' prime costs are ultimately reducible to wages,[5] we can see that the ratio of final (retail) prices of consumer goods to their prime cost will depend upon the *rate of net investment*, measured by the proportion of the total wages-bill (and hence of personal incomes) that is represented by the cost of new construction and new capital goods. (If the reason is not immediately plain, reference may be made for an explanation of this relation to the present writer's *Political Economy and Capitalism*, London, 1937, pp. 325–7, or his *Soviet Economic Development since 1917*, London, 1948, pp. 361–3; or in its application also to a capitalist economy to Mrs Joan Robinson's *Accumulation of Capital*, London, 1956, pp. 74–5.) If we reintroduce 'social consumption', then this ratio becomes dependent on the rate of new investment *plus* 'social consumption' as a proportion of national income (or rather of the total of personal incomes); further qualifications can be made in the relation if there is any substantial amount of individual saving out of personal incomes.[6]

The reason for what Dr Schlesinger calls 'the still current dogma'—the practice whereby this difference or gap between the

[5] Amortisation may be taken as roughly equivalent to current expenditures on capital maintenance or replacement.

[6] It is of course this relationship which renders nugatory the 'attempt to separate that part of net indirect tax paid by state enterprises which is properly factor income and that part which is truly tax', referred to in *Economic Bulletin for Europe*, U.N. Geneva, May 1957, p. 94: an attempt which is crucial to the 'adjusted factor cost' method of Professor Bergson and his school. Cf. the remarks of Professor F. D. Holzman in *Soviet Studies*, July 1957, pp. 35–6; and on the more general issue M. Kalecki, *Theory of Economic Dynamics*, London, 1954, p. 62.

level of retail prices and the level of industrial prices is siphoned off directly into the Budget, instead of being allowed to accrue initially as realised profits of State industry—was apparently an administrative one. The maximum incentive to cost reduction by the enterprise is evidently given when the whole (or a major proportion) of the results of such economy accrue in higher profit to enterprises. This is the case when the industrial selling-price which the enterprise receives for its output is fixed on the basis of 'planned cost' (*plus* a small profit-margin). If, however, the industrial selling-price received by the enterprise were to be related, not to production-cost, but to the final price at the retail stage, both the initial profit and presumably the percentage rate at which that profit was taxed would be high; consequently the addition to *retained* profit as a result of any cost-reduction (as well as the proportionate addition to total profit that this represented) would be much smaller. No doubt some complicated grading of the rate of profit-taxation could be devised so as to leave a larger percentage of retained profit beyond a certain level. But the method of taking 100 per cent of the 'gap' between the two price-levels by a turnover tax has the advantage of simplicity. It has also the further advantage of providing an easy means whereby retail price can be adjusted to particular scarcities.

Academician Strumilin seems to imply that it is irrational for the turnover tax to be levied on consumer goods alone; and that, since a commodity's 'value' consists not only of wages expended but also of its appropriate share of the 'surplus product' of society, the prices of producer goods as well as of consumer goods should be raised by the amount of their respective shares of this 'surplus product' (representing, i.e. net investment plus 'social consumption'). This he suggests should be done by setting an 'accounting (*raschotny*) price' for each product, to include, in addition to prime costs or direct expenses, a proportional share of this 'surplus product'; this accounting price being paid to the enterprise, but the element of 'surplus product' being skimmed off in the form of two sets of taxes or deductions (a 'deduction' for the fund of social consumption and a profit-tax for the investment fund).[7] Whether made

[7] It does not seem to be clear whether either or both of these are to have the form of the existing turnover tax or of a percentage tax on profit. One

exactly according to the Strumilin-method or not, the upshot of the change would be to raise the prices of producer goods relatively to wages: i.e. to make all constituents of input *other* than labour more costly to industries using them. To judge from the statement of Kronrod (cited by Dr Schlesinger), this change is prompted by the fact that the existing price-system encourages uneconomic use of capital goods and creates a bias towards saving labour at the expense of costly capital equipment, or alternatively of raw materials; in which case this discussion seems to be to some extent a direct sequel to the earlier one about calculating a coefficient of effectiveness of investment as a guide to choice between alternative technical variants.

But if this is the reason—the need to include a charge for scarce capital goods, any all-round increase in the supply of which would place a strain upon the limited current 'social investment fund'—the inadequacy of the remedy in the form in which it is proposed by Strumilin and Kronrod is at once obvious. (This proposal amounts to an equi-proportional mark-up all round on prime costs, since existing industrial prices, as we have seen, are based virtually on prime costs—Turetsky interprets it in the familiar Marxian notation as pricing at $c + v + \left(v \times \dfrac{s}{v} \right)$, but of course c would itself have been marked up in similar degree at a previous stage of production).[8] It is inadequate, firstly because the conditions of production of producer goods (output of Sector A) are sufficiently various to make an equi-proportional addition to their existing prices a very crude expedient. Their conditions of production differ as regards both their composition of capital (or ratio of capital to labour) and the turnover period of various constituents of their

[8] Sh. Turetsky, *Voprosi Ekonomiki*, 1957, No. 5, pp. 66–7.

of the critics of the proposal at any rate suggests that it would be inferior to the present method since it would blur the distinction between 'net income of the enterprise' (profit) and 'centralised net income of the State' (turnover tax) and hence weaken the incentive to the enterprise to cost-reduction (M. Bor, in *Voprosi Ekonomiki*, 1957, No. 3, p. 111). In an article in *Voprosi Ekonomiki*, 1956, No. 12, however, Strumilin seems to suggest that these might have the form of a tax proportional to the wage bill (p. 99).

capital; and what the logic of the Kronrod—Strumilin argument demands is some kind of general *agio* on capital—the all-round inclusion in the industrial selling-price of a charge proportional to the capital used (so far as this can be measured). Secondly, if there is a tendency to over-use of scarce capital goods when their price contains no specific capital-charge (over and above amortisation), then it follows, surely, that the prices of consumer goods should be adjusted according to the varying proportions in which capital (as compared with direct or 'living labour') is used in their production? (This should probably apply to the industrial selling-price; but it should certainly apply to the 'normal' price, taken as the standard or accounting price with which current retail prices are compared when the planning authorities are considering the distribution of investment between different consumer-goods industries.)

This is the *rationale* of those like Bachurin who claim that 'prices of production' and not the 'values' of Vol. I of *Capital* should be adopted as the norm; and it seems to me that they have logic on their side. In other words, analogous reasons to those used by Strumilin in his *Promishlenno-Ekonomicheskaia Gazeta* article for including in costs a charge for scarce natural resources[9] could be applied to the inclusion of a charge for scarce capital goods—or rather for things like buildings, plant and equipment in the degree to which they place a strain on the (limited) investible resources of society.

It is when one comes to determine the proper level of such a capital-charge that the problem becomes difficult, even intractable; and it may be remembered that the earlier discussion about choice between alternative investment projects came to a stop precisely at this point. The fact is that (apart from the well-known difficulties about valuing 'capital' without getting involved in circular reasoning) there exists no generally agreed principle for determining a 'true', or socially optimum, level of interest-rate, either among

---

[9] Cit. by Dr Schlesinger in *Soviet Studies*, July 1957, p. 95. It is true that Strumilin was here speaking of cost-*differences* in a diminishing returns industry. But (as Ricardo always recognised) there is an intensive as well as an extensive margin, and the rent-problem (depending on a difference between average cost and cost at the margin) derives essentially from scarcity of supply.

Soviet or 'Western' economists (anyone inclined to doubt this statement may be referred to J. de V. Graaf, *Theoretical Welfare Economics*, pp. 99–105; also cf. the present writer in *Soviet Studies*, Vol. II, No. 3, pp. 289 seq.). One can perhaps say that to include *some* interest-charge is better than to include none; though even this could be questioned—but probably one could safely say at least that to include some smallish capital-charge is better than to include none.

To avoid misunderstanding, one should perhaps add this in parenthesis: the difficulty of which we have been speaking is *not* because of the absence in a socialist economy of a market for capital, as Mises and his school would maintain. It is a difficulty that applies just as much to a capitalist economy: here an interest-rate happens to emerge, but there is no valid ground for supposing it to be an optimum rate from the standpoint of society as a whole.

Nor would the difficulty be surmounted by taking the actual difference between the level of retail prices for consumer goods and the level of industrial (cost) prices, and averaging this out over industry as a whole in order to find an appropriate profit-rate on capital. That is to say, the difficulty is not surmounted if we are looking for some 'correct' relation between the price-level of capital goods and the level of wages—'correct' in the sense of yielding the optimum degree of substitution of capital goods for labour in production and no more. [Cf., however, for a later and contrary opinion of the writer, below pp. 202 and n., 225n.]

However, if we are looking at the problem as being one of distributing a *given total* of investible resources, or a given total supply of capital goods, between various lines of production, then we have a different situation. The problem is then the purely relative one of comparing the social benefit to be derived from using those resources in one branch of consumer-goods industry and in another—investing them in expanding, say, the productive capacity of the woollen industry or of the furniture industry or of the food industry. This is question no. 2 of the three questions that we distinguished above. For this purpose it would be both proper and sufficient to take the difference between the current (retail) price of the product and its direct cost (Strumilin's 'surplus product'), provided that this were expressed as a ratio to the total capital involved in its production (and not simply to its wage-cost). A comparison of such ratios would then give an order of priorities, on the assumption that the object was to satisfy consumers' demands in their market expression to the maximum extent (there might be, of course, numerous exceptions to this, where one wished to modify the resulting market order of priorities for various 'social reasons'). One method of doing this would be to calculate for each commodity a 'normal' or standard price, in which an average share of the 'surplus product' (= sum of the current investment fund and 'social consumption') was included, expressed as a ratio to the capital involved. If the actual retail price of a product was above this standard, it would be in the list for expansion of its supply in subsequent investment plans; if its actual price was below the standard price, the presumption would be that it had little need of expansion. The price to the enterprise (*optovaia tsena*) could remain unaffected; this being based on planned cost as at present, with the difference between it and the retail price (less distributive costs) being covered by turnover tax.

One could not, of course, stop at introducing such a principle for the consumer-goods sector alone. One would have to work out analogous 'prices of production' for capital goods and all materials and components used by the former sector; with the difference that in this case these 'prices of production' would need to be, not merely planning-norms, but *actual* prices at which these producer goods were *bought* by enterprises and entered as constituents of cost in the industries using them in production. Again, these prices need not be the same as the prices *paid* to the supplying enterprise: the latter could be based on planned cost and the difference bridged by a turnover tax. But for consistency it would be necessary that the turnover tax should be so adjusted as to represent a uniform ratio to the capital employed in all cases—save for short-run departures from this uniform ratio to meet exceptional scarcities. It would be well, I suggest, to keep such departures from the rule rather exceptional in view of the well-known advantages of stability in the prices of producer goods. (Since these goods enter into the cost of industries that use them and may affect their investment decisions, short-term fluctuations in their prices may cause decisions about technique, location, etc., to be made that from a long-term standpoint are wrong decisions.)

Once the prices of capital goods have been regulated in this way, the choice of method of production by each enterprise, in so far as this concerns the type and amount of capital goods used, will evidently be decided—decided by what is profitable to the enterprises. For example, the choice between two alternative building materials, or between producing electricity from coal-burning plants or hydro-electric, will be governed by their comparative costs at existing prices (relative to their efficiencies); the least costly way of producing a given result being chosen. The price-level of capital goods relative to wages will also determine how far it is profitable for an enterprise to extend mechanisation, i.e. to substitute capital for labour in its methods of production; and it will affect such decisions as the amount of 'manning' of productive equipment or the size of the repair-staff employed, which may be a crucial factor in the length of life of equipment. All such decisions will affect the demand for capital goods coming from all branches of industry—from the consumer-goods sector (Sector B) and also from Sector A itself. Now, we have been assuming that the rate of investment (and hence, *ceteris paribus*, the total output of capital goods) is already given—that it has been determined in the Plan by an independent policy-decision. Accordingly, at any one time there must be one particular level of prices for capital goods (relative to the level of wages) that will make the aggregate demand for capital goods in any year equal to this supply. I can see no reason why this price should be one that involves the inclusion in it of the *same* rate of turnover tax (as a quasi-profit-rate) as is required in the consumer-goods sector. Of course, the demand for capital goods will to a large extent be directly controlled by the investment plan; and if the over-all rate of investment is centrally decided there are strong reasons for both the allocation between industries and the technical forms of investment to be centrally planned as well. In so far, however, as any of the decisions we have mentioned above are influenced by profitability to the enterprise, and hence by prices, it would seem to be essential that the appropriate rate of turnover tax (or profit mark-up) on capital goods should have the character of an 'arbitrary planning-price' (or, if you like, a 'trial-and-error price'), fixed at whatever level will bring the total demand for capital goods into equilibrium with the supply of them that the investment plan has decided to make available.

On a first reading of the published summary of the Soviet discussion it looked as though the crucial issue as between the use of 'values' and the use of 'prices of production' as a basis for price-fixing—the question of securing the most effective distribution of the current investment fund—was not brought out clearly. A reading of two contributions subsequently published *in extenso* in *Voprosi Ekonomiki* (1957, No. 3) shows that this first impression was wrong. A. Malishev, maintaining that 'in our conditions, it seems, the basis of price-formation must be the more developed, enriched, concrete form of value—price of production, with substantially another social content to what it has in conditions of capitalism', suggests that the prices of all goods, both means of production and means of consumption, should be based on their prime cost (*sebestoimost*) *plus* a uniform rate of profit, calculated in relation to all 'productive funds' (capital) employed in the branch of industry in question. The reason he gives is that different lines of production differ very greatly in the ratio of fixed capital to labour, in the proportion of circulating capital embodied in raw materials and in the length of their production-cycle (these he sums up as 'substantial differences in the relation of expenditure on stored-up to living labour'); that since the available resources for investment at any one time are insufficient to meet all the demands of technical modernisation and re-equipment, there must be some criterion for 'selecting the most advantageous variants' from among the mass of competing claims; and that the most serviceable economic criterion of the advantageousness of capital expenditure is a rate of profit, 'calculated in relation to all the basic and turnover funds of the enterprise'. 'In face of given prices of output and on condition that these prices are economically justified, any additional investment in basic funds' (fixed capital), to be justifiable, 'must raise or at least not lower the level of profit of the enterprise' below the given 'normal level' (arrived at by expressing the aggregate surplus product as a ratio to the aggregate capital employed).[10]

[10] I. Malishev, loc. cit., pp. 99, 103, 104; also cf. *Voprosi Ekonomiki*, 1957, No. 2, p. 73.

The reason which his critic, M. Bor of Gosekonomkommissia, gives for not accepting this criterion is instructive. He takes an example of two branches of industry producing ferro-concrete constructions and timber for building respectively. To produce 'an equivalent mass of materials' it is necessary for society to expend 100 and 140 hours of labour respectively. But because the production of ferro-concrete is highly mechanised whereas wood-working is not, the proportions in which this labour consists of 'stored-up labour' and of 'living labour' are respectively 80 : 20 and 20 : 80. 'Since prices of means of production, built according to Comrade Malishev's scheme, are higher than their value, an hour of stored-up labour will be priced higher than an hour of living labour'; hence 'in such a system of prices it may happen that it is economically more advantageous for society to produce timber than ferro-concrete constructions, although in actuality it is better to produce ferro-concrete constructions'.[11] This certainly puts the issue in a nutshell. Ferro-concrete would indubitably be better than timber if we reckoned an hour of 'stored-up labour' on a par with an hour of 'living labour', currently employed. But it would only be reasonable to treat them as being on a par, for purposes of economic accountancy, if the amount of labour one could employ in current capital construction were unlimited, if existing resources (stocks) of 'stored-up labour' were plentiful enough, as a result of quinquennia of past investment, to satisfy to the full all technical uses for it. Precisely because these conditions are not fulfilled, it is necessary that a rational system of economic accounting should place some premium on the use of 'stored-up labour' relatively to 'living labour' to ensure the most effective use of the former; and to this extent Malishev was clearly right and Bor was wrong. But what exactly this premium should be is not easy, as we have seen, to determine (nor is it easy to find a quantitative measure for stored-up labour, which is not a simple but a complex entity compounded of labour and time). However, once the rate of investment is determined, it should be possible, as we have also seen, to find empirically a figure for this premium which will equate the demand for additional stored-up labour with the current supply of such additions that the Plan has decided to make available.

[11] M. Bor, loc. cit., pp. 112–13.

To close with a brief mention of two incidental points. Firstly, how much importance are we to attach to Kronrod's proposition about the so-called equality of the sum of values and the sum of prices? Various views were expressed in the discussion as to whether this was to be taken as applying *only* to consumer goods, or in some sense or other to total output of both sectors. In the original context in which it was used, this was a statement about the average value of commodities (*all* commodities, whether consumer goods or capital goods) and the value of money under a commodity-money system (gold).[12] It is questionable whether this can have any relevance to the quite different context of Soviet economy today. It could be said still to have a possible meaning as a postulate about monetary policy (that in conditions of constant labour-productivity the price-level of goods sold to the population should be constant; this price-level being reduced only in the degree to which labour-productivity rises). But in a planned economy monetary policy cannot be separated from wage-policy and investment-policy. The significant relation is that of the price-level of consumer goods to wages, and this we have seen is dependent, not only on the productivity of labour in the consumer-goods industries, but also on investment-policy (if the rate of investment rises, the price-level of consumer goods must rise, *ceteris paribus*, relatively to money wages). What significance then can be assigned to Kronrod's equality? At any rate it does not seem capable of sustaining any such corollary as that, if the prices of producer goods are raised, those of consumer goods must fall equivalently, or *vice versa*.

Finally one should perhaps remark that for Soviet economists to be discussing price policy at all is a considerable advance beyond what were previously regarded as the proper frontiers of Political Economy. So long as prices were regarded simply as arbitrary planning instruments, it was not unnatural that price-policy should be treated as part of the technology of planning. Stalin drew a sharp dividing line between 'problems of the economic policy of the directing bodies' and 'problems of political economy';

[12] In the classical context in which Marx used it, the statement implied that gold was produced under conditions of *average* composition of capital (and turnover of capital).

including economic planning among the former and defining the latter as follows: 'Political economy investigates the laws of development of men's relations of production . . . To foist upon political economy problems of economic policy is to kill it as a science.'[13] It was scarcely surprising that economic writing thus divorced from policy-applications should confine itself either to description or to a few vague historical generalities. Now the dividing wall is down, and economists and economic discussion have a chance of generalising the experience and problems of three decades of planning into a theory of the functioning of a socialist economy.

[13] *Economic Problems of Socialism in the U.S.S.R.*, Moscow, 1952, p. 81.

Four

Soviet price-policy: a review*

Reprinted from *Soviet Studies*, July 1960 (Vol. XII, No. 1), by kind permission of the editors and publishers of that journal.

Despite its defects (the nature of which will emerge in the course of this review) this imposing and timely work is a great improvement on some of the rather dreary handbooks we have had in the past, describing this or that aspect of industrial or financial organisation. In addition to being fairly rich (if in places unevenly so) in factual detail, the book reveals a lively awareness of many of the requirements of a price-policy, as well as a refreshing empiricism. Indeed, it is a welcome change to find questions of price-policy discussed so fully and so frankly, after their remaining so long (up to recent years) a departmental mystery, excluded from the province of the political economist lest his scientific aloofness should be spoiled by dabbling (in Stalin's words) in what 'are not problems of political economy, but problems of the economic policy of the directing bodies'.

After two introductory chapters, which are largely concerned with stating the case for basing planned prices at the enterprise-level on planned production-cost, in the interests of *khozraschot*, and with a passing polemic (but naming no names) against the advocates of a radical price-reform in the price-discussions of recent years, the succeeding chapters deal with specific problems of price-fixing in the main sectors of the economy: fuel and power, metals and engineering, building materials, prices for agriculture and raw materials, transport and retail prices of consumer goods. Here the particular problems of each sphere are given due attention.

* Sh. Ya. Turetski, *Ocherki planovo tsenoobrazovania v SSSR* (Outlines of Planned Price-Formation in the U.S.S.R.). Moscow: Gosudarstvennoe izdatelstvo politicheskoi literaturi, 1959, 500 pp. 13r.

So far as any unifying principle runs through the book it is the importance of combining differential prices as between enterprises (allowing for 'objectively based' cost-differences between them) with uniform industrial selling prices (at the level of the *sbyt*, i.e. the sales agency), and moreover uniform prices to purchasers, wherever possible, 'free at station of consignment' (although, as we shall see, with some zoning where transport costs are high in relation to value). Although Professor Turetski appears as a conservative so far as defending the main shape of existing price-policy is concerned, he is not uncritical of deficiencies (as he sees them) in particular cases and is not unaware of the extent to which practice still falls short at many points of what he regards as the ideal. ('It is not always the case that the relationship of wholesale prices promotes a rational utilisation of the means of production, precludes superfluous transportation, and encourages replacement of old techniques by new.')

What is disappointing is the failure at any point really to come to grips with the fundamental question of what constitutes the *general* objective of price-policy, to which all particular objectives in this or that particular situation should be subordinated. True, there are plenty of references to the need for prices to be so fixed as to encourage a rational output-pattern on the part of producing industries and to encourage rational utilisation of supplies and transport services by purchasers. But such references remain either vague and imprecise or else too particularised (e.g. the need to economise on a 'deficit' metal or fuel or alternatively to promote the use of a 'non-deficit' metal for making spare-parts and tools); and when general principles are referred to they are apt to take the form of a list of policy-objectives, ungeneralised and unquantified —a list such as one may find in any policy-statement summarising targets. When in the opening chapter the author dismisses the proposal that the prices of producer goods (products of Group A industries), as well as those of consumer goods, should include a uniform ratio of 'surplus product to wages', he is content to stress merely the administrative difficulties of radically disturbing all prices, including retail prices. Here empiricism becomes a defect. In arguing against the advocates of marginal cost prices for mining, to allow for the effect of differences in natural conditions upon costs (he is talking specifically about ore-mining), he relies on the spurious objection that this would result in wide differences in the profits accruing to different mining enterprises. (The build-up of selling-prices to marginal cost could perfectly well be done, if necessary, by imposing an equivalent turnover tax at the *sbyt* level, as is in fact done in the case of oil and electricity.) Indeed, the argument at this stage seems to involve some contradiction (unless the reviewer has misunderstood something). The author himself has previously said that it is quite possible in such a case to combine 'uniform zonal wholesale prices (*optovie tseni*) on ores for metallurgy with differentiated prices for individual mines' (p. 144); and in dealing with fuel and power as a group he explains that, in view of differences in natural conditions and their effect on the costs of different sources of fuel and power, the prices of low-cost fuels like oil and gas as well as of electricity are raised above the levels of their own prime costs (*sebestoimost*) in order to bring them into line with the price of coal as the high-cost fuel (the instrument for doing this being a turnover tax levied on the former). If this is done on principle (and not simply as the out-come of empiricism) for fuel and power treated as a group of substitutes, the logic of it would seem to be the imposition, similarly, of a turnover tax (if at lower rates) on the various coal-field prices to raise them to the level of the highest-cost source of coal supply. (Cost per ton is only one *half* in Karaganda or Eastern Siberia what it is in the Donbas, and in terms of calorific units there is nearly a 1 : 3 cost-differential between the former and the sub-Moscow basin.) True, there may well be reasons for *not* doing this, such as the fact that additional demand in the future is likely to be satisfied from relatively low-cost mines in newly developed fields, and *not* from high-cost sources. But so far as I can see, Professor Turetski does not consider the question worthy of discussion and explanation; indeed one is inclined to doubt whether he is even aware of the problem in this form. His attention is occupied instead with the desirability of uniform (zoned) coal prices for each grade of coal (combined with dif-ferentiated transfer-pit-prices for groups of pits with similar cost-conditions), instead of the existing system of divergent coalfield prices.

The nearest he comes to enunciating a comprehensive principle is in connection with retail prices; and it would seem to be mainly this which prompts him to reject any automatic rule for linking 'prices' with 'values'. Quite rightly he insists that retail prices, both generally and in particular cases, depend 'not only on factors lying on the side of goods, but also on factors lying on the side of money (changes in the scale of prices), on relations of the distribution and redistribution of the social product'. By the latter he has in mind the level of money wages and of agricultural purchase-prices, and the level of State expenditures on such things as 'non-productive workers', defence and pensions. (Curiously, he nowhere explicitly mentions expenditure on investment, and hence the proportion of the productive labour force engaged on capital construction and in producing new capital goods—perhaps because the division of industries into Groups A and B does not lend itself to this kind of distinction, and the author thinks in administrative rather than in analytical categories.) Consistently with this, he emphasises that, if prices of Group A products (means of production) are raised (e.g. by levying turnover tax on them as well as on Group B) this will *not* enable retail prices of consumer goods to be lowered equivalently (with lower turnover tax-rates on consumer goods): indeed, the result must be to *raise* retail prices in consequence of the higher cost of means of production used in the production of consumer goods.

It follows that, while changes in labour-productivity (i.e. changes in 'value') are likely to exert an influence both on industrial costs and on retail prices (unless money wages change in step with productivity), there will be no direct or proportional connection between the change in productivity and the change in retail price. In the case of particular goods, even when their production-cost falls, it may not follow that their retail prices can be reduced, in view of 'the relationship of supply and demand in the case of individual goods' (the implication being that demand is very elastic and there is no early prospect of making good the 'deficit' in their supply). The author wisely adds that 'although the sum of money incomes can be directly influenced by State planning, the structure of people's demand for individual goods cannot be an object of direct State planning'; and that 'without deciding the question of the scale on which to lower the prices of individual goods it is impossible to decide correctly the problem of lowering the general level of prices in the country' (p. 411). Hence the importance of 'studying and knowing what influence the lowering of the price of individual goods will have on demand' (p. 413)—and there follow some examples of where too-uniform price-reductions in the early '50's led to unexpected results.

Evidently Professor Turetski thinks that this is quite inconsistent with proposals (made *inter alia* by Strumilin and Kronrod) for basing price-relations on value-relations as a 'normal rule'. It would be, of course, if such a rule were applied mechanically in each individual case, and not as a long-run *standard* at which to aim in adjusting relative outputs. He does not seem to have considered the possibility that retail prices might be determined in the way he describes, while at the same time on the *average* a like ratio of prices to cost (or rather of prices to wage-cost) was established for producer goods (Group A industries). But that is a question on which the reviewer must not strain the patience of his readers by digressing here.

One thing that emerges incidentally from the discussion of retail prices in this book is the fact that turnover tax is not thought of as an instrument of price-policy, but as its resultant—as a dependent, not an independent, variable in the problem. 'It is not the level of retail prices that depends on the turnover tax, but the turnover tax, its magnitude, depends on the distribution of the social product, on the structure of prices' (p. 29). In the textile industry (and subsequently over an increasing area of the light and food industries) this is explicitly recognised by the fixing separately of two sets of prices for each product and product-line, one at the level of the factory or enterprise, the other at the retail level, and by treating as revenue-obligation for turnover tax whatever is the difference in receipts between these two sets of prices (after allowance has been made for the planned costs and profit-margins of the wholesale and retail bodies). The reason for this change of practice was that previously, when turnover tax was levied at fixed rates, these rates were apt to apply uniformly over a group of products or product-lines or qualities, for which relative cost-differences were not necessarily the same as relative retail price-differences. Consequently profit-margins were apt to vary quite arbitrarily, and sometimes widely, on different items (with damaging effects on the fulfilment of the 'assortment plan'). The new arrangement is considered to make for more flexible adjustment of factory prices for different items and qualities in line with estimated cost-differences, consistently with more flexible (and independent) adjustment of retail prices in line with current supply-demand relationships.

When, therefore, visiting economists ask their Soviet colleagues whether turnover tax is treated as a mechanism for adjusting retail prices to conditions of demand, the answer is apt to be 'no', since the tax is rarely regarded in this way. (Cf. *Soviet Studies*, Vol. IV, pp. 57, 121–2, 273.) But it does not follow from such a reply that retail prices are rigidly geared to cost and that they only change as and when the latter changes.

Another problem which occupies Professor Turetski, where he thinks that there can be no simple relationship between price and cost, is that of price-differentials between grades of the same commodity. His discussion of this in the case of producer goods relates particularly to coke and iron ore (but there are similar examples in leather of what he calls a difference between 'value' and 'consumers' value', also in building materials such as cement). Here he has some acute observations to the effect that price-differentials should reflect the difference in productivity (or alternatively in costs incidental to use) to the *user*. For example, every 1 per cent lowering of the iron-content of a given weight of ore lowers the daily productivity of a blast-furnace by $2\frac{1}{2}$ per cent, raises coke-consumption by 2 per cent and raises also the labour-cost of a ton of pig-iron. Transport expenses are correspondingly increased by the greater weight of ore needed for a given quantity of iron-production. Hence 'difference in the iron-content of ores involves different expenditures per ton of pig-iron such that the wholesale price of different ores cannot be based on the individual costs (*sebestoimost*) of extracting them' (p. 143). An analogous case is that of two types of steel whose price-difference 'approximates to the equivalent of their substitutability . . . more strictly to the difference in their specific productivity' (p. 156). (In some other cases, e.g. cement, he stresses, however, the importance of encouraging the use of the higher-quality product, which implies that price-differences of grades should not only be less than their comparative cost but *less* than their productivity-differences—or the comparative advantage of using them. Similarly with the prices of old and new types of machines, he wants the latter to be priced lower than their cost would warrant as a stimulus to substituting them for the old.)

Some Western readers may hail this gleefully as a recognition of the 'bourgeois' principle of 'marginal productivity'. There is, of course, a theoretical answer to the apparent anomaly. If there are two substitutes (whether ores or fuels or metals or machines) for the same use and both can be increased in supply at unchanged cost, the one that has the lower cost relatively to the comparative advantage of using the two can and should supplant the other entirely, since from the social point of view it is on balance the more advantageous. If their prices do not reflect the respective costs of their own production, the comparison of cost with productivity in use will not be made, at any rate by the user, and the substitution of one for the other may not occur (unless the mining industry or machine-maker discontinues the production of that with the lower ratio of selling-price to cost). Only in the case where the supply of either or both of them is restricted by natural conditions will Professor Turetski's problem really arise as a long-term problem. Even then, if the supplies are variable at all, substitution of the more for the less advantageous is likely to be carried to the point where the ratio of costs at the *margin* is equal to the ratio of their productivities, or of their advantages in use.

Professor Turetski is presumably thinking in terms of the difficulty caused when different grades of (say) ore are compulsorily allocated to different iron and steel plants: the costs of these plants will be affected by this 'accident' of allocation. Difficulty arises if as a result their actual costs diverge from their 'planned cost'. But this difficulty could be avoided equally well by allowing for the effects on cost of using different ores when estimating the planned costs of various plants as by adjusting the prices of different ores in the way Professor Turetski advocates. It is difficult to see why, if an estimate of comparative advantages in use can be made for the purpose of fixing ore-prices, such an estimate cannot be made for the purpose of fixing the planned cost. At any rate, Professor Turetski's solution of adjusting ore-prices is in no way different from adjusting prices to meet short-period scarcities in relation to demand—a policy which, in the case of producer goods in general, he seems to reject. To adopt at all widely his method of fixing grade-differentials would seem to open a much wider door to 'exceptions' to the cost-principle than he would be willing, apparently, to contemplate.

A central theme of the book, as we have seen, is the need to combine differential prices at the level of production (to the extent that the planned costs of enterprises differ) with uniform prices to the purchaser. This means uniform delivered prices, which are set so as to allow for transport costs averaged out over all destinations, but the price charged on a particular consignment to a particular destination does not reflect the special transport costs which that consignment involves. True, this is modified in many (but not in all) cases by a zoning of prices according to distance from the source of supply. But the number of zones is not large (the largest apparently being twelve for timber, for cement and oil only five and for constructional steel only three), so that averaging of transport costs occurs over a wide area. This method of charging 'free at station of consignment' was first introduced in the middle and late '30's for consumer goods; it was extended to heavy industry only in the postwar period, and in 1955 covered about a third of its products.

The objection to uniform delivered prices is a familiar one: that they tend unduly to encourage long hauls and to discourage economy in transport by utilising nearer sources of supply. It is accordingly surprising at first sight to find the system so widely used in Soviet industry, and to find it so warmly advocated by Professor Turetski as a rational device. It might seem the more surprising in view of the constant appeals that have been made to reduce the extent of 'irrational long hauls'. Indeed, Professor Turetski's defence of this method seems inconsistent, at first sight, with his emphasis elsewhere on encouraging the maximum use of local materials.

What one has to remember is that the system was introduced in a situation of allocated supplies, and that it is in this context that

Professor Turetski is speaking of it. With strict allocation of supplies the purchaser has no option as to the source from which he draws them; and accordingly the fact that the price does not vary with distance cannot affect the choice of source through any action on his part. On the other hand, it will be to the interest of the supplier (usually the *sbyt* organisation), in so far as he has a say in the matter, to economise on transport costs by reducing the extent to which he supplies customers at a distance. (As Professor Turetski points out, 'the *sbyt* or wholesale trading organisation suffers loss in face of too distant and irrational hauls, and equivalently makes an above-planned profit if it can obtain more rational and shorter and economical ways of transporting products to their point of consumption', p. 92.) There have, indeed, been complaints of favouring near-by consumers and discriminating against distant users of a product. With greater decentralisation of the supply system, however, and more latitude for industrial enterprises to contract for their supplies directly, the situation is altered. The source from which given supplies are drawn may no longer be beyond the purchaser's influence; and if he wants to be 'choosey' and to get his supplies from a distance instead of from near-at-hand, there is every reason why he should pay the additional cost of so doing. The fact that different enterprises in the same industry may incur different costs for their fuel or raw materials or components is no more of an objection than is the fact that enterprises pay more if they opt for a higher grade of fuel or raw material. In each case, the one that incurs the higher cost can be presumed to do so (in so far as the choice rests with him) because he estimates that there will be some compensating advantage. If decentralized supply-arrangements at the discretion of enterprises are to become more common, it looks as though Professor Turetski will have to reconsider his advocacy of uniform delivered-prices.

It may be remarked incidentally that, if one thinks it right for transport costs to be included in the final selling-price, as well as production costs proper, one must not be surprised to find the relationship between the prices of various grades or of various products differing between zones, as sometimes happens where there are price-zones and the ratio of transport costs to production cost differs for these various grades or products. This is quite as it should be; and Professor Turetski seems to approve of it in the case of zonal differentiation of retail prices for such things as milk and butter (p. 463). There is also a table (p. 131) showing how the zonal differentials for different kinds of oil-products differ quite considerably and have been widened since 1955; and of this he seems to approve. But this approval does not seem to be extended to all analogous cases of producer goods.

If one switches one's attention to the production-end of the double set of prices (uniform to the purchaser, differentiated to the producers), one meets another type of problem. The prime object of this principle that Professor Turetski treats as crucially important is to further the operation of *khozraschot* at the factory level—to stimulate intra-factory efficiency and cost-reduction. Some have advocated, however, that in the interest of quality and assortment (and in the consumer-goods sector to further the adaptation of supply to consumers' demands), prices to the enterprise should be adjusted to selling-price so as to increase the incentive (*via* a widened profit-margin) to produce things that are in short supply. This kind of price-flexibility obviously conflicts with a rigid adherence to Professor Turetski's principle; and while the stimulating of cost-reduction may be important and deserve high priority, it is not the only objective of policy. Measures for stimulating the production of the right things also deserve attention. In the case of consumer goods the latter objective has special importance. One can well understand why in recent years stress has been laid upon eliminating arbitrary differences in profit-margins on different product-lines and making profitability more uniform. But to remove pointless and harmful differences does not mean that one should never create such differences when there is good reason to do so. Perhaps there is a case for only doing so exceptionally; but it would be a pity if the possibility of using prices in this way were to be excluded by too rigid adherence to the rule that factory selling-prices must be related to (planned) cost. This would be as unfortunate as the opposite mistake of allowing the selling-prices to purchasers of various products (especially in the case of producer goods) to diverge too much from their long-run cost-relationships. This kind of problem, presented by rival policy-objectives, Professor Turetski does not seem to face up to. Perhaps this is due to a too-ready assumption that the matter of *what* to produce can be both decided and effectively controlled from the centre, whereas *how* to produce it must be left to the enterprise. Experience seems to have shown that no such rigid line can be drawn.

We have said that there is much detailed information in this work, on various aspects of price-policy, which one could go on summarising for some time. Some of this is of interest for its own sake; some only so far as it fits into a larger pattern. One learns, incidentally, that in electricity tariffs there is a uniform all-Union lighting-charge for domestic use, and a lower charge for industry, together with some exceptional (preferential) tariffs (this differential between domestic use and industrial being consistent with the two price-levels for things sold retail and things sold to producers; a similar discrimination existing in freight-rates on the railways). Mention is also made of two-part tariffs for large industrial users; but there is no mention of the peak and off-peak problem or of price discrimination designed to deal with it (unless a passing reference, on page 136, to the peculiarity of electricity as a product that its consumption has to coincide with its production is intended as a recognition of this problem). We learn that in the case of railway tariffs there is no close correspondence of charges with the operating costs of different kinds of traffic (e.g. differentials between the transport of Donbas coal and of sub-Moscow coal; a 40 per cent preference on mineral fertilisers; mineral waters are more favourably treated than vodka or brandy); although since the changes of 1939 and 1949 there has been less arbitrary discrimination in rates geared to particular policy-objectives, such as favouring key objectives of the current plan, opening up new regions, etc., and charges on distance have been graduated to discourage long hauls. Even in 1953, however, differences in tariff-scales on the railways for different items ranged as widely as 17 to 1, compared with an estimated cost-differential of no more than 4 or 5 to 1. By 1955 the former difference had been narrowed to 11 to 1. In both water and road transport differences in tariff-scales are much narrower. We also learn that unification of tariffs for different types of transport, especially for railways and water transport, are still a matter for the future. In the chapter on agriculture there is a good

deal of interesting detail about collection-prices and their variations between zones and cultures, together with some data about
the movement of collection-prices for various crops. Here the
price-structure as it existed up to 1953 comes in for special criticism
as harmful both to the growth and the desirable pattern of agricultural production; and the view that one cannot calculate costs
of production in agriculture and hence relate prices to them is
rejected as 'unscientific' and a source of mistaken policies.

There are signs that the book was composed, in the main, before
the 1957 changes in industrial administration. The author has
evidently done what he could to adapt his description to those
changes (e.g. substituting Sovnarkhoz for Ministry in various
places). One has the feeling, however, that his adaptation of the old
picture to the new may be incomplete and that in certain directions,
at least, the new organisation may have created more changes in
price-policy and its problems than the book has been able to catch
up with. Whether this is so or not only time can show. What
emerges fairly clearly is that the position as regards both the
principles of price-policy and their implementation is far from
rigid, probably less so than at any time since the 1920's.

Five

Some further comments on the discussion about socialist price-policy

This appeared as a contribution to *On Political Economy and Econometrics: Essays in Honour of Oskar Lange*, Warszawa, 1964, and is reproduced here by kind permission of the publishers (Polish Scientific Publishers).

It would be superfluous to summarise for Polish readers either the traditional price-system as it has prevailed in the Soviet Union and in other socialist countries or the discussion of recent years about its merits and defects. As is well known, a central feature of this traditional system is the so-called Dual Price-System under which the prices of consumption goods sold retail to individual consumers are generally constructed on a different principle (and on a higher level, in consequence of the turnover tax) from those of producers' goods passing between industrial enterprises within the socialist sector. It is not the intention of this paper to dwell upon the main alternatives proposed in the course of discussion, whether the introduction of the 'value principle' as a uniform general rule for price-formation, or alternatively the principle of 'price of production' as the appropriate 'form of transformed value'. Still less is it the intention to traverse those more abstract formulations with which the discussion in its early stages was surrounded; if only because matters of correct pricing have manifestly to be approached from the standpoint of the concrete needs of the actual functioning of a socialist economy, and not settled *a priori*. A few observations, however, about this traditional price-system and the past discussion of it will not be, perhaps, entirely superfluous.

Firstly, there does not seem to be any valid ground for criticism (I would venture to suggest) merely because there is a difference of price-levels as between consumption goods and producers' goods. The reason for gearing the latter to prime cost (i.e. to *sebestoimost* plus a small 'planned profit-margin') was evidently that this best accorded with the basic aim of *Khozraschot*—to give the maximum incentive to price-reduction on the part of the enterprise. Granted that this was a correct basis for the pricing of producers' goods, it followed (for reasons that are now sufficiently familiar) that the price-level of consumption goods must be at a level substantially *above cost* (to the extent that net investment and also non-productive expenditures by the State were being undertaken) if a chronic condition of excess demand, or 'goods shortage', in the retail market was to be avoided. A convenient instrument for bridging this gap between retail prices and cost was, of course, a turnover tax,[1] which had the additional advantage of easy and potentially flexible adjustment to the particular supply-demand situations of particular commodities.

It follows from what has just been said that the retail price-level of consumption goods could not be reduced simply by extending the allowance for surplus product (whether *via* turnover tax or in some alternative way) to producers' goods as well—even if this should involve some lowering of turnover tax rates on consumption goods (by the amount of the higher price of producers' goods entering into *sebestoimost*). So far, at any rate, as the ratio of retail prices to *wage*-cost is concerned, this manifestly cannot be altered, given the rate of investment and non-productive State expenditures.[2]

The crucial weakness of the traditional price-system would seem to be its failure to encourage a proper and sufficient economy of capital equipment. Indeed, one could express it more strongly and say that it provides an inducement to industrial managements to be profligate of fixed capital, both in the sense of failing to economise sufficiently in its use and upkeep (e.g. undermanning, scanty repairs and even maintaining an undue amount of reserve-

---

[1] The alternative to this was a steeply graduated profits-tax.
[2] Cf. the present writer's *Essay on Economic Growth and Planning*, London, 1960, pp. 91–2, 101.

capacity) and of having a chronic bias towards the choice of more capital-intensive methods of production than the economy as a whole can really afford. This is for the reason that cost is interpreted exclusively as prime cost (i.e. wages *plus* 'constant capital used-up'). A contributory reason is the narrowness of the customary profit-margin, or difference between the industry's (or enterprise's) selling-price and cost as interpreted (*sebestoimost*); since this narrowness places a large premium[3] upon reducing *sebestoimost* at all cost—i.e. at the cost of using, and over-using, the most expensive forms of equipment. This might be met by including in cost some allowance for the use of capital equipment (additional to amortisation),[4] and relating the performance of an industry or enterprise, for accounting and financial purposes, to the relation between profit and the total of basic and turnover funds (instead of between profit and *sebestoimost*). Alternatively it might be met by widening the profit-margin or gap between selling-price and cost (thereby reducing the *proportional* addition to the margin to be gained from any given effort or expenditure designed to lower prime cost). But this would meet the objection that it would seriously weaken *Khozraschot* by making profit too easy of attainment.

One reflection which this consideration provokes, and one to which economists might do well to pay some attention, is that there is not *one* type of efficiency problem, to which everything is reducible (as economists with their myopic focus upon marginal adjustments in the allocation of resources have so often assumed in the West). There are, in fact, several distinct types of efficiency problem, and their several requirements may well stand in conflict.

One could take as an example of this the kind of circular production-flow associated essentially with any growth-process and abstractly represented in the famous von Neumann model. In such a process 'productive consumption' predominates over personal consumption; outputs being used as inputs for further production; capital goods being destined for the making of more capital goods rather than for the consumption-goods sector. Apart from necessary subsistence for workers, it is all a process of self-expansion

---

[3] In the shape of the resulting proportional increase in the profit-margin.
[4] Such as, for example, the rK included in Professor V. V. Novozhilov's proposed formula for what he terms 'national economic cost'.

within Marx's Department I. This stands in contrast with the 'straight-line process' whereby certain initial factor-inputs finally emerge as outputs for individual consumers, as has been the conventional economists' picture since the days of Jevons and Menger. In such a circular process optimum allocation principles derived from Paretian tangency-conditions are irrelevant. What is important is the keeping of this circular production-flow moving smoothly with the minimum of interruption. During the period of industrialisation the planning problem essentially consisted of this; and since the flow was composed of a series of transfers within the State sector, it was handled by a combined system of planned output targets and their related supply-allocations, such as can be derived from data about input and output norms within a matrix of material balances. It may be noted, however, that in so far as aggregated technical coefficients are formed as an average of non-uniform coefficients of a number of enterprises, a certain amount of flexibility or 'play' lies concealed within the averaged technical norm, and with it an efficiency-problem of a different (and in a Paretian sense more 'orthodox') type enters in—a matter to which we shall come later when we speak of Kantorovitch.

Another type of conflict between different efficiency criteria is that between optimum conditions defined within a purely static context and the requirements of growth, and the conditions favourable to each, about which we have spoken elsewhere.

The problem regarding fixed capital which we have mentioned above might be held to be of minor importance so long as decisions about investment in fixed capital are centrally planned. This seems, indeed, to have been the attitude adopted in the period up to the middle '50's when major strategic questions of rapid industrialisation and growth held the centre of the stage, and the main function of the price-system was to harness enterprises to perform efficiently the operative functions that fell within their province (and were mainly concerned with financial elements involved in *sebestoimost*). The problem we have mentioned assumes greater importance, however, in the degree to which investment decisions become decentralised. Experience seems to show that, even when the planning of investment is highly centralised, the viewpoint and interests of an enterprise exert a considerable influence *de facto* upon investment decisions. At any rate, control over the usage of plant and equipment and its day-to-day upkeep and maintenance cannot fail to be vested in the enterprise and its management.

This consideration (to which we shall return) leads us immediately to a second type of observation. The question has been much debated (at various levels of abstraction) as to why the actual prices at which commodities exchange within the socialist sector should matter at all for the efficient operation of a planned economy—or, in other words, why the 'law of value' should influence production at this level at all. The prices at which products pass between socialist organisations and enterprises are purely 'transfer prices' and have a role and meaning only for purposes of book-keeping and control. Provided that there is an adequate system of *accounting prices* on the basis of which planning decisions are made, why should these actual transfer-prices exert any influence on industrial efficiency? In focusing, therefore, upon *actual* prices, was not the price-discussion guilty of adopting a mistaken focus?

The standpoint implied in this question includes a certain element of truth is so far as it emphasises that for certain purposes and in certain contexts it may well be *accounting* prices (used for planning purposes) of which we ought to be thinking, and that such accounting prices[5] need not be identical with the actual prices used in the book-keeping of enterprises (as Professor Lange long ago pointed out). This is a matter to which we shall also return. At the same time, there is an answer to this objection, which consists in saying that those who make it are guilty of over-simplifying the actual problem when they degrade the importance of *actual* prices. The latter are not solely important for book-keeping and control; for reasons already mentioned they play (and must inevitably play) a crucial part in the system of economic incentives to enterprises as operative units in the economic field. As such they have a crucial function to perform (as the inventors of *Khozraschot* appreciated). It remains true that any discussion of their appropriateness or inappropriateness, if it is to be realistic, must be

[5] In so far as 'price correctives' are used for the purpose of decision, then of course accounting prices that are different from actual prices are in effect being used.

strictly subordinated to this function (limited, though important) which they perform. But a picture of a planned economy in which every decision affecting output and investment is centrally planned, on the basis of 'ideal' accounting prices only, is obviously a chimaera.

One difficulty with regard to fixed capital is to make any charge for it effective as an incentive. A charge or tax laid upon an enterprise in proportion to its fixed capital (and entered as an item in its cost) will have no force as an inducement to economise if its existence is merely an excuse for an equivalent rise in its selling-price.[6] The only way in which such a charge can provide an inducement to avoid it (by economising on the amount of fixed capital in use or by making existing equipment last longer) is if the selling-price is fixed *independently of it*, either by ignoring such a charge altogether or taking as basis some postulated 'normal' amount of it (like the 'planned *sebestoimost*' which is used as the basis for price-fixing at the enterprise-level under the traditional type of *Khozraschot*)—a 'normal' from which the actual may diverge, thereby yielding a *plus* or a *minus* in the accounts of the enterprise. For various reasons this is probably easier to do in the case of short-period costs than of long-period costs; and if a proper stimulus is to be given to innovations as well as to economies in use of equipment, the period over which selling-prices remain unadjusted for cost changes must be the *same* with respect to changes in short-period costs as to long-period costs.[7] One of the attractions of the Lieberman-proposals, discussed in *Pravda* in the course of September and October 1962, is that according to them

---

[6] This point was, indeed, noticed by a writer in *Voprosi Ekonomiki*, 1963, No. 5, p. 107, V. Batyrev; but this writer seems to be wrong in saying that if prices remain at their former level there will be no inducement to introduce new technique. There will be such an inducement if the resulting economy of prime cost (*sebestoimost*) *exceeds* the cost of the additional capital (when the latter is assessed at the standard coefficient of effectiveness of investment)—subject to the proviso mentioned in the next footnote.

[7] Otherwise, for example, a cost-reducing innovation involving capital expenditure in order to achieve a reduction of prime cost would not be attractive to an enterprise if in the year following its introduction prices were revised downwards in consequence of the lower *sebestoimost*.

qualification of an enterprise for bonus would be based on its profit-position *in relation to the total capital employed* (in the shape of basic and turnover funds); this profit-position being measured over a period of years. As such it has the advantage of providing a unitary or 'synthetic' index of achievement. A possible difficulty, however, is that if the period of time over which results are measured and selling-price stabilised is too long, many enterprises (or even whole lines of production) may accumulate profits too easily and too largely: a profit-position which will itself reduce the pressure on them to economise and induce in them a conservative rather than an adventurous mood.

At this point some may raise the objection that if the notion of cost is to be extended in this way, on grounds of expediency in operating *Khozraschot*, reason demands that it should be extended still further. A charge for use of capital, it may be said, is a recognition of the scarcity of investible resources (due basically to limited productive capacity of capital-goods industries) to meet all possible demands for technical re-equipment and extension; whence arises the need to economise on plant and equipment. But why should not recognition be given also to other types of scarcity: for example, scarcity of natural resources, the use of which has, again, to be economised because they cannot be reproduced, at least not at all easily or quickly? There may be, indeed, a case for making some allowance in costing and pricing for enduring, as distinct from temporary, scarcities; as has been hinted at in some proposals of Academician Nemchinov. There are those, however, who go much further than this and declare that at any given time what is relevant for economic calculation is the prevailing supply-demand situation, and that for purposes of planning calculations and economic incentives alike all prices should reflect these current scarcity-relationships. This they can only do if they are *market prices*, equilibrating current demand and current available supply.[8] I shall henceforth refer to this type of market price as 'short-period prices', to distinguish them from what economists have tradition-ally spoken of as 'normal price' (in a long-period context)—Adam

[8] This is equivalent to saying that costs, when reckoned at these prices for all constituent inputs, are so-called 'opportunity costs', expressive of the value of foregone alternatives when the cost in question is incurred.

Smith's 'natural value', Marx's 'value' and 'price of production'.

This was essentially the standpoint of most of the economists participating in the prewar debate (in Germany and Austria, Britain and U.S.A.) about so-called 'economic calculation' or 'the pricing-problem' under socialism, in particular of those who advocated various types of decentralised market or quasi-market mechanisms.[9] It is the standpoint also of many, if not most, 'Western' commentators today on Soviet economy and on recent discussion in socialist countries about price-policy.[10]

There is, I think, no dispute regarding retail prices of consumption goods: these are, and must be, short-period prices (unless there is to be rationing, or symptoms of damaging disequilibrium in the retail market such as shortages and queues). This follows from the fact that the retail market is a market in the full sense; which in turn follows from the nature of the wage-system under socialism, with the existence of individual wage-differences (according to kind and quantity of work performed)—differences which can only exert their full effect as production-incentives if the recipients are free to spend their wages as they please. There may be disagreement about the practical expediency and the difficulty of changing them at frequent intervals; but in principle opinion seems now to be fairly unanimous as to the importance of adjusting the prices of different products and grades to the peculiarities of the respective demand-situations.[11]

Where there is serious difference and dispute is regarding the application of any such ideas to producers' goods, or means of production, which, instead of being sold to individual consumers, change hands within the socialist sector. Are the prices of these to be adjusted as short-period prices or to be based upon some interpretation or other of long-period value or normal cost? An element of the former is, of course, introduced as soon as prices of 'deficit'

[9] Cf. W. Brus, *Ogólne problemy funkcjonowania gospodarki socjalistycznej*, Warszawa, 1961, Rozdzial V.

[10] Cf. Joan Robinson, *Exercises in Economic Analysis*, London, 1960, Part V; A. Nove, *The Soviet Economy*, London, 1961, *passim*.

[11] E.g. S. Turetsky, *Ocherki Planovogo Tsenoobrazovania v SSSR*, Moskva, 1959, pp. 401–18, on the lessons learned from the Soviet price-reductions of the middle '50's.

products (whether fuels, building materials or steels) are raised in order to encourage economy in their use, or the prices of close substitutes (e.g. fuels) are brought into alignment, irrespective of their costs; and to this extent traditional practice has sanctioned the notion of supply-demand prices as applied to producers' goods.[12] Some writers have advocated more extended use of this practice.[13] But its exceptional application, whether exceptions are narrowly or broadly defined, remains different from its adoption as a general principle. In the latter case 'market autonomism' would tend to become, indeed, the regulator of production, as regards both the output and the productive consumption of all means of production (as many who have advocated such a system have intended).

Leaving aside the question as to whether such a system of continually changing (with changing supply-demand situations) short-period prices could be reconciled with central planning of output-targets, there is, I think, a practical argument of considerable weight against the expediency of applying short-period prices to producer goods, or means of production. This is that most of such products represent durable objects of investment; and decisions regarding their use are essentially long-period decisions to which long-period considerations, not transitory and short-period, apply. Admittedly this consideration directly relates mainly to means of production that are 'instruments of labour', not 'objects of labour'. But even in the case of the latter (e.g. fuels or some metal ores) the use of them, and substitution between them, is conditioned in many cases by installed equipment appropriate to their use, and such installation involves long-period considerations. In turn decision as to installation of equipment will be influenced by the prices of these goods: indeed, its profitability will in all cases depend on the future price-trends of all the inputs as well as the outputs for which the equipment is designed and intended. The adoption of 'scarcity prices' for such products might in many cases result in the

---

[12] The notion of 'users' value' has even been mentioned by quite conservative writers in connection with price-differentials for different grades or qualities (cf. ibid., pp. 176–80). Once introduced, this seems to open a rather wide door.

[13] E.g. A. Kulikov, *Voprosi Ekonomiki*, 1957, No. 9, p. 80.

generation of the very kind of 'cobweb fluctuation' in their prices and output that is characteristic of many markets in the capitalist world.

The notion that the only prices that are relevant for rational economic calculation are short-period prices partly arises, I suggest, from the habit of conceiving the problem too narrowly as consisting simply in allocating *given* supplies between various alternative demands. But once the problem is widened to include the alteration and adaptation of supplies themselves as inputs, one cannot then proceed further without some standard 'normal' price with which the current short-period market price can be *compared*. True, such a standard or normal could be a purely *notional* price, not an actual one. But in so far as any of the decisions about supply-changes are taken decentrally at lower levels, these decisions are bound to be influenced in some degree, as we have seen, by actual prices. Investment decisions, in fixed capital at any rate, are essentially concerned with events and valuations in the future, over the period of the physical length of life of the project in question. As a simple example one might take the decision whether to install a coal-fired or an oil-fired boiler plant—what is relevant to this is not the *present* relative supply-demand prices of oil and coal (which may be due to quite transitory, and in a sense 'accidental', circumstances) but the trend of oil and coal prices over the next ten or twenty years. One can take it for granted that the function of planning is to correct and eliminate discrepancies between supply and demand that arise in the short-run from unforeseen contingencies (where it cannot prevent them by anticipatory action) and thus to re-establish an equilibrium relationship between them. It is accordingly with the latter, and with social cost interpreted in relation thereto, that investment decisions should be concerned.[14]

[14] An analogous point obtruded itself into recent English discussion about marginal cost pricing in its application, e.g. to the pricing of coal, in the form of the contention that it is long-period marginal cost (not marginal cost in the short period) that is relevant; cf. I. M. D. Little, *The Price of Fuel*, Oxford, 1953, esp. pp. 10–18.

Someone may at this point interject: but will not oil and coal prices ten years hence be *short*-period prices, and not classical normal values? The only meaning I can give to such an objection is that at any given date

Emphasis on this type of consideration indicates the need to base the prices of means of production (by contrast with consumption goods) on social cost interpreted in a long-period sense such as we have been referring to. For the reasons stated earlier this does not mean basing them on *sebestoimost* alone, as does the traditional price-system; but it involves the inclusion in price of some allowance for social surplus product (proportioned to the use made of society's capital funds in any line of production), and probably also for the rents, or quasi-rents, of other fairly long-enduring scarcities as in Nemchinov's suggestion. Prices constructed in this way would have the advantage both of stability (over considerable periods) and of relevance for long-period planning and decision-taking. Such a solution need not preclude the existence of some 'exceptional' price-mark-ups in the case of deficit-commodities, where the current deficit was unlikely for some reason to be at all quickly overcome, or in order to bring prices of close substitutes into alignment in cases where, again, the supply-structure of these substitutes was not subject to rapid modification (such as would effect the replacement of high-cost or inferior substitutes by low-cost or superior, as with oil and electricity and coal or plastics and metals). Turnover tax would probably be the appropriate mechanism here for constituting these special mark-ups.

A possible objection which may be raised here is as follows. 'Natural' or 'long-period' value is no more than a theoretical abstraction: at most it can be regarded as something lying *behind* the phenomena of prices, whether it be Adam Smith's 'natural value' or Marx's 'value' or 'price of production'. If prices are made

---

the prevailing supply-demand relationship will be affected by some 'accidental' (and hence unforecastable) factor. It is obvious, however, that planning cannot take account of what is unforeseeable (apart from noting the possibility of its occurrence) and can only plan in terms of what can be foreseen. What can be foreseen and controlled about any future situation in a planned economy is the degree to which the supply of various products can be adjusted to the pattern of demand for them; and it is only in relation to such foreseeable situations that investment decisions are taken. From the nature of things there will always be *some* element of contradiction between *ex ante* design and *ex post* result. But planning greatly reduces this contradiction by comparison with the operation of a free market system.

identical with this, where is the operative mechanism whereby mutual adjustment of supply to demand occurs: an adjustment which has traditionally occurred in market systems precisely *through the divergence* of current market price from this long-term norm? To this objection there is, I think, a simple answer: namely, that such adjustment does not depend upon divergences between market price and cost; it can take place (and always has done in some degree) through the flow of orders consequent upon movements of stocks. In the very short run it is nearly always stocks that bear the brunt of any disequilibrium between demand and current supply; stocks being run down in the one case and accumulating above their normal level in the other. In a planned economy this can, surely, be regarded as the 'normal' method of adjustment, especially within that circular production-flow of which we spoke above; price-adjustments being necessary only in the case of particularly stubborn supply-inelasticity. Once stated, this seems obvious enough. But it can be obscured by preoccupation with the traditional theory of a competitive market.

To enter into the contingent question as to how the pro-rata allowance for surplus product (or charge for use of social investment funds) for inclusion in cost-price is to be determined would take us too far afield. It must suffice to say that one possible method is that suggested by Professor V. V. Novozhilov (of Leningrad). The present writer has suggested elsewhere that the appropriate allowance for inclusion in prices generally (including the prices of means of production) is that part of the price-mark-up in the case of consumption goods (approximately measured by the average rate of turnover tax upon them) which is attributable to the rate of investment.[15] This would leave consumption goods alone to

[15] *Essay on Economic Growth and Planning*, Chapter VI. The argument in favour of this solution cannot be repeated here: in brief, it was that the resulting price-structure would be consistent with, and conducive to, choosing the technique in each sector or industry which maximised the investment-potential of the economy, and hence growth. In an article in *Kyklos*, Vol. XIV, 1961, Fasc. 2, pp. 144 seq., I tried to show that this solution would be similar to Novozhilov's method of arriving at his r (in his 'national economy cost price' of $rK + S$)—provided that the output-plan was so constructed as to maximise growth in relation to any given wage-level.

bear (as it were) social expenditures *other* than investment; and to this extent some element of the dual price-system would remain (i.e. there would still be a differentiated, and not a uniform, rate of surplus product, or of profit, as between the two sectors of consumption goods and means of production). But this is to present the matter in a very abstract fashion.

This discussion of so-called short-period prices leads us inevitably to Kantorovitch, since his *o.o. otsenki* are analogous to short-period prices in the sense in which we have spoken of them: i.e. they reflect the scarcities of the given situation at a given time. They are applied to the problem of how best to allocate given resources between various uses or productive employments (in all his problems there is at least one scarce resource). But while analogous they also have some difference from the kind of market autonomism referred to above. Firstly, they are (or at least are capable of interpretation as being) *accounting* prices, for use in taking planning-decisions. Secondly, his application of them is usually within a given framework: a framework of output-targets and supply-allocations set by planning at higher levels. Hence his optimal 'solutions' are always contingent on the latter, and the extent to which his *otsenki* provide automatic answers to planning problems is circumscribed and limited. True, he does generalise his conclusions (as we shall see) and suggests that his *otsenki* could, and should, be made a basis, in principle, for reforming actual prices. To this we shall return later and see whether analogous objections to those we have raised against short-period scarcity-prices apply here also.

For readers not closely acquainted with the work of Kantorovitch the following summary of his method may not, perhaps, be out of place. As is now well-known, Kantorovitch's *Method of Decisive Multipliers* (literally: 'solving multipliers') was first published in 1939 (in a monograph series of Leningrad University). The multipliers implied a set of 'shadow prices' which when used gave the optimal result as the least cost or highest net value solution. These he christened 'objective conditional estimates' (*otsenki*, or estimated ratios), commonly abbreviated to the three initial letters '*o.o.o.*'; and he has since developed them most ingeniously into a general price-theory. But to begin with he is careful to distinguish his *o.o. otsenki* both from prices and from values, emphasising in his very name for them their essential contingency —their dependence in each case on a special context and the particular problem framed thereby. (I am referring here to his book published by the Academy in 1959.)[16] In his first, and elementary, example he takes a number of groups of enterprises producing two types of product, each enterprise-group having a different comparative cost, in labour, of producing the two products. The general 'assortment plan' is given, defining the proportions in which the two products are required. 'The optimal plan', he writes, 'is that in which the assigned assortment programme is observed and the products are manufactured in the largest quantity. To this plan, evidently, will correspond also the lowest prime cost of production'. The solution is, of course, that enterprise-groups should be severally concentrated on the product for which they have the higher productivity-ratio, leaving one group marginally producing some of each. The *o.o. otsenki* correspond to the comparative labour cost of this marginal group; and when the products are valued at this ratio both total product and the output (and hence profitability) of each enterprise-group will be maximised when specialisation is according to the optimal plan. ('These *otsenki* are such that if one starts from them, it turns out that in the optimal plan the principle of profitability is observed: i.e. in this plan each enterprise produces that type of product for which the size of the net production of the enterprise is greatest'—p. 35.) The case is then extended to more than two products.

The second chapter considers the case of two productive factors, first labour and electricity and then labour and machines, with the second of the two factors in each case as the scarce and limiting factor; and a series of 'tasks' with different technical coefficients, each capable of being performed in two variants, one less energy-intensive (and in the later example, less machine-intensive) than the other. The objective is maximum fulfilment of the production programme, defined as the most 'tasks' performed without exceeding the limits of the given resources (the tasks being arranged in a certain order of importance). The *otsenki* in this case represent a

[16] *Ekonomicheskii Raschot Nailuchshego Ispolzovania Resursov*, Moscow, 1959.

ratio between the factors, for example kilowatt-hours of electricity to hours of labour, and depend on the equivalence-ratio, or substitution-ratio, in the marginal case—in the task for which there is only just enough of the scarce factor.

In the machine-case he derives a so-called *prokatnaia otsenka*, or hire-price for a machine-day (the machines in his example are, of course, homogeneous). This is virtually expressed in wage-units (its money-value depending on the wage), and is defined as the economy in prime cost per machine-day from substituting machinery for labour under marginal conditions. When this *prokatnaia otsenka* for machinery is included in cost, the method used for each job in the optimal plan comes out as the cheaper; and in the marginal case, of course, the cost of mechanised and un-mechanised production is equal. Transition from *otsenki* for par-ticular machines to a general investment-coefficient is then made in the same manner as Novozhilov's coefficient is derived—by giving investment-priority to those with larger hire-price ratios.

Finally the notion is applied to land—three grades of land and three kinds of crop; the programme of crop production being given and minimising of labour expenditure being the object. By analogy with the previous cases, rent per unit of product is equal to the labour saved when it is used on superior land; rent being here referred to alternatively as 'indirect labour': i.e. the *additional* labour that would be required if production were under the least favourable conditions. Kantorovitch maintains that it is the sum of direct and indirect labour expenditures that should be mini-mised, and not the former alone; and it may be noted that in a number of places he stresses as a corollary of this that the optimal result does not correspond to a minimising of *sebestoimost*.

It is easy enough to see how this method could be applied to a number of partial plans, devoted to particular problems in par-ticular contexts (moreover, in cases where the products and/or factors involved can be measured in physical units). It may be less easy to see how it can be generalised into a global price-system. His method of making this transition is interesting because it could represent (so it seems to the present writer) a different method to Professor Oskar Lange's 'trial and error' accounting prices, and one quite reconcilable with central planning (Kantorovitch remarks:[17] 'in place of the action of competition on a market, competition of plans and methods in the process of planning calculation'). In the first instance his method would be applied presumably to limited problems at a local level; within the framework of output-targets and supply-allocations set at higher planning levels. Each of these local solutions would yield its system of *otsenki*; and differences in them would indicate the need (and point the direction) for some reshuffling of plans at higher levels, within the framework of which these partial solutions and their *otsenki* were developed. In this way, by a series of mutual adjustments between local solutions and higher plans, a tendency would develop in the direction of uniformity of *otsenki* through successive approximations, or at least towards the removal and levelling of major discrepancies in such *otsenki*.[18]

All this is in the realm of accounting prices; and as regards accounting prices I cannot see any valid ground for criticism of such a method. But in addition to treating them as such, Kantorovitch evidently intends, as an ultimate result, that actual prices should be adjusted accordingly. Indeed, in the final chapter of his 1959 book we find him criticising his colleague Novozhilov's effectiveness-coefficient because this uses actual prices instead of his ideal *otsenki*. Here, I think, so far as this is part of his intention, the proposal is subject to a similar kind of objection to that which has been levelled above against the 'market autonomism' of universal short-period prices. His criteria for devising optimal plans at the *general* level would always be derived from what were essentially short-period situations, and they would be mirrors of the transitory scarcities of today or of yesterday; whereas planning, at any rate planning of long-term investment and development, must be forward-looking and geared to situations that can be expected to come into being in the future (situations which will themselves depend in part on what long-term planning decides to do).

[17] Op. cit., p. 169.
[18] It may be noted that this method is substantially the same as the 'two-level planning' elucidated by J. Kornai and Th. Lipták in *Econometrica*, January 1965, on the basis of Hungarian experience (an article which appeared after the present article was written).

Now Kantorovitch has an answer to this which is, I think, valid so long as one confines oneself to the realm of *accounting* prices. For long-term planning, he says, one should use a *different* set of prices (which he terms 'a dynamic system of *otsenki*') from those appropriate to short-term planning—different, i.e. for making five-year or fifteen-year perspective plans from those used for drawing up the operative plan for next year. It is certainly one of the advantages of planning that it can operate with a number of accounting prices *for the same things* (which the market can only do, of course, in those comparatively rare cases where conditions make possible an organised futures market). But this answer can*not* be transferred to the realm of actual prices, since there cannot normally be two systems of actual prices coexisting for the same things, in view of the function prices have to perform under *Khozraschot* in governing incentives to enterprises. The most that seems possible would be the announcement of probable price-changes some time ahead. But could one seriously conceive of this being done at all firmly for some *years* ahead?

Six

Soviet transport: a review*

Reprinted from *Soviet Studies*, October 1959 (Vol. XI, No. 2), by kind permission of the editors and publishers of that journal.

This new monograph in the series of the Harvard Research Centre takes as its subject, not a particular industry like Gardner Clark's study of iron and steel, but the transport system as a whole (which, as we shall see, means essentially railways). On this there is quite an extensive literature; and one is surprised how much detail the author has been able to accumulate and at his diligence in piecing together and recording it. (How much of it, one wonders, would be accessible to a Ph.D. student embarking on such a subject in this country? One guesses that very little would be.) The amount of statistical information set out here in charts and tables is impressive (although there is some repetition, and occasionally charts are overdone and add little to our perception, as with the successive charts for traffic in various commodities in Chapter 9). Indeed the author himself is at pains to underline in his Introduction the plenitude of information, and to add that the familiar myth about Soviet development being 'an enigma' 'actually has reflected insufficient scholarly attention to the Soviet record' and that 'in recent years topic after topic has been clarified through careful winnowing of primary source material available in Western libraries'.

To some extent, perhaps, the author's diligence has overborne a sense of proportion regarding the amount of detail it was advisable to lay before the reader in the text. Although he has relegated a great deal to appendices, and more than a quarter of the

* Holland Hunter, *Soviet Transportation Policy*. Cambridge, Mass.: Harvard University Press, 1957. xxiii + 416 pp. $8.50.

book consists of appendices and notes, an even more rigorous selection of essential from inessential would have been welcome and several of the main chapters would have been improved by more ruthless pruning of the detail packed into them. As it is, a reader may be forgiven if he sometimes nods and loses the wood for the trees.

For an American study the work is surprisingly objective and almost (if not quite) free of those genuflections to the Cold War which seem to be *de rigueur* for many American researchers in Soviet studies. During a visit to the U.S.S.R. shortly before its publication the author submitted galley-proofs to the scrutiny of Soviet railway experts and records their criticism of it, especially of his scepticism about the prospects of developing river transport. (The claim on the dust-jacket, however, that the author was enabled 'to appraise its accuracy through a month's tour in the U.S.S.R.' remains an odd overstatement.) None the less, and in the circumstances perhaps unavoidably, a faint air of remoteness remains. Although he is sceptical of claims made for planned coordination of transport services, he is ready to give credit where he deems credit is due (if on occasions a bit apologetically) and the general tone of the work is soberly factual.

Dr Hunter starts by considering the effect on transport of Soviet policy towards industrial location. Shifting the location of industry towards the underdeveloped eastern regions could be expected eventually to be transport-economising because it tended to bring industries nearer to raw materials. But the initial effects of such a policy were to increase both the volume of traffic and the average length of haul. Actually there was comparatively little eastward shift of industry until the late '30's; developments in the '20's (e.g. the Goelro plan) and the early '30's being mainly concentrated near the old centres of population. As the author notes, the First Five-Year Plan allocated 'approximately two-thirds of total investment to the established centres of European Russia'.

The increased traffic of the early '30's was mainly for other reasons—consequent on the large volume of construction and movements of population, independent of location. This increased traffic, however, was able to be carried with relatively modest investment in new lines, largely as a result of the policy of so-called 'super-magistrals' (super-trunk-lines), by intensive investment in key-lines of existing track so as to convert them from low carrying-capacity to high carrying-capacity lines (reducing gradients, improved ballasting, heavier rails, etc.). During the whole of the First Five-Year Plan period steel was extraordinarily scarce and relatively little investment in railways could take place. After the transport crisis of 1932–3 (when there was an estimated 20 million tons of goods traffic awaiting transport), much more steel both absolutely and as a proportion of all uses was put into railways, and by 1935 they were taking as much as 30 per cent of the country's steel output. Between 1928 and 1940 operating efficiency on the railways (as measured by 'gross freight ton-kilometres per freight train-hour') more than doubled.

In a chapter on 'Soviet Railroads in World War II' the author takes as text the 1939 forecast of the Vilna railway expert Piotrowski that in a war the Soviet railway system would collapse, and proceeds to show why (as with so many other forecasts of its kind and date) this did not happen, despite the loss of some 40 per cent of railroad by German occupation (though a much smaller proportion of locomotives and rolling stock). Part of the explanation given is the considerable amount of railway building between 1941 and 1944 (including emergency construction of an extensive north–south lateral line behind the front, on the edge of occupied territory) and 'the really impressive performance' of railway maintenance and construction, and part the fact that average traffic-densities actually fell during the war years.

As regards the last point, it is not quite clear what the force of this is as a 'reason' (a reason why 'the gloomy forecasts of outside observers were not proved wrong—they simply were not put to a test'). Manifestly it is quite possible for average traffic-density (i.e. total traffic in ton-kilometres divided by length of line) to *fall* and at the same time the density on any particular part of the railway network to *rise*: it is possible if previously traffic-density on the latter has been below the average for the system as a whole. If, then, the high-density part of the system is cut off by enemy-occupation, the strain on the remaining network may be enhanced even though total traffic is diminished in greater proportion than the length of available line. This is indeed what happened; and

Dr Hunter himself cites figures to show that traffic-densities in unoccupied territory rose considerably, especially on the main trunk lines connecting the Urals and Siberia with the front (e.g. Cheliabinsk to Moscow). How then does this afford an 'explanation' for Piotrowski, who had denied that Russian railways could stand the strain of higher densities? What Dr Hunter may, of course, mean, is that the previously low-density lines had more reserve-capacity than previously high-density lines in the west (although this does not necessarily follow) and that a concentration on the former of the traffic that remained did not involve an increase of strain in the relevant sense. But he does not say this in so many words; and one cannot help suspecting that he may have fallen a victim to thinking in over-all averages.

In the postwar period recovery of the transport system was surprisingly rapid and was virtually complete by the end of 1948. Between 1948 and 1955 traffic more than doubled; this increase once again greatly exceeding 'the expansion of railroad facilities' (rolling stock increasing by no more than 30 per cent, although most of this increase was of greatly improved type and capacity). Meanwhile the actual length of line in operation grew by less than 5 per cent; and in relation to investment-projects in new lines under the two postwar Five-Year Plans, Dr Hunter emphasises the extent to which many of them were in fact postponed either in start or in completion, the quinquennial list of planned projects constituting little more than 'an agenda from which actual construction projects have been drawn'. Over the whole period 1928 to 1955 traffic-density on Soviet lines increased about $6\frac{1}{2}$ times.

A chapter on the relation between growth of industrial output and growth of goods traffic (complete with scatter-diagrams and fitted trend-lines) reaches the tentative conclusion that 'additional output has led to additional freight traffic in a systematic way, and the forces tending to increase the traffic–output ratio seem to have been at least as strong as the government's drive to reduce it'. The author finds, curiously enough, that 'both in 1928–40 and 1949–55 increments of industrial output have been associated with proportionate increases in freight traffic'.

In the concluding chapter he asks the question whether transport is likely to be 'a retarding influence on industrial expansion in the next decade or two', and answers it in the negative. This answer is based on two contentions: (a) that the ratio of traffic to industrial output, even if it rises (as he thinks it may on balance), will not rise very much (for one thing, greater regional self-sufficiency may tend to reduce it); (b) that the average capital–output ratio for Soviet railways is likely to decline (as he thinks that it has done in the postwar period up to 1955) rather than rise. If this is correct, the proportion of total investment that has to be devoted to transport (which is under 10 per cent in both the Fifth and the Sixth Five-Year Plans) is unlikely to rise.

This claim rests on some evidence marshalled in an earlier chapter entitled 'Railroad Capital–Output Relations'. The reviewer has no wish to question the commonsense conclusion that hitherto traffic has expanded faster than has the capital equipment of the railway system, and that there is no special reason for expecting it to cease to do so in the future. But he does feel inclined to be sceptical of the manner in which the author generalises from the evidence and of the particular categories in which he does so. Solemnly to call the relation between increasing equipment and increasing traffic a capital–output ratio (and an 'incremental' one to boot) can only have point if one thinks that this ratio refers to some significant technological relationship between equipment and its full-capacity performance. One is rather tempted to suppose that Dr Hunter has gone through the motions of fitting his evidence into the mould of so-called capital–output ratios (there are even hints that he would, if he could, translate 'incremental' ratios into a long-period 'envelope' supply-curve) mainly because the notion happens to be fashionable among economists. But how much, I wonder, is gained by doing so—except possibly a few illusions? There are some good textbook examples in this chapter of how the apparent value of this ratio at any one time (and of changes in it over time) may be indicative of little else but the degree of utilisation of equipment. (Of this difficulty Dr Hunter is well aware; indeed he underlines it: 'capital–output ratios computed from actual output data rather than from capacity data . . . may be highly misleading'.) In railways there is always some element of excess capacity somewhere in the system; and this one might have supposed would be a reason for using the notion of a capital–output ratio here with great circumspection if at all. The notion becomes all the more blurred when qualitative changes in equipment are occurring. Not only does such change introduce problems of measurement (and hence of meaning); not only is capacity–output changed to an extent to which the figures of investment-cost and output-change give us no clue; but the change that we are observing is probably a once-for-all change, a unique 'historical' event, that provides no basis for extrapolating any observed relationship into the future. (We are probably *not* moving along a 'production function' or even a long-run 'envelope cost-curve', as Dr Hunter would like to think we were.) Again, the author seems to be not unaware of such difficulties (e.g. 'new technology will invalidate old relationships'); yet he persists in taking such computations more seriously than they deserve.

A chapter is devoted to other forms of transport than railways; but the information about these is scanty. The fact emerges that the amount of traffic carried by railways has increased more than proportionately to traffic carried by these other forms. Today railways take 84 per cent of all goods traffic and river transport under 10 per cent; timber and oil each accounting for about a third of river transport. One had expected to learn more about the general principles governing charges for goods traffic, especially in view of the emphasis on cost as a basis for charges in the discussion preceding the revised scales of 1949. We are told something about variations according to distance (discriminating against very short and very long hauls), but little more. Presumably on this subject available data are still deficient. Similarly one might have expected to hear something about the use of investment criteria.

Some interesting details emerge from comparison with other countries, particularly America. In a chapter on 'Soviet Railroad Operations' the author points out (quoting Professor Khachaturov) that Soviet railways use heavy equipment (like the American but unlike the European system) but with much higher average traffic-densities than American railways; thus borrowing features from both the American and the European type. However on many secondary lines Soviet railways still operate with light equipment. While the goods-train population per mile of line in U.S.S.R. is more than three times that of U.S.A., the proportion of goods wagons that are heavy four-axle wagons is still (or was in 1955) under 60 per cent, and the average weight of rails only 85 lb. per yard compared with 104 lb. in U.S.A. The average daily mileage of both locomotives and wagons is substantially higher than in U.S.A.; on the other hand average gross and net train weights were lower than in U.S.A. (61 per cent of the American level gross and 83 per cent net) and 'net ton-miles per freight train-hour' were only two-thirds of the American level. The author's summing-up is that 'the present system, with all its differences from accepted American practice, is already a remarkably effective one'.

An isolated detail is of some interest as indicating the retarding influence of two wars upon economic development: the iron and steel devoted to building Soviet tanks in the Second World War 'would have been sufficient for 60,000 kilometres of railroad line'.

Dr Hunter's monograph will prove a valuable source-book for future students of the Soviet economy. It has an extensive bibliography and a short but efficient index. Footnotes unfortunately are placed, not at the foot of the relevant page, but inaccessibly at the end between bibliography and appendices where one gives up trying to find them. In addition to forty-five charts in the text, there are seventy-nine tables of figures (together with explanatory notes) in Appendices.

Seven

Notes on recent economic discussion

Reprinted from *Soviet Studies*, April 1961 (Vol. XII, No. 4), by kind permission of the editors and publishers of that journal.

There is one aspect of recent developments in economic thought and discussion in the U.S.S.R. that perhaps deserves more emphasis than it has received: the degree of interconnection between several apparently distinct discussions which have been going on for a number of years, and the extent to which these discussions have had their roots in actual problems arising in the Soviet economy. Although the more recent debates may have consisted in a reassertion of what had previously been unorthodox views, discussion of all these questions started within the framework of Soviet planning practice and /or within the framework of Marxist thought. Deriving its special character and interest, as it does, from this fact, it cannot be dismissed as simply 'importing from the West' as some in the West would like to do, and to be properly understood must be considered in its own context. The three main discussions of recent years have been those concerned with calculating the effectiveness of investment, with price-policy and with the use of mathematical techniques (about which Dr Zauberman wrote in the July 1960 issue of this journal). The first of these goes back a long way, as far, at least, as the famous Strumilin article of 1946 on 'The Time Factor in the Planning of Investments'; and this itself was in part a critique of coefficients already devised for use in certain economic departments, and especially in transport.[1] Most of the initiative in raising these issues

[1] T. S. Khachaturov's *Osnovy ekonomiki zheleznodorozhnovo transporta* (Economic Principles of Railway Transport), in which such coefficients are explained and referred to as having 'been found absolutely necessary in planning practice', is of the same date as the article of Strumilin.

and also in framing relevant concepts and methods seems to have come, indeed, from the practical men, while economists and economic theory lagged behind (*vide* the remark of I. S. Malishev: 'Life does not wait until theoretical economists have succeeded in answering this question; and therefore technicians and project-makers have been obliged to decide it for themselves'— *Obshchestvenny uchet truda i tseni pri sotsializme*, Moscow, 1960, p. 326).

The second debate seems to have started (in non-public form) during the discussions on the new Textbook of Political Economy in or around November 1951, was reanimated in 1956 and 1957 in a public form and has continued intermittently ever since. Dating the start of the third is less easy. For long it was evidently discouraged by the prevailing view that Marxist political economy, since it was essentially a study of the 'social relations of production', was concerned only with the *qualitative* aspect of social phenomena. Attention to the quantitative aspect of economic relations was apt accordingly to be frowned upon as 'formalism'. (Cf. Nemchinov's statement that 'some economists began incorrectly to regard economic science, and particularly political economy, as a science only of qualitative economic laws, leaving out of sight the huge significance of theoretical methods of analysis of the quantitative aspect of economic laws', in *Voprosi Ekonomiki*, 1960, No. 6, pp. 13–14.) It is now clear that in Gosplan a cloud was early cast over the use of mathematical models in planning by their association with the unrealistic and over-optimistic *Genplan* of the period of the first Piatiletka, the shadow of which continued to fall as late as 1956, when a vice-chairman of Gosplan approvingly repeated Kuibishev's condemnation of the 'statistical-arithmetical deviation in planning'.[2] Since 1956, however, there has been a quickened interest, both in the Central Statistical Department and in Gosplan (partly stimulated, no doubt, by the increased use of electronic computers) in the refinements of input–output analysis and also in the methods of Kantorovich, with an increasing number of articles on such questions in the economic journals. This interest culminated in the scientific conference of April 1960 on mathematical

[2] G. Sorokin, *Planovoe Khoziaistvo*, 1956, No. 1, p. 43. Cf. M. Kaser in *Value and Plan*, ed. G. Grossman, p. 216.

economics (at which Nesmeianov, the President of the Academy, was present and spoke), followed by a resolution of the Council of the Academy on the promotion of study and research in the subject and by the formation of a special Scientific Council of the Academy to take charge of this work.[3] Mathematical economics seems to have graduated as a scientific discipline in its own right.

The connection between the effectiveness of investment discussion and the price discussion may not be immediately obvious to others than economists. The link between them is that the coefficient of effectiveness, relating as it does the saving in prime cost (or operating cost) to investment cost, although it is essentially a measure of a technical relationship, is a measure that is expressed in terms of prices. Hence it will be contingent upon the structure of relative prices. For example, two technical projects under comparison may involve the use of different materials in their construction, and their comparative investment cost, which forms one term of the coefficient, will be affected by the relative prices of these materials. That participants in the debate were fully aware of this is evident from Strumilin's reference to it in his 1946 article, and more recently by Khachaturov's remark that deviation of prices from 'values' may result in an 'untrue expression of actual effectiveness'.[4] One of the most recent writers on price-policy is even more forthright about the connection: 'Both these problems present two sides of one and the same phenomenon. They are indestructibly linked and cannot be decided in isolation one from the other' (Malishev, op. cit., p. 76).

This connection can be illustrated by taking one of the forms of calculating effectiveness that is mentioned in the official *Tipovaia*

---

[3] Cf. article by Nemchinov on 'Mathematical Methods in Economics and Planning' in *Vestnik Akademii Nauk SSSR*, 1960, No. 8, pp. 62–8.

[4] *Planovoe Khoziaistvo*, 1959, No. 8, p. 80. Cf. also Strumilin's remark at the scientific–technical conference of June 1958 on the subject, that 'these problems [about prices and value] are particularly real for calculating and planning the effectiveness of capital investment in new technique', *Ekonomicheskaia effektivnost kapitalnikh vlozhennii i novoi tekhniki*, ed. T. S. Khachaturov, Moscow, 1959, p. 67; also L. V. Kantorovich on the same occasion: 'Questions of analysis of capital investment are most closely linked with questions of price formation', ibid., p. 228.

metodika issued last year.[5] This is the so-called 'index of profitability', which is defined as 'the relation of the difference between the yearly production of an enterprise in wholesale prices (of the enterprise) and its prime cost (*sebestoimost*) to all capital investments according to the formula:

$$E_r = \frac{Ts - S}{K}$$

where Ts = yearly production in wholesale prices
S = yearly production at prime cost (*sebestoimost*)
K = general sum of capital investment (including the change in size of working capital)'.

The numerator of this fraction is obviously dependent on the price of the product of the enterprise in question relatively to the level of wages. The denominator will depend, as we have said, upon the prices of the particular equipment or constructional materials of which the particular investment consists.

Not unnaturally it is the advocates of 'prices of production' (in the sense of Marx's Volume III) as a pricing-principle who have most stressed the connection between these two discussions—notably Malishev, whom we have quoted, Z. V. Atlas and L. Vaag and S. Zakharov.[6] Once, indeed, some 'normal' coefficient of effectiveness has been established, it is easy enough (as we shall see in a moment) to translate it into a second element in price, in addition to the S of the above-quoted formula.

Since the renewed interest in mathematical economics centred round input–output analysis and linear programming methods, there might seem to be no very evident connection with the other two discussions. The former is related to the use of material balances in planning and the latter to the finding of optimal solutions to a series of particular problems, such as transport problems

[5] *Tipovaya metodika opredeleniya ekonomicheskoi effektivnosti kapitalnykh vlozhenii i novoi tekhniki v narodnom khozyaistve SSSR*, Gosplanizdat, Moscow, 1960, p. 8.
[6] Z. V. Atlas, 'On Profitability of Socialist Enterprises' in *Voprosi Ekonomiki*, 1958, No. 7, and 'Profitability and Value in Socialist Economy' in *Voprosi Ekonomiki*, 1960, No. 10, p. 71; L. Vaag and S. Zakharov, 'On Calculating What is the Economical' in *Voprosi Ekonomiki*, 1960, No. 7, pp. 103 seq.

or the loading of machine-tools or the distribution of crops within a given area of farmland. But as writers on linear programming have frequently emphasised, the optimal solutions with which they deal have implicit in them sets of 'shadow prices'; moreover, Kantorovich has explicitly developed a price-theory from his method of calculating 'direct and indirect labour expenditures'.

If I have understood it rightly, this amounts to a kind of marginal cost theory of pricing, whereby value is calculated in terms of the labour required at the margin of use of any scarce factor.[7] (This would presumably involve the incidental accrual of various kinds of surplus or rent above wage-cost, to be taxed in some way into the Budget, by means of either the profits tax or a turnover tax— or possibly a tax proportioned to the amount of scarce factors used.) The discussion about whether it provides a basis for the general structure of prices (as distinct from a calculating-device for yielding particular solutions in a special context) also seems to bear some analogy with discussions among economists in this country as to whether it is 'marginal cost' in a short-period sense or long-period marginal cost that is relevant to pricing. The critics of Kantorovich's price-theory[8] appear to have argued that it is based on a situation of scarcities existing at a particular date which is not (or may not be) relevant to long-term planning decisions, since the latter will refer to a situation in which those scarcities will have been modified. This reminds one very much of the arguments around the divided report of the Ridley Committee, ten years ago, about price-policy in the British coal industry: in particular, the argument that what was relevant to price-policy was not the *existing* difference between the average cost of coal and its cost under the least favourable conditions then prevailing in the industry, but what this difference was likely to be several years hence when the National Coal Board's policy of developing new (low-cost) pits and closing old (high-cost) pits had borne fruit.[9]

[7] Alternatively, the additional labour required to *replace* a unit of the scarce factor elsewhere if this were withdrawn and transferred to the use in question.

[8] E.g. A. Katz, 'On an Incorrect Conception of Economic Calculation' in *Voprosi Ekonomiki*, 1960, No. 5, pp. 107–18.

[9] Cf. I. M. D. Little, *The Price of Fuel*, esp. Appendix to Chapter I.

It must be acknowledged, I think, that this kind of answer to the Kantorovich proposals has considerable weight. It does not seem, however, to dispose of the problem entirely, since there are some crucial scarcities that are not so quickly removed by new investment. About enduring natural scarcities (even if modifiable within limits by investment policy) there does not seem to be much dispute between the parties ('differential rent' is acknowledged as being a category of socialist economy). But what about capital, or rather the 'investment potential' of the economy as a whole? Does not this constitute a basic and enduring limiting factor in the economic situation, for so long at any rate as the productive powers of society are in need of development by means of a high rate of investment and a high rate of growth? And if so, should not this limitation find an expression in the price-structure?

True, as the process of investment continues, the accumulation of capital and the technical equipment of industry develop, and in this respect the situation in the economy at large changes, just as it does in a particular industry such as coal. But technical knowledge is also changing (and therewith making new demands upon investment), as is the standard of life and probably also population. Until the productive capacity of the capital-goods sector of industry has reached a certain relative size (relative not only to the rest of the economy but to the social need for new investment), its output-potential will always constitute a crucial limit to what can be planned (e.g. how capital-intensive the technical projects in which the economy can afford to indulge). It follows from this that a principle of 'maximum economy of labour', in terms of which the protagonists of the value-principle in pricing-policy have apparently been thinking, cannot be accepted *simpliciter*. It must necessarily be interpreted subject to a certain investment-constraint; otherwise the principle would lead always to the choice of the most labour-saving technique, yielding the highest possible productivity of labour. This is obvious enough once stated; what is less obvious is how these two distinct elements in social cost, a measure of this investment-constraint and the wage-cost of any given output, are to be related.[10]

[10] Curiously, Malishev, although he emphasises that 'the general scale of accumulated income in the country is always restricted by definite

It is his explicit derivation of a category of cost-price from a coefficient of effectiveness of investment that gives special interest to Professor V. V. Novozhilov's contribution to the symposium, *Primenenie matematiki* (reviewed by Dr Zauberman in July 1960).[11] This category of cost-price he calls *narodnokhoziaistven-naia sebestoimost* because its perspective is that of cost at a national or social level—from the standpoint of the national economy as a whole. It bears an obvious analogy with 'price of production' as championed by Malishev. In his editorial Postscript to the symposium, however, Academician Nemchinov speaks of it as a 'new, very important conception', which is a 'more perfected form of transformed value than prices of production'; noting certain differences between them, in respect to which he thinks that the advantages lies with the former. (It may be said that these differences do not seem to be very fundamental, with one exception, perhaps: namely, that while the 'average rate of profit' to be included in prices of production is usually derived from 'the relationship between total surplus product and the value of basic and turnover funds', the equivalent quantity included in Novozhilov's cost-price, being derived from the effectiveness of investment, 'does not express that part of surplus product which is spent on the upkeep of non-productive spheres'.)[12]

The special interest of Novozhilov's contribution is the manner in which he derives his 'second element' in price (additional to prime cost) from the effectiveness of investment measured on a social scale. This he does consistently with his concept of 'inversely

[11] Incidentally, it is not clear to the present writer why Dr Zauberman should treat Novozhilov's advocacy of 'prices of production' under socialism 'as a classic of the *refutation* of the Law of Value' (loc. cit., p. 10). Prices of production were an essential part of Marx's theory of value: the argument is simply regarding the applicability of this value-category to socialism as well as to capital.

[12] *Primenenie matematiki*, pp. 479–80. The latter happens to be the interpretation adopted elsewhere by the present writer (*An Essay on Economic Growth and Planning*, Routledge, 1960, p. 97).

---

limits', seems to yield too much to his opponent (M. Bor) by defining 'the problem of finding an optimal combination of living labour and stored-up labour' as consisting in minimising 'the sum of living and embodied labour' (op. cit., pp. 247–8, 251).

related cost' or 'differential expenditures' (similar to Kantorovich's 'indirect labour expenditures'). Whenever any requisite of production is present in insufficient quantities to meet all possible demands upon it, the use of it for one purpose must involve depriving some other use of it; hence this other use will have to resort to an inferior method of production, involving a lower productivity of labour (the additional labour accordingly needed to yield the same end-product being the measure of the 'inversely related cost' or 'differential expenditure' in terms of labour). It is, therefore, the sum of these 'indirect' (or 'inversely related') and direct expenditures of labour that needs to be minimised, and not the latter alone. In the case of capital goods or instruments of production, Professor Novozhilov starts from the assumption that their availability at any one time is limited (has to be treated as a 'constant magnitude' in the problem of planned allocation)—limited, i.e. by the investment-history of the past and the existing output-capacity of the capital-goods sector. Hence the 'inversely related cost' of using them in any one direction is measured by the extra labour which their absence elsewhere imposes; and the latter can be seen to be expressed by the effectiveness-ratio of an equivalent amount of investment in capital goods elsewhere (since this ratio measures the saving in prime cost which results from higher labour-productivity due to a unit-quantity of additional investment).

His method of arriving at the new category of cost-price can be summarised as follows. Suppose that the various alternative investment projects in each industry are available, and are arranged in a list, for example according to ascending order of expense (it must also be tacitly assumed, I think, that the output plans of the various industries are given, at least provisionally). It will generally be the case that increasing expense is associated with the promise of lower operating cost when the project is in use (if in a particular case increased expense is not associated with any economy in operating cost, it will not be worth including in the list; and if any project promises the same operating costs as others in the industry but is cheaper initially, it will presumably be substituted for the latter). As one moves down the list for each industry, the effectiveness-ratio of additional investment (relating additional expense to greater operating efficiency) will alter. Let us further suppose that the total investment fund to be allocated in any plan-period is given, and that this is allocated between industries in such a way that the effectiveness-ratio at the margins of these industries is kept approximately equal. Then there will be one set of such allocations which exhausts the investment fund, without residue or deficiency. In this situation the effectiveness-ratio will have a certain value at the margin (approximately equal in all industries), and this will be taken as the standard minimum ratio, in the sense that projects yielding a lower marginal ratio than this will be rejected.

This ratio has the now-familiar form of

$$\frac{S_1 - S_2}{K_2 - K_1}$$

where $K_2 - K_1$ represents the difference in investment cost of two projects (e.g. a newly equipped plant compared with a pre-existing one of older type) and $S_1 - S_2$ the prime (or operating) costs in the two cases. Then writing the standard effectiveness-ratio (arrived at in the way described in the last paragraph) as r, Professor Novozhilov's new type of cost-price is $rK + S$. It is to be noted that r will here be the *standard* minimum ratio for the economy as a whole; whereas K and S will represent the investment cost and prime cost respectively in the case of the particular product in question.

At first sight it might seem as though such a cost-category would lack any objective validity, since it would vary with every variation in the price-level of capital goods (the constituents of K) relatively to the level of wages (to which S is ultimately reducible). This is not so, however, as regards the *general* price-level of capital goods relative to wages (variations in the prices of particular capital goods relative to one another are a different matter). Reflection will show that rK as a magnitude is independent of the units in which K and S are expressed; since the larger *in general* is K relatively to S, the smaller will be r, and conversely. Hence rK is in effect a measure of a technical relationship: that between a given (proportional) increase in investment-outlay and the resulting (absolute) increase in labour-productivity.

Professor Novozhilov then proceeds to show[13] that once his type

[13] *Primenenie matematiki*, pp. 113–15.

of cost-price has been established, it can be directly used in choosing the optimum technical variant, where choice between a number of alternative methods of producing a given output is involved. This is for the reason that the cost of a certain output (when calculated on this basis) will come out lowest when it is produced under the method of production that yields an effectiveness-ratio of r.

Thus, if there are three technical variants under consideration, such that

$$K_1 < K_2 < K_3 < K_4 \text{ and } S_1 > S_2 > S_3 > S_4$$

and

$$\frac{S_1 - S_2}{K_2 - K_1} > \frac{S_2 - S_3}{K_3 - K_2} > \frac{S_3 - S_4}{K_4 - K_3},$$

then it will follow that, if

$$\frac{S_2 - S_3}{K_3 - K_2} = r,\ rK_3 + S_3 < rK_4 + S_4$$

and also $\leqslant rK_2 + S_2$ and $< rK_1 + S_1$. 'In this formula the product Kr expresses the normative effect of the investment of K, i.e. the minimum economy of labour which an investment of K must yield for it to be included in an optimal balance. Similarly $S + Kr$ is the sum of prime cost (*sebestoimost*) and the normative economy of labour from projected investments.'[14]

The official *Tipovaia metodika*, which we have mentioned, includes as one of its suggested methods a cost-price that is essentially the same as Novozhilov's. This is written as $C_i + E.K_i =$ minimum, where K_i stands for the capital investment relevant to a particular variant, C_i for the prime cost of annual production under this variant and E for the 'branch normative coefficient of effectiveness'. It is recommended for use in complex cases where 'several variants' have to be compared. An example is attached to illustrate its use, as follows:

1st variant $K_1 = 1,000$ thousand rubles. $C_1 = 1,200$ thousand rubles

2nd variant $K_2 = 1,100$ thousand rubles. $C_2 = 1,150$ thousand rubles

3rd variant $K_3 = 1,400$ thousand rubles. $C_3 = 1,050$ thousand rubles

[14] *Primenenie matematiki*, p. 114.

Then, if the 'normative coefficient of comparative effectiveness' is ·2, the cost under the three variants will amount to:

$$(1) \quad 1{,}200 + (·2 \times 1{,}000) = 1{,}400$$
$$(2) \quad 1{,}150 + (·2 \times 1{,}100) = 1{,}370$$
$$(3) \quad 1{,}050 + (·2 \times 1{,}400) = 1{,}330$$

and the third is the favoured variant.[15]

Although the analogy between this type of price and 'price of production' is obvious enough, what is less clear is the extent to which they will yield the same result. This mainly depends upon how the rate of surplus (or of profit), to be included in price of production, is determined—a point on which the advocates of such a pricing-principle have not always been very explicit. The Novozhilov r is one way of calculating it. But it is only one way among several;[16] and, if r or its equivalent is derived in some other way, as basis for a set of prices of production, it does not follow that the ratio of surplus (or profit) to prime cost under the latter will be the same as the ratio of the Novozhilov rK to S. In which case the technique that appears as the most profitable will not be the same in the two cases. If rK (as well as S) is actually debited as a cost to whatever unit (e.g. the industrial enterprise) is taking the relevant decisions, then that technique which yields the lowest $rK + S$ will yield the largest profit, whatever the level of the

[15] *Tipovaia metodika*, pp. 11–12.
[16] Another way is to take the actual ratio of surplus to prime cost (or wages) in the consumer-goods sector, after excluding the influence of 'non-productive consumption', and to apply this ratio *also* to the pricing of all capital goods (the solution advocated in the present writer's *Essay on Economic Growth and Planning*, Chapter VI; further, on the connection between this model and Novozhilov's cost-price cf. a forthcoming article by the writer in *Kyklos*, 1961, No. 2). Yet another is to average out the total surplus product emerging in the consumer-goods sector as a uniform rate over *all* capital (whether used in the production of consumer goods or of capital goods)—the solution which most Soviet price-of-production-ists seem to have in mind. Again, in either of these two cases 'surplus product' may be so defined as to allow for 'non-productive consumption' (or 'social consumption', as Strumilin has called it) *as well as* investment (as noted by Nemchinov, cited above).

selling-price of output, *if* (but *only* if) individual prices are proportional to $rK + S$. Such proportionality would not, however, be consistent with a uniform (as well as a different) profit-rate; hence such a set of selling-prices would not constitute a set of 'prices of production' in the strict sense. *A fortiori*, if rK is *not* debited as an actual cost to the responsible decision-unit (e.g. if enterprises are only debited, as at present, with their prime costs, and rK remains a purely accounting category) the technique that yields the lowest $rK + S$ will not prove the most profitable; what is most profitable depending upon the ratio of selling-price to prime cost (and only at one such ratio coinciding with a minimising of Novozhilov's cost-price).

The conclusion we reach, therefore, is that Novozhilov s cost-price, if regarded as an actual pricing-principle, is one of a family of 'prices of production', each member of the family differing in the precise results it yields according to the way in which the value of r is derived or determined.

For the authors of *Tipovaia metodika* the Novozhilov-type of cost-price is no more than a calculating device; and Novozhilov himself seems to claim for it no more than this (at most, he leaves the question open as to whether it is to be treated as an accounting-price only or as an actual selling-price). This is in contrast with Malishev and other sponsors of 'prices of production', who maintain that actual prices, both of capital goods and consumer goods, should (at least 'normally') be constructed on this basis. At present one cannot say that there is much sign of any general price-reform of this latter kind being round the corner. But there are signs of a tendency, at least, to move in the direction of cost-prices of the Novozhilov-type as an accounting basis for investment decisions. Thus, in addition to the example of the profitability-index which we have cited from *Tipovaia metodika*, there is the example, already some two-and-a-half years ago, of an engineering conference convened by economic councils of the Moscow region which made a formal recommendation to Gosplan and to the Ministry of Finance that profitability should in future be calculated according to two indices: not only in relation to prime cost but also in relation to the total basic and turnover funds; and that as a general criterion for judging the financial results of economic activity the *latter* should be given precedence.[17] It is possible that an increasing use of accounting-prices of this type may lead to some local experimentation (e.g. by regional economic councils) in the fixing of such actual prices as are subject to local control. But whether this will spread to nationally-fixed prices (at the level of Republics or of the Union) and attain the dimensions of a general price-reform it is too early even to guess.

However, the influential (if still labelled 'discussion') article by Nemchinov[18] which arrived at the time of writing speaks confidently of a reform of *optovie tseni* as being overdue. The change which it advocates is from their present basis in *sebestoimost* (*plus* no more than a nominal profit-margin) to the new type of cost-price as advocated by Novozhilov (although he is not here mentioned by name). The latter is to be arrived at by working out 'norms of profitability' (*rentabelnost*) for various branches of industry, and adding these to the averaged *sebestoimost* of enterprises.[19] In the way in which these 'norms of profitability' are to be calculated he parts company with the price-of-productionists to the extent of rejecting the idea of uniform norms in favour of some differentiation between industries. This is because he believes that they should allow, not only for the amount of fixed and circulating capital employed, but *also* for any relevant elements of economic rent due to natural properties or situation (e.g. in extractive industries and also, apparently, situation-rent in other cases). In other words, these norms for each branch of industry should be based on (1) the size of its 'basic and turnover funds' through an effectiveness-coefficient (the r discussed above), (2) the presence of differential rent-elements. (Retail prices, *per contra*, should continue to be 'market prices', based largely on supply-demand considerations, taking into account demand-elasticities, etc.)

One cannot help remarking the analogy between these proposals

[17] Cit. Z. Atlas in *Voprosi Ekonomiki*, 1960, No. 10, p. 71; also Malishev, op. cit., p. 285. Malishev adds that 'this is very well understood by practical workers in contrast with some of our theoretical economists'.

[18] 'Value and Prices under Socialism' in *Voprosi Ekonomiki*, 1960, No. 12, pp. 85–103.

[19] As regards the destination of these profits: these are to be partly payable (it is suggested) into the Enterprise Funds of the various enterprises and partly taxed into the Budget.

(which have something of the appearance of a 'reconciliating position', unyoked as they are to any of the clearly defined *doctrinaire* standpoints) and those represented in the *Tipovaia metodika* in which the effectiveness of investment debate has reached a provisional conclusion. Perhaps the setting up of some economic commission or inter-industrial enquiry to examine the problem may be the next step.

Eight

Kantorovitch on optimal planning and prices

This article-review was written for *Science and Society* (New York), Spring 1967, and is reproduced here by kind permission of the editors of that journal.

One of the troubles for many people about the discussion of the so-called 'operation of the law of value in a socialist economy' has been the question of terminology. To those unaccustomed to this, the discussion has often seemed baffling; and clarity has not been helped by some terminological confusion among participants in the discussion themselves.[1] Economic students in the West, moreover, reared as they have been on the 'equilibria' of a (supposedly) free market process, have generally been victims of very over-simplified notions about the role of prices in a socialist economy. To avoid confusion, one or two preliminary explanations should, perhaps, be made before we deal with the proposals of Kantorovitch about prices and their relation to the earlier discussion and to changes at present in contemplation.

Firstly, the socialist debate about the 'operation of the law of value' (or 'the role of commodity relations', as it is now more usually called) was essentially concerned with the part to be played by the market, and by market forces and influences in a planned economy—whether a quite significant role, or on the other hand a negligible and dwindling one. One can now appreciate that, apart from the retail market for consumers' goods (which has always been a free market in the ordinary sense, outside emergency-

---

[1] Cf. the examples cited by Prof. W. Brus in *Studies in the Theory of Reproduction and Prices*, ed. Falkowski and Lukaszewicz, P.W.N., Warszawa, 1964, pp. 301–5.

periods of rationing), this largely depends on how much independence is assigned to the enterprise, under conditions of *khozra-schot*; since the more decisions (e.g. about output and investment) are taken at the level of the enterprise, the greater inevitably will be the influence of prices.[2] The old debate was conducted at a very abstract level; argument was largely in *a priori* (and often dogmatic) terms; it was essentially concerned with what may be called the general framework and setting of price-policy rather than with detailed questions of particular prices.[3] The discussions and changes of the last few years have, however, transferred the whole matter to a quite different and much more practical plane; as a result of which one can say that the question is being answered by the demands of practice and by the actual experience of running a developed socialist society. Today discussion of such matters runs increasingly in terms of: 'what does experience show to be necessary for solving the actual problems of a socialist economy?'

Secondly (as may be seen to follow from what has just been said), the statement that 'the law of value operates under socialism' is *not* necessarily intended to mean that individual prices should coincide with 'values' in the sense of Volume I of *Capital*—even if some have interpreted it in this way. Indeed it carried (let us repeat) no specific implication for a detailed price-policy. During the Stalin-period the need for 'deviations of price from value', for specific reasons of planning policy, was always recognised; and since then, under its *aegis*, there have been advocated various 'modified' or 'transformed' forms of value, such as 'prices of production'.

Thirdly, experience has made it clear that prices, in the sense

---

[2] Thus relative prices of inputs will affect what appears to be the least-cost combination of inputs to be used, while the relative prices of different sorts of output will influence (from a balance-sheet standpoint) the commodity-assortment to be placed on the production-agenda.

[3] Stalin, indeed, in a now-notorious aphorism even denied that price-policy properly belonged to the province of political economy. Such a separation is of course untenable; but, in so far as his intention may have been (possibly) to stress the practical and empirical setting of price-problems, and the wrongness of trying to decide them *a priori* by general reasoning about 'social relations of production', etc., there was something to be said for this standpoint.

of relative valuations or equivalences, perform a variety of functions in a socialist economy, not a unique one; and one could even speak of a number of different *categories* of prices according to the functions they perform. For example, they may perform a purely informational, or record-keeping, function and serve as a means of statistical aggregation (i.e. for aggregating qualitatively different output-items into a more comprehensive total, covering, e.g. a whole branch of industry for the purpose of passing up statistical information to higher levels). They may be purely 'accounting-prices' used in constructing some index or coefficient for the purpose of taking certain centralised decisions, such as investment-decisions, within a Ministry or planning-office. Or they may be the actual prices *paid* to some *khozraschot* organisation, such as an individual enterprise, influencing its balance-sheet net income (and hence probably its production-policy)—prices which may be different, again, from the prices at which the product in question is *sold* to consumers of it (whether other industrial enterprises or individual consumers).[4] Then there are retail prices at which consumers' goods are sold to individual citizens (giving real value to money wage-payments and wage-differentials, and hence closely connected with wage-policy): prices which have to be supply-demand equilibrium-prices if disorganisation is to be avoided in the retail market in the shape of queues and shop-shortages, or alternatively mounting stocks of unsaleable wares. These latter correspond most closely to 'prices' as the reader of economic textbooks in the West knows them. Clearly, any given set of principles or rules is unlikely to apply uniformly to all these different categories of prices: what suits one function may not suit another, and conversely.

Moreover, even when one is speaking of equilibrium prices one has to remember (what is often forgotten) that there are several distinct kinds of equilibrium-price, each relating to a distinct context. This has been recognised since the days of Adam Smith, who first distinguished what he called 'natural price' (= cost of production) from 'market price' (which fluctuates from time to time according to transitory and changing relations of demand to

---

[4] The difference being due either to an 'averaging' of the (differing) prices paid to differently-situated enterprises at the level of the branch or selling-organisation (*sbyt*), or to the imposition of turnover tax.

supply). Marshall was later to distinguish between what he termed 'long-period' and 'short-period' equilibria (with the prices appropriate to each situation) and between variants of each type. Each of these may be said to constitute a distinct 'category' in the theoretical sense; and while these categories are not unconnected with each other, it is unwise to transfer generalisations appropriate to one category to another and different one, at any rate without careful qualification to allow for difference between the situations. Of course, the idea that conditions of production were fundamental (in a causal sense) was crucial to Marx's method of analysis of the problem of value and price:[5] in this sense there can be a connection between the categories and one of them be said to be 'derivable' from another—but only with due attention being paid to modifying conditions. When, for example, one is concerned solely with market-price in its contingent and short-period context, one will be speaking mainly, if not exclusively, in terms of those demand-supply relationships that are the stock-in-trade of economic textbooks in the West; a Marxist, when speaking at this level will not sound all-that-different from a 'bourgeois' economist, and it is simple-minded to be surprised at the resemblance.[6]

Actually Marxists in the past have seldom bothered much about

[5] As Prof. V. V. Novozhilov expressed it in a recent article, 'prices are always derived from value, but only in some historical conditions are these derivatives equal to value'; and he goes on to speak of prices (in the sense he is speaking of, i.e. 'optimal prices', corresponding to an optimal plan) as being determined by 'the differential (marginal) expenditures of socially necessary labour', in the sense of the *'transformed* expenditure of social labour required by an increment of production of a given good'. *Ekonomika i matematicheskie metodi*, 1966, No. 3, p. 331.

[6] There has been some simple-mindedness on both sides: on the one hand those who immediately accused the advocates of a more concrete and realistic approach to the question of particular prices of importing bourgeois ideas of marginal utility; while Western economists and 'Sovietologists' have cited statements of writers like Novozhilov and Kantorovitch as evidence that Marxism was in retreat before what they chose to call 'marginalism'. Partly, this was a failure to distinguish formal elements in a theory from economic content. The notion of 'marginal' increments or decrements comes, of course, from the differential calculus and is no monopoly of the school of marginal utility theorists; and the kind of formal apparatus associated with the notion of marginal changes will tend to come into the picture whenever one deals in a mathematical

what are nowadays called 'micro-economic' questions about particular prices in a particular context. This was because they were primarily concerned (and rightly so) with 'macro-economic' questions concerning the movement of capitalism, distribution of income between classes and so forth. Moreover, their emphasis was on the extent to which macro-relations were both the framework for and a determining influence upon micro-relations (whereas 'bourgeois' economists have sought *per contra* to derive macro-relations, e.g. income-distribution, from micro-). Marx only reached the category of 'market prices' at a fairly advanced stage of his unfinished Volume Three. In the period of dogmatism in the Soviet Union political economy was conceived of as mainly *qualitative* (concerned, e.g., with social relations of production) and devoted scant attention to quantitative questions at all. It is only in the past decade that Marxist economists have been forced to deal with questions of particular prices by the practical needs of a developed socialist economy.

This may seem a long-winded preamble to a review of the work of Kantorovitch, for some time known to specialists and now available in an English translation.[7] The author is the distinguished Russian mathematician who invented what is now known (both east and west) as Linear Programming: an Academician and a recipient last year (along with Novozhilov and Nemchinov) of a Lenin Prize. As Academician Nemchinov said in his Preface to the Russian edition:

> With the level of development of the national economy and the exceptional complexity of internal economic relations, the problem of

[7] *The Best Use of Economic Resources*, by L. V. Kantorovitch, with a Preface by V. S. Nemchinov; English edition edited by G. Morton, trans. by P. F. Knightsfield, London and New York, Pergamon Press and Harvard University Press, 1965, $15. This is a translation of *Ekonomicheskii Raschot Nailuchshego Ispolzovania Resursov*, published in Moscow by the Academy of Sciences Press, 1959.

manner with so-called 'extremal' problems (i.e. with maximising or minimising). On this cf. V. V. Novozhilov, *Matematicheskii Analiz Rasshirennogo Vosproizvodstva*, Trudi Nauchnogo Soveshchania o Primenenii Matematicheskikh Metodov, 4–8th April 1960, Tom II, Academy of Sciences Press, Moscow, 1962, pp. 4–5.

finding the best possible system of planning would become insurmountable without a radical improvement in methods of economic calculation and the utilisation of the latest computing techniques. The use of modern mathematical methods in the organisation and planning of production provides a real and very efficient method of improvement. It is therefore not surprising that linear programming as an independent discipline first emerged in the Soviet Union. Important results in this field were achieved in 1938-9 by the author of this book, L. V. Kantorovitch, and published by him in a number of works beginning in 1939. The first of these contained fundamental advances and determined the content and further development of this discipline: it examined the mathematically new type of 'extremal' problems; it evolved a universal method for their solution (method of solution multipliers) as well as various efficient numerical algorithms derived from it; it indicated the more important fields of technical-economic problems where these methods could be most usefully applied; and it brought out the economic significance of indicators resulting from an analysis of problems by this method which is particularly essential in problems of a socialist economy.

The author starts by introducing us to a number of fairly simple and elementary (but crucial) problems. Firstly, he takes the case of two articles, which the plan requires to be produced in a given 'assortment' or ratio to each other, and a number of factories, with fixed productive capacities but different conditions of production (i.e. their labour productivities differ, and the *ratios* of their productivities measured in terms of the two articles differ). The problem is how to allocate the output-plan for the two products between the various factories so as to maximise total output while maintaining the prescribed 'assortment'. An analogous type of problem is that of allocating various machines, of differing efficiencies for various jobs or operations, between these operations so as to maximise the total volume of operations performed in a given time or with a given quantity of labour. In the second chapter he considers the problem of choosing between different methods of production for different 'tasks' in a situation where the productive resources available are limited (which is the situation confronting the makers of any short-term plan). The simplified example he takes is where there are only two limiting factors of production, namely 'labour and some other factor which increases labour productivity', such as electrical power or machinery ('we analyse the problem in its pure form when the scarcity cannot be changed by man and the factor must be used economically'). Later in the same chapter he takes the case of land of different qualities and three different crops, required in certain definite quantities according to the planned target: how to allocate the available land between the crops in such a way as to fulfil the plan with the least expenditure of labour? Following this comes the now-familiar transport problem: with limited rolling stock and various points of origin and destination, the problem is how best to allocate existing wagon-capacity to different consignments and routes so as to minimise transport cost.

What, then, is the connection between operational problems of any of these kinds and the question of valuation or prices (which is the leading theme of the third and final chapter of the book)? In comparatively simple examples, such as those that are dealt with in chapters one and two, an optimal solution can generally be found by direct inspection. But in more complex cases this is no longer possible and one can only proceed from any arbitrary or random solution to an optimal one with the aid of some computational rule. This is where the Kantorovitch 'multipliers' come in. These multipliers are in effect valuations or prices (commonly called 'shadow prices'). In the present work they are called *otsenki* —'objectively determined *otsenki*'. 'The superiority of the methods based on *otsenki* consists in making it possible to avoid direct comparison of all the [feasible] plans'; the latter being obviously 'impracticable in more complex cases in which millions of solutions have to be compared'. In the above-mentioned case of factories with different labour productivities and two outputs required in a ratio or assortment, the relevant *otsenka*, or valuation-ratio, is given by the relative labour-cost of producing the two outputs in the 'marginal' group of factories that is assigned to producing some of each (i.e. this group of factories has no pronounced advantage in producing one or the other when the two outputs are valued at this ratio). As the author is at pains to emphasise, when (but *only* when) relative prices are so fixed will the optimal pattern of output prove to be the most profitable for each and all factories to undertake and total output be maximised.

Thus the *otsenki* or valuation-ratios are derived from the optimal plan, and once they are found (by a series of approximations, or by a so-called 'iterative procedure') they serve as indicators of what is the optimal plan.

Again, in the case of the two methods of production, one more labour-saving than the other, a 'hire-valuation' for electrical power or for a machine as a scarce factor is calculated. This is equal to the man-hour /kilowatt hour equivalent in the marginal operation where both methods are used (i.e. the man-hours of labour saved by using one kilowatt-hour of additional electrical power); or alternatively, in the machine case, equal to the saving of manual labour-cost (measured in wage-units) per additional machine-day in the operation where both methods are used indifferently. In the agricultural case of crop-distribution between lands of different quality a 'differential rent' (per unit of product) is calculated for each grade of land; this being equal to the additional labour needed to grow a unit of the crop in question on the poorest type of land.[8] The latter is called 'indirect labour'; and the cost of growing any particular quantity of a crop (for the purpose of choosing the least-cost use of land) is calculated as the sum of the so-called direct (or actual) and the 'indirect' labour. (The *rationale* of doing this is that the 'indirect' labour represents the *cost to society as a whole* of using a scarce resource, since it measures what some *other* line of production is deprived of in the way of labour-saving by not being able to use it: optimal usage of the scarce resource requiring that the result of using it for any specific purpose should cover the cost of this deprivation.) Professor Kantorovitch concludes:

> The hire valuation [i.e. for a machine] represents in itself a specific form of differential rent—a rent for equipment. The difference consists in that equipment, as distinct from natural resources, can be reproduced. However, this difference becomes only apparent in long-term planning; in short-term planning reproduction of equipment within a short time is not possible and for this reason the difference is not obvious (p. 101).

[8] This will be different for different crops. The answer is that (in the assumed circumstances) the largest *proportional* difference should be taken; the optimal crop-plan giving priority in allocating land to that use in which its differential or comparative fertility is greater.

It is easy to see how such a method can be used for given problems within a special (short-period) context, such as how best to allocate machine-tools within a factory between jobs, or different factories within a branch of industry, or to work out a transport plan or a crop-distribution plan within a farming region. Here there is no controversy. All such problems are set within the framework of given resources (either carried over from the past such as plant and equipment or perhaps allocated by the plan, in the case of fuel, power and raw materials) and of given output targets. Says Kantorovitch in chapter two:

> The planning and allocation problems envisaged here relate to comparatively short periods of time (a year, a quarter, a month)—*problems of short-term planning* and of operational economic solutions. . . . In the existing situation and a given period, the composition of the final product is determined. . . . Starting from these requirements and the available means (labour-force, equipment, methods of production in use or known) an optimal plan has to be constructed, a plan which will ensure the highest possible final output of the required composition (pp. 122–3).

And again: 'Relative costs—the valuation of costs—are used basically *not for deciding what to produce but how to produce*' (p. 138).

What may be less easy to see, and has proved more controversial, is how these results can be generalised to the level of the economy as a whole, and the calculated ratios or *otsenki* made the basis of actual prices—both accounting prices used for the purpose of certain *ad hoc* calculations and actual prices paid to enterprises and affecting their decisions under *khozraschot*. It is this that his critics have denied in the past, and probably continue to deny. Even Academician Nemchinov in his Editorial Preface to this work felt constrained to deny the author's claim to 'universality of the proposed method of economic calculations based on his objectively determined valuations (*otsenki*)', while conceding their usefulness 'in a strictly limited sphere'. (Whether he would have modified this negative assessment six or seven years later we shall unfortunately never know.)

There is no doubt, however, about the author's intention in the matter. He makes it abundantly clear that he conceives of his *otsenki*, not just as an *ad hoc* calculating device, but as the proper basis for *actual* prices of means of production generally (and even of skilled labour in specially short supply); and that he seeks to generalise his method to the task of optimal planning on a national scale, including long-term planning, the allocation of investment and choice of new construction projects, to which he devotes his third chapter. As he puts it:

> The methods of planning described here will be of value, in so far as they will make it possible to coordinate general planning with the planning and economic accounting of individual factories more easily and accurately. The analysis carried out in the drawing up of the national economic plan will, as a result of establishing objectively determined *otsenki*, furnish individual factories with a summary of the whole situation, in an extremely convenient form which should be used as a guide. For instance, a metal works in solving the problem as to whether it is worth substituting three tons of aluminium for one ton of lead need not analyse production and consumption of lead and aluminium on a nation-wide scale, but be guided simply by the *otsenki* given, and calculate whether such a measure results in a reduction of expenditure (p. 149).

This he justifies by the need to effect an identity between the outlook of the individual *khozraschot* unit (i.e. the enterprise or factory) and the needs of an optimal national plan; and it is in this claim that his proposals are most closely in tune with the latest economic reforms and the discussion of them during the past two years.

He has some severe criticisms to make of the existing price-system, which he says leads to wrong choices being made, whether the prices in question are used as indices for centralised decisions or as criteria for decentralised decisions by individual enterprises.

> In principle prices should approximate to *otsenki* . . . even an approximate agreement of prices with *otsenki* would mean that both prices and valuations reflected hire cost, rent, etc. . . . . This would result in a change in price relationships in comparison with existing prices—in particular, a certain relative increase in prices for those types of output (and of services) in the production of which large, specialised and also scarce equipment are being used, namely, prices of metal, petrol, coal, cement and railway transport (p. 135).

A particular example that is stressed (p. 60) is that of 'electricity in territories with a tight energy balance' which is undervalued in existing tariffs. For this reason 'many measures calling for an increase in consumption of electrical energy and clearly inadvisable with the available supply, produce, according to the calculations, a reduction in cost and seem advantageous. Conversely, other measures resulting in an economy in electrical energy do not appear advantageous on the basis of such calculation.' Such a discrepancy between actual price and 'real value' is stated to be 'generally characteristic of the prices and tariffs of the majority of factors whose production involves the use of large-scale equipment'.

We seem to be confronted with yet another kind of price—a novel type of animal—different from those we have known hitherto: one that can be derived only when the particular plan among feasible plans which is optimal has been discovered, and one that when it is arrived at will both indicate what is optimal in methods of production and ensure that optimal methods are maintained.[9] It is relevant also to remember that there will be a *different* optimum for each *different* set of final output-targets. The price in question is an 'equilibrium' price in the sense that when the planned output is being produced with optimal methods of production, the total money value of anything that *is* produced exactly covers total cost (and fails to cover total cost in the case of anything that is *not* produced or is produced by non-optimal methods). But since no *actual* plan, still less a plan in its actual execution, will ever succeed in being completely optimal (at best an approximation thereto), if only because of the imperfection and inprecision of available information (repeatedly stressed by Kantorovitch) and of unforeseeable elements in any future situation, these 'optimal' prices will never be identical with actual equilibrium-prices in the usual (market-price) sense of what equates the quantities demanded in any given period with available supplies. (They will only be identical in an ideal situation where everything matches perfectly.) In the case of retail prices Kantorovitch explicitly recognises this

---

[9] In one sense, I suppose, it could be maintained that this kind of price is not really new, since economists ever since Walras have sought to identify prices under 'perfect competition' with 'optimal prices' in an analogous sense. But this 'identification' was nothing more than a mirage.

discrepancy: they need to be true demand-supply equilibrium-prices (sometimes called 'clear-the-market prices').[10] The same may apply to some 'other prices' which he does not specify (agricultural ones?); and even as regards 'wholesale (*optovie*) prices' within the State sector, 'they too need not strictly agree' with the optimal *otsenki*, 'since frequent changes in these prices are for various reasons not desirable' (p. 135). He also mentions as exceptional cases large indivisible units of equipment with spare capacity: here the hire-valuation for equipment might even be zero (pp. 205, 214).

Yet in another sense these optimal *otsenki* will be (and could hardly avoid being) influenced by current demand-supply situations. Again this is recognised: they 'reflect those deviations which are due to temporary deficiencies or to the existence of reserves of one type of equipment or another or to an abrupt increase in the demand for the given type of output, etc.' (p. 135). In the case of an electrical power plant, its 'hire-valuation', and hence the proper price to charge for electricity, will differ according to whether the plant is being used to full capacity or is not; and similarly with other types of equipment and also materials in more or less scarce supply. The 'ideal' answer no doubt is that the price in such cases would depend on whether the capacity (or the material) was over-used or under-used *when everything was optimally adjusted*, including the demand for the plant or the material in question. But in imperfect actuality, where no more than a *tendency towards*, or an approximation to, optimal adjustment can be hoped for, prices and costs could also never be more than approximations to the ideal *otsenki*. In other words they would inevitably reflect in some degree actually existing supply-demand situations, affected by transitory, short-period influences and events (including 'accidental' deviations from the plan).[11] In this sense they would always be some kind of hybrid between short-period equili-

[10] The difference between them and cost would presumably be bridged by a turnover tax.
[11] This element of duality is, indeed, pointed out by Professor V. V. Novozhilov in the first-quoted article of his above (loc. cit., pp. 335–8). There may be temporary deviations of what he terms 'demand price' from 'supply price'.

brium (or 'market') prices, as we know them, and the optimal *otsenki*.

This does not seriously matter, of course, if we are not looking for precision, and if we view the matter as one of continually moving *towards* an optimum through a series of approximations and by a process of mutual adjustment between plans and prices. In any given (non-optimal) situation one would have at least an indication of the *limits* within which an 'optimal price' would lie; and this information would enable one at least to correct glaringly non-optimal features of current plans. Kantorovitch makes it clear that it is by some such trial-and-error method of successive approximation that at the general level he envisages the movement towards an optimum in both plans and prices being reached. Moreover, he stresses that there is a variety of ways in which in practice his ideal *otsenki* can be arrived at; that what he presents is 'only a bare preliminary scheme' and that its practical realisation 'presents a problem of the highest complexity and requires the development of special methods'.

In short, we have to accept, I think, that *otsenki* remain an ideal and are unlikely ever to be realised in practice. The prices that prevail in actuality are bound to be non-optimal in some degree, and to this extent to be false guides in choosing methods of production. The question is *what* degree—whether of a magnitude large enough to matter or small enough to be insignificant in the larger picture. If we are 'purists', who insist on the optimum and nothing less, this may appear as a serious objection. But 'purism' in such matters is rather foolish; and most would be content to eliminate major cases of inefficiency and be able to recognise and work towards an improvement. The present reviewer has inclined to the view that what is important (especially in relation to growth) is to get the macro-price-relations approximately 'right', and that if this be done micro-price-relations can mostly be left to look after themselves. Kantorovitch would certainly add to this the requirement that the prices of all major inputs, especially where these are close substitutes and there is room for choice, should be as nearly optimal as is possible.[12]

[12] This would imply something *other* than an equal rate of profit on capital in different lines of production; since the price of temporarily

One of the ways in which the process of successive adjustment could work is hinted at by the author (pp. 147–8, also 226) without being worked out at all fully. It was suggested a few years ago by the present writer, in some comments on Kantorovitch, as an alternative (and in a sense opposite) to the prewar proposal of the late Oskar Lange; and it has since been dignified with the name of 'two-level planning' by two Hungarian writers.[13] In the Lange trial-and-error process, it will be remembered, it was variable prices (accounting-prices) that were fixed by the top-level authorities from time to time and 'given' to the lower level: i.e. to industries and industrial enterprises who fixed their output-quantities accordingly. In this scheme there was no general output-plan worked out centrally at the top level. This process could be reversed, and in a form consistent with centralised planning of output; *quantities* being fixed centrally instead of prices.[14] The top-level authorities could issue output-targets (at least, in general terms), as is the current practice, together with supply-allocations of main fuels and materials needed to fulfil them. The lower level would then be instructed within this framework of targets and allocations to work out their local and sectional plans for optimal fulfilment: i.e. for choosing the least-cost method of reaching their targets. To each of these local or sectional plans would correspond its set of optimal prices—prices which would diverge as between localities or industries to the extent that the initial top-level plans were 'arbitrary' or non-optimal. These very divergences would

[13] For the present writer's remarks see above, pages 205–6. In Hungary the idea was worked out in a mathematical form (together with a proof that the adjustment-process was convergent) by J. Kornai, and also published in an article entitled 'Two-Level Planning' by Kornai and Lipták in *Econometrica*, January 1965. The prewar work of Oskar Lange referred to was *On the Economic Theory of Socialism*, University of Minnesota, 1938.

[14] In practice, of course, some compromise between the two alternative methods could be (and probably would be) used, with *some* prices, at least, fixed centrally and *some* quantities left to lower-level determination.

scarce inputs would include a differential 'rent' of their scarcity—which explains why he rejects 'prices of production' as a solution, while thinking that they might be an improvement on the existing practice by raising the prices of things made with expensive equipment.

indicate the need, and point the direction, for subsequent adjustments in the output-targets and supply-allocations of top-level plans; and the process of mutual adjustment would continue until a rough uniformity of the *otsenki*-valuations arising from lower-level solutions had been attained. This illustrates what Kantorovitch means when he speaks of 'competition among plans and methods in the process of planning calculations, instead of competition on an actual market' (p. 150). Its practicability depends, of course, on the process of mutual adjustment between quantities and prices converging easily and fairly quickly; and whether it does so is something which remains to be proved.

When one comes to long-term planning, with large-scale investment decisions which set the structural framework for future development, an additional difficulty comes to the fore. The prices relevant to such decisions will be prices related to the situations of *future years*; and to the extent that development is taking place, these situations and their related prices will be different from present ones. Nor will present prices (to the extent to which they reflect fortuitous events and transitory scarcities) necessarily be sound indicators of future trends. It will be a matter of reaching, not only a set of ideal prices corresponding to an optimal production plan, but a set of prices corresponding to what *will be* the optimal production plan and production methods of some imperfectly foreseeable future year or series of years. Kantorovitch recognises this difficulty, and postulates that for long-term planning not the same but a different set of optimal prices will be needed—special 'dynamic *otsenki*', or series of *otsenki*. Of these he speaks (p. 175) as 'a system of valuations of all types of output and factors of production for each period'. We have seen that he devotes his third and final chapter, entitled 'Expansion of the Production Base', to this problem. Evidently, the mutual adjustment process between plans and prices will be equivalently more complicated in the dynamic long-term case. About this the book is quite frank:

> an optimal long-term plan, even an approximation to it, can hardly be constructed straight away in its final form. Evidently its construction must involve a process of successively drafting and improving the plan, in a whole series of stages in which the plan itself

and its indicators, together with the initial data and tasks, are simultaneously refined (p. 220).

In making decisions about long-term investment (e.g. in deciding between different technical variants of a constructional project, some more expensive but yielding more future output than others), the use of a coefficient or ratio of effectiveness[15] is essential. But unless this is calculated in terms of optimal prices or *otsenki*, it can be misleading and result in faulty investment decisions being taken—and once taken these may well be irrevocable. Yet even if we have these ideal valuations (or something close to them), they are likely to change over time in a manner that is partly unforeseeable: 'when the relative valuations change in the course of time these changes must be allowed for in the calculation of the efficiency of capital investments' (p. 170). Hence 'it is immeasurably more complicated' in the case of long-term investments to allow 'with any satisfactory degree of accuracy and reliability' for changes likely to occur within the relevant time-period, 'and for this reason the calculation of the ratio of effectiveness of investment is much more difficult' (p. 183). To this extent, the notion of an optimum, whether of prices or of plans, is a utopian ideal which in practice can never be reached—at best some approximation to it is possible. For example, in a particular case (or even generally) this calculation will be affected if the overloading of electricity generating plant (and hence the 'true price' of electricity), or alternatively the scarcity of some key metal or metals, is likely to be increased by developments over the coming decade or to be eased. As regards unforeseen changes, Kantorovitch says: 'In applying a system of optimal planning a plan actually in operation over a number of years will inevitably not be optimal since changes in the situation and new data require continual changes of plan, and therefore the planned solutions already operating are frequently not optimal'—and as examples of new data he instances 'appearance of new requirements; appearance of new products, replacing old ones; the appearance of new and improved techniques' (p. 215).

[15] Sometimes referred to as the 'period of recoupment' of an investment, which is the inverse of the effectiveness-ratio as customarily defined.

We should not, however, over-emphasise the difficulty of unforeseeable events in long-term planning. It should be possible to reach a pretty fair approximation to optimal efficiency if calculations start from existing prices (and effectiveness-ratios) as a basis, provided that one is careful to correct them for the more obvious cases of transitory or 'accidental' influences (e.g. temporary scarcities, due to sudden demand-shifts or past misjudgments of demand, supply-changes due to newly discovered products or processes). The approximation will be further improved if allowance is made for price-shifts likely to result from major developments projected in the coming period. It is one of the major advantages of a planned economy that at least the macro-framework of development is known for as long ahead as long-term planning can project, and interrelated decisions can be coordinated accordingly; whereas in a so-called 'free market' system this is all a matter of guesswork and speculation. In so far as the prices used in long-term planning calculations for gearing together the constituent parts of the strategic framework are *accounting*-prices, there is no reason at all why these should not be different ones (as the book suggests) from those used in current short-term planning. So far as *actual*-prices (influencing the actions of *khozraschot* organisations) are concerned, it is more difficult to envisage any mechanism whereby future (and guaranteed) prices diverge from current ones, except in the form of indicative price-trends (inevitably somewhat tentative in character and perhaps in the form of upper and lower 'price-limits') issued in the case of certain main staple products for the guidance of industries. But this very difficulty of affording a firm and reliable basis for 'decentralised' long-term decisions at lower levels may well be a reason for retaining centralised planning of all major investment decisions, even if a major part of current (i.e. short-term) output-decisions, within the macro-framework of productive capacities and their development, were decentralised, as it has been the tendency of recent change in the socialist countries to do. The indices utilised for these investment decisions could then be based on special accounting-prices (or 'corrected prices') that were different from the prices actually used in the framing and carrying-out of short-term plans (where productive capacities in existence could be taken as given).

For the mathematically inclined reader one should add that the book under review concludes with two longish mathematical appendices, eighty pages in all, in which the advocated methods are set out in a more rigorous and formal manner. In the course of the first of these one meets this passage:

> until recent times mathematical analysis was not only rarely used in economic problems, but it was even necessary to contend with definite objections to its use. Such objections cannot be accepted as justifiable. . . . Equally unjustified is the prejudice against mathematical methods because of their partial use by bourgeois economic schools. Clearly, the precedents of the incorrect use of mathematics for purposes different from ours cannot prevent Soviet scientists from using mathematical methods in economic problems in a way which is correct and of advantage in the building of communism (pp. 296–7).

We must be grateful to the translator for rendering this work into recognisable English; and on the whole the translation is clear and readable. Yet unfortunately it is not impeccable, and at times there are flaws which obscure the sense of the original.[16] This seems to be attributable largely to unfamiliarity with the context of discussion and the usage of some of its technical terms. A minor and not very serious example (possibly a defect of team-work?) is that the word *Syezd*, the stock term for Congresses, whether of Soviet or Party, is in some places (pp. xxii, xxviii) rendered as 'Session', with 'reports' to it (by Brezhnev, etc.) called 'papers'; whereas a dozen or so pages later (e.g. p. 11) 'Congress' correctly appears. It is not very helpful to have *shturmovshchina* rendered as 'rush work' without any indication (by footnote or parenthesis) that a very special type of problem is being referred to (storming to reach the quantitative plan-target in the final weeks of the plan-period). It is not easy for the non-specialist reader to appreciate that the special coefficient (or ratio, or norm) of effectiveness of investment is being referred to when this is translated throughout simply as 'normal efficiency'; nor does it help understanding for

[16] For example, in the first sentence of the passage from Nemchinov's Preface cited above we find: '. . . without a fundamental appreciation of quantitative methods' instead of 'without a radical improvement in methods of economic calculation'.

realizatsia on page 167 to be called 'completing' (the object of investment at the end of its period of service)—here the translator cannot, one feels, have understood the argument in question. But there is one example, I am afraid, where the point of a contrast is completely destroyed (p. 232) by rendering *khozraschot* as 'national economic account', when the point is to contrast using a price for accounting purposes at higher planning levels and using it as an actual price paid to an enterprise at the *local* level. At least this latter example has the virtue of explicitly mentioning the original term used.

Six

Introduction to an Italian Edition of *Capital*

Karl Marx, *Il Capitale*, Libro Primo, trad. Delio Cantimori, Editori Riuniti, Roma, 1964. The English version (which is being simultaneously published by the journals *Science and Society* and *Marxism Today* on the occasion of the centenary of the first publication of *Das Kapital*) is reproduced here by kind permission of Editori Riuniti.

Das Kapital is, I suppose, the most controversial work on Political Economy ever to have been written. The subject of more and sharper controversy even than was Ricardo's *Principles*, it has probably met with wider extremes of praise and denigration than any other work of its kind. More frequently refuted than most economic theories—and when not being refuted it was as often as not in academic circles ignored—it has survived to be accepted over a large part of the contemporary world as the authoritative interpretation of capitalist society. Even in the last decade of the nineteenth century a foremost critic could say that 'Marx has become the apostle of a wide circle of readers, including many who are not as a rule given to the reading of difficult books' (Böhm-Bawerk). Despite the passion his doctrines have aroused, however, there are those among his academic critics who have estimated his intellectual contribution soberly. Joseph Schumpeter, for example, in his monumental *History of Economic Analysis*, says of Marx that 'the totality of his vision, as a totality, asserts its right in every detail and is precisely the source of the intellectual fascination experienced by everyone, friend as well as foe, who makes a study of him'; and elsewhere that 'at the time when his first volume appeared there was nobody in Germany who could have measured himself against him either in vigour of thought or in theoretical knowledge'.

The two concepts that have been the special centres of controversy have been those of property-income as surplus-value, or the fruit of exploitation, and of the historical development of capitalist society towards revolutionary transformation into socialism. The former could be regarded, perhaps, as a development of the so-called 'deduction theory' of profit to be found in Adam Smith (where it was no more than a surplus theory in embryo, and some would say no more than a hint); or possibly as a more rigorous and systematic version of ideas already current among the so-called 'Ricardian socialists'. The latter concept, in itself an application of Marx's general view of history and of the role of class conflict as the motive-force of historical change, sharply contrasted with prevailing views of economic progress; since these, even when tinged as they often were with fears about the approach of a 'stationary state', held no inkling of an historical role for the working class. Such a role was quite foreign to bourgeois conceptions, and its introduction was at once transforming and to traditional notions distinctly shocking.

Proper understanding of both these concepts depends on an appreciation of the boundaries of political economy as Marx envisaged them. The tendency of modern economic analysis since the last quarter of the nineteenth century has been to narrow its focus to a study of the exchange-process, i.e. of the market and of market equilibrium under various hypothetical conditions. In gaining precision of formulation it has achieved a fairly drastic narrowing of scope and of range. Conditions of production have been narrowed and faded down to the assumption of given supplies (or supply-conditions) of disembodied productive factors and of given technical coefficients or so-called production-functions; and in so far as any kind of process of production appears, it does so implicitly as a unidirectional flow of primary factors into final consumer goods (in terms of which the so-called 'imputation' of prices to intermediate goods and factors—the Austrian School's *zurechnung*—alone makes sense). Anything to do with property-ownership, or any distinction between the propertied and the propertyless, is relegated to the category of social or sociological factors, excluded from the domain of economic theory *per se*, and not affecting the formal structure of that theory (merely affecting, perhaps, the value of some of the variables involved). As is well-known, the shape assumed by a theoretical model is itself a selection of the facts and the events to be studied; hence however impeccable or elegant its logic it can represent a biased selection which may distort our vision of the real world, instead of illuminating it. One result of the increasing formalisation of economic theory in recent decades has been to render its analysis of market equilibrium almost entirely quantitative in character, leaving little or no room for qualitative *differentia*, and certainly no room for *differentia* of a so-called socio-economic kind. What Marx called the 'fetishism of commodities' is thus able to ripen behind this imposing façade to an unnatural degree. It is hardly surprising that a relationship such as 'exploitation' or the characterisation of income as a 'surplus' should cease to have any meaning within this context; and that even so sympathetic a critic as Mrs Joan Robinson should dismiss the notions of exploitation and surplus value as moral judgments masquerading as economic concepts.

By contrast, Marx conceived the bounds of political economy more widely than this—as indeed was true of classical political economy, without in its case such explicit formulation. For him the 'social relations of production' were included as well as the 'productive forces' and the conditions of exchange. This followed from his historical approach to the analysis of capitalist production and his historical conception of the mode of production as the basis of a given society and 'the true source and theatre of all history'. Qualitative characterisation of relationships was as important as was a solution of the quantitative problem of value and of the derivation of prices from values. From the standpoint of causation, especially of movement and change, such characterisation was essential; and a constant preoccupation of his analysis was 'to penetrate through the outward disguise into the internal essence and the inner form of the capitalist process of production' behind the market appearance with which the *epigoni* were content.

If we take the terms 'exploitation' and 'unpaid labour' at a socio-economic description of a relationship (and not *per se* a moral epithet), then it is hard to see how its correctness can be disputed. Few if any would, I think, question the description of the income of feudal lords as having its source in the appropriation of a part of what was produced by others—the product of 'a subject peasantry' to use the historian Marc Bloch's phrase. (Marc Bloch says: 'whatever the source of the noble's income he always lived on the labour of other men'.) Surely, anyone who denied this would be concealing or distorting a major feature of an economy based on serf-labour? To apply a similar characterisation to property-income in a capitalist society is to assert that in this respect it bears a major analogy with previous types of class society, and this *despite* the fact that all economic relationships have a contractual form governed by the market. In other words, owners of capital continue to 'live on the labour of other men', even though politico-legal compulsion to work for a master is replaced by the economic compulsion which a propertyless status involves. Are not those economists the word-jugglers and the obscurantists who have sought to deny such a proposition with the aid of various types of 'productivity theory', conjuring their denial by imputing the activities of a machine or the chemical properties of land to the passive *rentier* who happens to be their owner?

Some have supposed, wrongly I think, that the characterisation of profit as surplus value is somehow derived from the labour-theory of value; the two standing in relation to one another as the premise and conclusion of a syllogism. Thus the two theories are sometimes regarded as inheritors of Lockean notions of natural right—the natural right to own the product of one's own labour. This is, I believe, an incorrect interpretation. Rather was it a case (as Marx himself explained it in *Value, Price and Profit*) of reconciling the fact of surplus value with the classical notion that in a regime of free trade and free competition all things exchanged at their values: a reconciliation which he achieved by separating labour-power from labour; the former being a commodity which itself had a value, depending upon the value of what was needed for its replacement, or for subsistence. If there was some premise from which the notion of surplus value was derived as a conclusion, this was the definition of 'producer' and of 'productive' in terms of human activity.

The theory of value of Marx stood essentially in the classical tradition, although in its formulation by different writers of the classical school there were ambiguities and some lack of clarity, as well as the well-known differences between Adam Smith and Ricardo on this matter. There is no doubt that it was Ricardo who stood closest to Marx—an affinity which we can appreciate the more now that we have Ricardo's unpublished and previously unknown paper on 'Absolute and Exchangeable Value'.[1] What this theory of value essentially did was to explain conditions of exchange in terms of conditions of production, and hence in the final analysis to represent the prices of production as determined (in the 'normal case' and under conditions of free and perfect competition) by the amount of labour which their production cost, together with the technical conditions of their production as expressed in what Marx termed the 'organic composition of capital'. This derivation of exchange relations from conditions of production was, again, wholly consonant with his general conception of history, and with the leading role played in this by the mode of production. It was, indeed, a direct application of this historical conception, and represents the organic link between the two that enables one to speak of his economic theory as being in this sense *historical* and which illustrates the essential unity of his thought.

It is precisely this claim that the structure of prices can be derived from conditions of production that has evoked the most strenuous denials from economists of the subjective, or utility, school. And the charge that Marx's attempt to demonstrate this (and hence his theory of profit as surplus value) foundered on a crucial contradiction was what enabled his leading critic, the Austrian von Böhm-Bawerk, to proclaim confidently 'the close of the Marxian system', thereby leaving the field open for an explanation of prices and incomes simultaneously in terms of Utility (*vide* Böhm-Bawerk's own well-known theory of interest on capital as dependent on the different subjective valuation of present and

---

[1] Published in Volume 4 of *Works and Correspondence of David Ricardo*, ed. Sraffa, Cambridge, 1950. The paper is unfinished, its writing having been interrupted by Ricardo's fatal illness and death.

future goods). In Volume I of *Capital*, as is well-known, Marx tackled the problem of surplus value on the assumption that commodities exchange at their values. At this stage his analysis is concerned only with the most *general* features of capitalism, and it is on these that he fixes attention. Expressing it in modern terminology, one could say that analysis is conducted at this stage at the most macroscopic level. He is not concerned at this stage with individual products and industries, but with the 'social relations of production' which determine how the total product, viewed as a whole, is divided between the classes. It is only in Volume III, at a later stage of approximation, that he concerns himself with more of the detail of the picture—that he introduces conditions affecting the relations between different industries and comes closer to *differentia* that become visible and important at a more microscopic level of examination. In particular, he takes account of differences in the technical conditions and in the so-called 'organic composition of capital' in different lines of production, combined with the necessity (given conditions of capital-mobility between industries) for a uniform rate of profit on capital, irrespective of where capital is used. Under these conditions, for reasons which are sufficiently familiar, 'prices of production', as the normal (or long-term equilibrium) prices at which products exchange, diverge from values; profit being equalised by a process of 'redistribution of total surplus value' between different branches of industry.

In subsequent Marx-*kritik* it was upon the relation between these prices of production and the Values of Volume I that attention came to be focused. The theory of surplus value was constructed on the assumption that commodities exchanged at their values; yet it transpired in Volume III that exchange in capitalist society was on the basis not of values but of prices of production which diverged from values. What then was left of the theory of surplus value and all that was pendant on it? This was 'the Great Contradiction' which, according to Böhm-Bawerk, lay at the core of the Marxian system and was the source of its inevitable dissolution. ('The Marxian system has a past and a present, but no abiding future.') What point was there in speaking of two levels of approximation, or two stages of analysis, if the second could not be derived (given the additional data introduced at this second stage) from the first? This could not be done in the manner indicated by Marx; and if it could not, then Marx's theory provided neither a theory of profit nor a theory of prices; and an explanation both of profits and of prices must be sought elsewhere. It was demonstrably untrue that conditions of production determined conditions of exchange.

In subsequent discussion of this question the problem of deriving prices of production from values (or of the later approximation from the essential data postulated in the earlier approximation) was called the Transformation Problem. This discussion was both intermittent and recondite; it was confined to a mere handful of *cognoscenti*, and was very little known either among Marxists or among non-Marxian economists. But on the outcome of it the force of Böhm-Bawerk's apparently telling criticism of the theoretical structure built up in the three volumes of *Kapital*, and especially in the first and third, can be said to have turned. On this issue Böhm-Bawerk,[2] usually so perspicacious, had contented himself with a disdainful dismissal of the particular solution indicated by Marx, and had not stopped to enquire whether the character of the problem was such as to make it likely or unlikely that an alternative solution to it could be found. It is, indeed, clear that Böhm-Bawerk's method of argument was altogether too simple for the nature of the problem in question, and that he had really no notion of complex determination implied in the proposition that 'the values stand behind the prices of production' and 'determine these latter in the last resort'. It is true that the particular arithmetical examples which Marx uses to illustrate the derivation of prices of production from values are inadequate and incomplete— a fact of which he himself was aware (as evidenced in a passage in the *Theorien über den Mehrwert*).[3] Moreover, the simple contention that 'on the average' prices of production and values, profit and surplus-value came out equal, was quite insufficient. Like much else in Volumes II and III this was unfinished work, and in this unfinished state it was open to some, at least, of the objections which Böhm-Bawerk and later Bortkievicz levelled at it. This

[2] In *Zum Abschluss des Marxschen Systems*, 1896.
[3] *Theorien*, Vol. III, pp. 200–1 and 212; also cf. *Capital*, Vol. III, Eng. ed. Kerr, Chicago, pp. 190, 194.

incompleteness consisted in the fact that only the outputs were transformed into prices of production, while all the inputs (including labour-power) continued to be expressed in terms of value. Obviously this is not sufficient: as Marx himself saw, the inputs themselves must also be transformed into price terms (the elements of constant capital and wages as the price of labour-power, which itself depends upon the price of workers' subsistence, or so-called wage-goods). If inputs are so transformed, both the rate of profits and the prices of output will be affected thereby. It follows that the rate of profit will not be the same (except in a special case) as the rate of profit that was formed out of the surplus value of the value situation (by averaging); and in Marx's arithmetical examples it would be different from the rate of profit with which he constructed his prices of production. But it does *not* follow that the new rate of profit cannot bear a definite relation to the old rate of profit (i.e. of the value situation) and hence to the rate of surplus value as defined in the theory of surplus value. Nor does it follow that in this situation of complex interdependence, where output prices depend on input prices and output prices reciprocally influence input prices, a single set of magnitudes cannot be found for all the variables which satisfy the postulated conditions. The solution if it can be found will be like the solution to a set of simultaneous equations, and the possibility of finding one will depend, formally, on similar conditions.

It was the merit of Bortkievicz in the first decade of the present century to have shown that such a solution was, indeed, possible in the simplified case of three sectors or industries, producing respectively elements of constant capital (the Department I of Marx's reproduction schema at the end of Volume II), wage-goods and luxury goods consumed exclusively by capitalists.[4] This he did

---

[4] L. von Bortkievicz, 'Marx's Fundamental Theoretical Construction in the Third Volume of *Capital*', and 'Value and Price in the Marxian System' in *Jahrbücher für Nationalökonomie und Statistik* and in *Archiv für Sozialwissenschaft*, 1907 (both articles appearing in the same month of July); trans. into English respectively in Paul Sweezy's ed. of Böhm-Bawerk's *Karl Marx and the Close of his System*, New York, 1949, and in *International Economic Papers*, No. 2. Bortkievicz's solution had, however, been anticipated (as he himself acknowledged quite handsomely) by the Russian writer W. K. Dmitrieff in a little-known work of 1904 (a 're

with the aid of the condition (a condition of so-called 'simple reproduction') that the outputs of each category were equal to the incomes devoted to their purchase (namely, replacement expenditures on constant capital, total wages and total surplus value). It was a curiosity of this Bortkievicz-solution that it was independent of the conditions of production of the third sector producing for capitalists' consumption: the solution depended exclusively on the conditions of production in the other two sectors.[5] This, he claimed, was not just a formal result, but demonstrated that profit was the fruit of exploitation (or as he preferred to put it, in the manner of Adam Smith, it had the nature of a 'deduction') and had nothing to do with the productivity of capital.

> If it is indeed true that the level of the rate of profit in no way depends on the conditions of production of those goods which do not enter into real wages, then the origin of profit must clearly be sought in the wage-relationship and not in the ability of capital to increase production. For if this ability were relevant here, then it would be inexplicable why certain spheres of production should become irrelevant for the question of the level of profit.[6]

This Bortkievicz-solution in terms of three sectors was, in essence, a three-industry, three-product solution. Alternatively it could be thought of as yielding the *average* price of production for each sector and hence demonstrating that these average prices could be derived from the *data* of the value-situation (i.e. conditions of production measured in terms of labour), while leaving the individual prices of particular prices *within* each sector undetermined. It was intuitively obvious, of course, that if a solution were

---

[5] Or, more strictly speaking, 'on those amounts of labour and those turnover periods which concern the production and distribution of the goods forming the real-wage-rate' (Bortkievicz).

[6] 'Value and Price in the Marxian System', Eng. trans. in *International Economic Papers*, No. 2, p. 33; cit. in the present writer's *Economic Theory and Socialism*, London, 1955, p. 280.

---

markable work', presenting 'something really new', according to Bortkievicz). Dr Sweezy deserves the credit for starting a discussion of this solution (in his *Theory of Capitalist Development*) among English-speaking readers.

possible for the three-product case, it could be found in all probability for any larger number of products. For some time, however, an actual demonstration of this remained lacking—a lack which may perhaps be regarded as an adverse reflection upon the 'creative Marxism' of Marxist economic thinkers of the period. The first such demonstration (to the knowledge of the present writer) that a more general solution was possible for any number of commodities—for the n-product case—was provided by Francis Seton (of Oxford) in an article in the *Review of Economic Studies* for 1956–7.[7] The conclusion was that his analysis had shown the 'logical superstructure' of Marx's theory 'to be sound enough': a demonstration which some may think acquires additional conviction from the fact that the writer was at pains to dissociate himself from the implications of Marx's theory of surplus value.[8] Such a demonstration (worked out, indeed, in its essentials many years earlier) is also implicit in the equations which form the crux of the derivation of prices from conditions of production and the ratio of profits to wages in Part One of Piero Sraffa's *Production of Commodities by Means of Commodities* (cf. esp. Chapter II). The upshot of discussion over more than half a century accordingly is that Marx was quite correct in supposing that prices of production as the actual 'equilibrium prices' of a competitive capitalist economy could be regarded as being determined by the conditions and relations of production, including in the latter the basic exploitation-ratio which in value-terms is expressed as the rate of surplus value. The logical structure of Marx's analysis of capitalist production, and the unfolding of this analysis from the level of value-theory of Volume I through to the theory of prices in Volume III, remains intact after a century of vehement, sometimes acute but more often far-from-understanding, criticism. And in its qualitative characterisation of the essentials of capitalist society and of its driving-force, can there be much serious doubt that it provides an insight that no economic writing of other schools has done?

[7] Volume 24, 1956–7, pp. 149–60. The article is entitled 'The Transformation Problem'.
[8] He considered a denial of factor-contributions other than those of labour, on which the doctrine of surplus value rested, to be 'an act of *fiat* rather than of genuine cognition', ibid., p. 160.

A mere Introduction cannot do justice to the numerous special aspects of these three volumes that are deserving of comment; and the present Introduction would become tedious if it attempted to do so. One general remark, however, about Marx's method can perhaps be made: namely, that while his interest and purpose in this work were primarily theoretical, he resembled Adam Smith in the extent to which he mingled theoretical generalisation and abstract reasoning with historical data of a most concrete and detailed character. This was manifestly part of the central design of the work and was fully consonant with his general attitude towards the relation of theory to actuality: the combination of the two served to reveal the general in the particular and to establish the categories of his thought as representations of the essence of real activity, not abstractions empty of life. Thus we have in parts of Volume I richly factual excursions into reports of early-nineteenth-century factory inspectors and government 'blue books' about working conditions and the payment of wages and the effects of machinery; also the well-known historical *data* on the methods of 'primitive accumulation' in Part VIII. In Volume III there are the historical excursions into different forms of rent and the distinctive types of social relations of which they are the expression; into Merchant Capital, rich in detailed hints and suggestions (it is here that we find the brief reference to the 'two roads' of transition to bourgeois methods of production; also the pregnant phrase about 'the way in which surplus value is pumped out of the direct producers' constituting always the explanation of the 'relation between rulers and ruled'); also *data* about interest and credit with its references to Thomas Tooke's famous *History of Prices* and *An Inquiry into the Currency Principle,* to official enquiries into the financial crisis of 1847–8 and to evidence before the Select Committee on Bank Acts.

But one cannot pass over altogether without mention three topics which, in addition to his theory of value and surplus value, have been the subject of comment and controversy. First, there are his references to the impoverishment of the working class in Chapter XXV of Volume I: the chapter entitled 'The General Law of Capitalist Accumulation'. This is the origin of the so-called 'tendency to absolute impoverishment of the working class' which has occasioned so much questioning and discussion, both as regards its correct interpretation and its accordance with statistical evidence about the trend of wages.[9] Secondly, there are the chapters in Volume III on the Falling Rate of Profit and on counteracting tendencies. These occasioned much debate as to the place this tendency has, if any, in his theory of periodic crises and in his conception of the long-run historical destiny of the system as a whole; also on whether he conceived it as necessarily overbearing the influence of the counter-tendencies (a matter on which he is silent, and at any rate offers no proof that it must in all circumstances be the more powerful).

Thirdly, there is the famous schema of reproduction in the third part of Volume II: a set of arithmetical tables which depict in a two-sectional or two-departmental form the equilibrium relations needing to be observed under conditions of 'simple reproduction' and 'expanded reproduction' respectively, and in doing so indicated the improbability of such conditions being maintained except 'by accident' in a system characterised by 'anarchy of production'. The two sectors or departments were those producing respectively means of production and means of consumption; the former for replacement of (or under expanded reproduction additions to) constant capital within each department (i.e. to meet the needs of 'productive consumption'), and the latter to cater for the personal consumption of capitalists and wage-earners. In each department the gross output was broken-down into its main value-constituents, namely using-up of constant capital (raw materials, plant and equipment), expenditure on wages (variable capital) and surplus value. It followed, of course, that in simple reproduction (with zero saving) the gross output of Department I (means of production) must equal the sum of the used-up constant capitals of both departments. Correspondingly, the gross output of Department II (means of consumption) must equal the sum of the wages and surplus value of both departments. Hence, exchange between the two departments must consist of an amount of means of production from I equal to the replacement-needs of constant capital

---

[9] I have given my own opinion about its interpretation in *Teoria economica e socialismo*, Roma, 1960, pp. 365–72, and will not make any comment here.

in II against means of consumption from II equal to the sum of wages and surplus value in I. Unless this equality is maintained ($s + v$ in I $= c$ in II), there will be excess production in one of the two sectors without a market in the other. The equilibrium conditions for 'expanded reproduction' were a more complex extension of these conditions. Since the publication of the *Grundrisse der Kritik der Politischen Oekonomie* (*Rohentwurf*) of 1857–8 which contains a preliminary version of the schema, we know that this notion of setting out the structural interrelationships of production in a tabular form was present to Marx's mind at a relatively early stage, before the actual publication of his *Kritik der Politischen Oekonomie* (in 1859). It is interesting to note, moreover, that the schema in the *Grundrisse*, in its breakdown into sectors, distinguishes production of raw materials and of machinery among means of production, and among means of consumption between production of necessaries for workers and surplus products (or *surplus-produzent*) for consumption out of surplus value.

It can be readily seen that the schema constitutes an embryonic, two-sector form of a modern input–output matrix, of which the totals of rows and of columns bear a necessary relation to one another. This analysis is, indeed, the actual ancestor of the latter, since it directly inspired the Soviet method of balances in the 1920's, and as we now know the basic idea of the more complex input–output matrix of Leontief was derived from these balances. One could say, indeed, that much of present-day thinking about dynamic problems not only represents a long-overdue return to the focus in which economic problems were envisaged by the classical economists and by Marx, but is inspired directly or indirectly by the Marxian method, in particular by his structural analysis of reproduction.

The reproduction schema was also the centre of attention in the various discussions between rival interpretations of Marx's theory of crisis, most notably in Rosa Luxemburg's theory, which started from a critique of the theory of expanded reproduction and laid emphasis on the so-called problem of 'realisation' of surplus value. Similarly with the strongly opposed theory of Tugan-Baranovski, which stressed the possibility of a non-contradictory process of expanded reproduction. In a certain sense it is true that the under-consumption which formed the emphasis of certain theories is simply another facet of overproduction. This would be true, for example, of the equilibrium relationship between the two sectors, which we have just mentioned: from one side the failure to observe this relationship could be regarded as deficiency of demand, and from the other side as an excess of supply. But this is merely to say that any exchange-transaction has two sides. What is really important is the *source* from which any rupture of the equilibrium conditions of exchange originates. If pressed further, the two-facet notion can constitute an illusory way of reconciling what are real differences of emphasis regarding the originating factors, and tend to blur essential features of Marx's approach. As in other parts of his theory, the bias latent in his analysis here was certainly to focus upon causal factors within the structure and relations of production rather than upon factors within the process of circulation or exchange *per se* or than upon demand-factors which have their roots in the psychological propensities of individual consumers.

It was in November 1866 (as Franz Mehring tells us) that 'the first bundle of manuscript' of Volume I of *Das Kapital* was sent off to Hamburg, to 'a publisher of democratic literature' called Otto Meissner. This was followed five months later by the remainder of the manuscript which was taken to Hamburg by Marx in person. The final proof-sheets were corrected on 16th August 1867—'at two o'clock in the morning' as he told Engels—and returned to the printer. The Preface to the first German edition is dated 25th July of that year; publication was early in September.

This first volume was the product of work over nearly two decades—work interrupted and rendered intermittent both by illness and by political preoccupations, including the foundation of the First International. His acquaintance with the English economists of the classical school dates back to his days in Paris in the middle '40's (after the closing-down of the *Rheinische Zeitung* which he had edited). But intensive study and writing about political economy and capitalism dates from his domicile in London from 1850. Here it was that he made the Reading Room of the British Museum his workshop; his writing being mainly done at home—at first in the cramped Soho lodgings occupied by his family for six years and after that in modest but somewhat more capacious and pleasing surroundings in the neighbourhood of Haverstock Hill. Already in April 1851 we find him writing to Engels: 'I am now so far that I have finished with all the drudgery of economics. After that I shall work on my book at home and pitch into some other science in the Museum. It is beginning to bore me. The science of political economy has made no fundamental progress since the days of Adam Smith and David Ricardo.' But this mood was not to last for long, and he was very soon back at the study of the history of political economy in the British Museum. His intention of completing work on the book at an early date, however, was frustrated. 'Especially is the time at my disposal,' he explains, 'cut down by the imperative necessity of working for a living.' In December 1857 he writes: 'I am working like mad all through the nights at putting my economic studies together.' This produced, as a kind of interim product or first instalment, the *Zur Kritik der Politischen Oekonomie* in 1859. But again nine years later it is: 'as for my book, I am working 12 hours a day at writing out a fair copy' (Letter to Kugelmann, 15th January 1866); and a few months afterwards he complains: 'I cannot work productively more than a very few hours a day without feeling the effect physically. . . . Besides that my work is often interrupted by adverse external circumstances' (Letter to Kugelmann, 23rd August 1866).

It seems to have been by the beginning of 1866 that the design of the first volume, and the intention of publishing it separately, took shape in his mind. In that year he writes to Kugelmann that 'my circumstances (physical and external interruptions without intermission) make it necessary for the first volume to appear separately, not both volumes together, as I had at first intended' (Letter of 13th October 1866). He goes on to explain how 'the whole work is divided':

BOOK I   The Production Process of Capital
BOOK II   Circulation Process of Capital
BOOK III Form of the Process as a Whole

adding that 'the first volume contains the first two books'. According to Mehring, it was between January 1866 and March 1867 that the final writing of the manuscript for Volume I was done.

As is well-known, Marx was not to complete the other volumes during his lifetime. These were to bear the subtitles 'The Process of Circulation of Capital' and 'The Process of Capitalist Production as a Whole', and were to be published by Engels, Volume II in 1885 two years after Marx's death, and Volume III in 1894. These parts of the manuscript were left on his death as incomplete drafts and in some cases only notes, which Engels pieced together in the two volumes as we know them. 'At best one single manuscript (No. 4) had been revised throughout and made ready for the printer'. In his Preface to Volume II Engels describes this material as 'fragmentary' and 'incomplete in various places', unpolished as regards language—'careless, full of colloquial, often rough and humorous, expressions and phrases'; 'thoughts were jotted down as they developed in the brain of the author'; 'some parts of the argument would be fully treated, others of equal importance only indicated', while at the end of chapters were often 'only a few incoherent sentences as milestones of incomplete deductions'. It was in this Preface, incidentally, that Engels gave a foretaste of what Volume III would contain by saying: 'As a matter of fact, equal capitals, regardless of the quantity of actual labour employed by them, produce equal average profits in equal times. Here we have, therefore, a clash with the law of value, which had been noticed by Ricardo himself, but which his school was unable to reconcile.'

Rosa Luxemburg's comment[10] on these two posthumous volumes is worth quoting:

> In these circumstances we must not look to the last two volumes of *Capital* to provide us with a final and completed solution of all economic problems. In some cases these problems are merely formulated, together with an indication here and there as to the direction in which one must work to arrive at a solution. In accordance with Marx's whole attitude, his *Capital* is not a Bible containing final and unalterable truths, but rather an inexhaustible source of stimulation for further study, further scientific investigations and further struggles for truth.

His work on the history of economic thought, upon which we

---

[10] In the passage she contributed to F. Mehring's *Karl Marx: the Story of his Life*, Eng. trans. by Edward Fitzgerald, London, 1936, p. 371.

have seen that he had started in the early '50's, was not to appear even during the lifetime of Engels, who was to outlive Marx by some twelve years. At one time this work was intended as a sequel to the *Kritik*, and was described by the heading of 'critique of political economy'. Later it was designed to form the fourth volume of *Das Kapital*; and the manuscript of it apparently formed part of the general manuscript of 1861–3, and to have been written between January 1862 and July 1863. It was left for Karl Kautsky to publish it as *Theorien über den Mehrwert* in 1905. More recently the manuscript of this work was purchased by the Marx–Engels–Lenin Institute in Moscow, which, after reworking the manuscript, issued in 1954 a new edition, according to a different pattern from that of Kautsky, and one said to be closer to that of Marx's original design.

Index

38999

ST. MARY'S COLLEGE OF MARYLAND
ST. MARY'S CITY, MARYLAND